CAMBRIDGE LIBRARY COLLECTION

Books of enduring scholarly value

British and Irish History, Seventeenth and Eighteenth Centuries

The books in this series focus on the British Isles in the early modern period, as interpreted by eighteenth- and nineteenth-century historians, and show the shift to 'scientific' historiography. Several of them are devoted exclusively to the history of Ireland, while others cover topics including economic history, foreign and colonial policy, agriculture and the industrial revolution. There are also works in political thought and social theory, which address subjects such as human rights, the role of women, and criminal justice.

Three Seventeenth-Century Yorkshire Surveys

Originally founded in 1863 to promote interest in the history and archaeology of the Huddersfield area, the Yorkshire Archaeological Society expanded its purview in 1870 to cover the whole of Yorkshire. In 1884 it began publishing its Record Series, which aimed to make historical information available through the reprinting of original documents, diaries, letters and charters. First printed for the society in 1941, this work comprises three seventeenth-century surveys. The first, introduced and edited by Thomas Stuart Willan (1910–94), addresses the manor of Wensleydale, and the remaining two, introduced and edited by Ely Wilkinson Crossley (1863–1942), are concerned with the areas – then known as lordships – of Middleham and Richmond. Providing details of property and land ownership, tenancies, dispute resolution, and farming, this work remains a valuable resource for local historians as well as scholars of seventeenth-century British history and historical geography.

T0364312

Cambridge University Press has long been a pioneer in the reissuing of out-of-print titles from its own backlist, producing digital reprints of books that are still sought after by scholars and students but could not be reprinted economically using traditional technology. The Cambridge Library Collection extends this activity to a wider range of books which are still of importance to researchers and professionals, either for the source material they contain, or as landmarks in the history of their academic discipline.

Drawing from the world-renowned collections in the Cambridge University Library and other partner libraries, and guided by the advice of experts in each subject area, Cambridge University Press is using state-of-the-art scanning machines in its own Printing House to capture the content of each book selected for inclusion. The files are processed to give a consistently clear, crisp image, and the books finished to the high quality standard for which the Press is recognised around the world. The latest print-on-demand technology ensures that the books will remain available indefinitely, and that orders for single or multiple copies can quickly be supplied.

The Cambridge Library Collection brings back to life books of enduring scholarly value (including out-of-copyright works originally issued by other publishers) across a wide range of disciplines in the humanities and social sciences and in science and technology.

Three Seventeenth-Century Yorkshire Surveys

EDITED BY
THOMAS STUART WILLAN
AND ELY WILKINSON CROSSLEY

CAMBRIDGE
UNIVERSITY PRESS

CAMBRIDGE UNIVERSITY PRESS

Cambridge, New York, Melbourne, Madrid, Cape Town,
Singapore, São Paolo, Delhi, Mexico City

Published in the United States of America by Cambridge University Press, New York

www.cambridge.org
Information on this title: www.cambridge.org/9781108059619

© in this compilation Cambridge University Press 2013

This edition first published 1941
This digitally printed version 2013

ISBN 978-1-108-05961-9 Paperback

The Anniversary Reissue of Volumes from the Record Series of the Yorkshire Archaeological Society

To celebrate the 150th anniversary of the foundation of the leading society for the study of the archaeology and history of England's largest historic county, Cambridge University Press has reissued a selection of the most notable of the publications in the Record Series of the Yorkshire Archaeological Society. Founded in 1863, the Society soon established itself as the major publisher in its field, and has remained so ever since. The *Yorkshire Archaeological Journal* has been published annually since 1869, and in 1885 the Society launched the Record Series, a succession of volumes containing transcriptions of diverse original records relating to the history of Yorkshire, edited by numerous distinguished scholars. In 1932 a special division of the Record Series was created which, up to 1965, published a considerable number of early medieval charters relating to Yorkshire. The vast majority of these publications have never been superseded, remaining an important primary source for historical scholarship.

Current volumes in the Record Series are published for the Society by Boydell and Brewer. The Society also publishes parish register transcripts; since 1897, over 180 volumes have appeared in print. In 1974, the Society established a programme to publish calendars of over 650 court rolls of the manor of Wakefield, the originals of which, dating from 1274 to 1925, have been in the safekeeping of the Society's archives since 1943; by the end of 2012, fifteen volumes had appeared. In 2011, the importance of the Wakefield court rolls was formally acknowledged by the UK committee of UNESCO, which entered them on its National Register of the Memory of the World.

The Society possesses a library and archives which constitute a major resource for the study of the county; they are housed in its headquarters, a Georgian villa in Leeds. These facilities, initially provided solely for members, are now available to all researchers. Lists of the full range of the Society's scholarly resources and publications can be found on its website, www.yas.org.uk.

Three Seventeenth-Century Yorkshire Surveys
(Record Series volume 104)

The first of three surveys in this volume focuses on the manor of Wensleydale in 1613–14. It was edited by T.S. Willan FBA (1910–94) during the early part of his career at the University of Manchester; he was later appointed professor of economic history and held the post from 1961 to 1973. The survey appears to have come to his attention through his cousin, W.H. Willan, a partner in a firm of solicitors in Hawes, North Yorkshire. The present whereabouts of the manuscript edited by Willan are not known. However, another version, which includes field names, is to be found among the records of the Office of the Auditors of Land Revenue at the National Archives, where it has the reference LR 2/195. Professor Willan also contributed an article on 'The parliamentary surveys for the North Riding of Yorkshire' to the *Yorkshire Archaeological Journal*, 31 (1934), 224–89.

The 1605 surveys of the lordships of Middleham and Richmond were edited by E.W. Crossley FSA (1863–1942), who was honorary secretary of the Yorkshire Archaeological Society from 1906 until his death. The provenance of the document is unknown, but it was presented to the Society in 1928 by the Yorkshire Tykes' Club, a dining club composed of the male members of the Society's council. The document has the archival reference MS509.

THREE SEVENTEENTH-CENTURY
YORKSHIRE SURVEYS

THE YORKSHIRE ARCHÆOLOGICAL SOCIETY

FOUNDED 1863   INCORPORATED 1893

RECORD SERIES

VOL. CIV

FOR THE YEAR 1941

THREE

SEVENTEENTH-CENTURY

YORKSHIRE SURVEYS

EDITED BY

T. S. WILLAN AND E. W. CROSSLEY
M.A., D.Phil.   F.S.A.

PRINTED FOR THE SOCIETY

1941

MADE AND PRINTED IN GREAT BRITAIN
BY
JOHN WHITEHEAD AND SON LTD., LEEDS

PREFACE

MANOR OF WENSLEYDALE.

I am indebted to my cousin, Mr. W. H. Willan, for permission to print the Survey of Wensleydale, which is the property of Messrs. Willan and Metcalfe, Solicitors, Hawes, and to my brother, Mr. J. J. Willan, for permission to consult the Broderick valuation which is in his custody as Clerk to the Aysgarth Rural District Council.

While this work was in the press Mr. C. T. Clay kindly drew my attention to the fact that Christopher, second son of John Colby of Bowbridge (Introduction, p. xv), by his wife Jane, daughter of Alexander Moore, was Dean of Middleham from 1681 to his death in 1727 (Dugdale, *Visitation of Yorkshire*, ed. J. W. Clay, iii, 434).

T.S.W.

THE LORDSHIPS OF MIDDLEHAM AND RICHMOND.

The MS. Survey of these two lordships is the property of the Yorkshire Archæological Society, having been presented to that body in 1928 by members of the Yorkshire Tykes' Club. Mr. Willan has subjected the Survey of Wensleydale to a painstaking and intensive analysis. Those of Middleham and Richmond are, however, published only as a record, but it is hoped that they will be useful as a basis for closer examination by students of social and economic history.

The term "lordship of Richmond" is here used in a very restricted sense as compared with the area covered, at an early date by the honor which included not only the whole of Richmondshire but lands in other counties as well.

When Mr. Willan offered his paper on the Survey of Wensleydale to the Society for publication it was thought that the three Surveys covering districts which were contiguous to each other might well be printed together, and that they would make a suitable volume for our Record Series.

A separate index of field names is printed at the end of the book.

E.W.C.

INTRODUCTION

I

A Seventeenth-Century Survey of the Manor of Wensleydale.

Edited by T. S. Willan.

(i) THE MANOR OF WENSLEYDALE.

The manor of Wensleydale " consisted of the possessions of the abbey of Jervaulx in the forest of Wensleydale north of the Ure. In 1086 4 carucates in the place known as Fors were held of Count Alan by Bodin. His nephew Acharis son of Bardolf granted 1½ carucates here to found the abbey of Charity. Hugh son of Gernagan, probably a tenant of Acharis, granted a like amount. This was the nucleus of the abbot's possessions on this side of the river. The monks removed to East Witton in the time of Hervey son of Acharis, and founded there the abbey of Jervaulx. The old building was known as Dale Grange, and in 1301–2 the abbot paid subsidy for it and for the hamlets of Skelgill, Cams House, Simonstone, Cotterdale and others. The whole estate now began to be known as the Manor of Wensleydale, the alternative name (*i.e.* the manor of Dale Grange) being due to the fact that the courts were held by the steward of the abbey at Dale Grange."[1]

At the dissolution of the monasteries and the attainder of the abbot of Jervaulx, the manor of Wensleydale was worth £68 13s. 4d. p.a. It was granted by Henry VIII in 1544 to Matthew Earl of Lennox and Margaret his wife, but returned to the Crown in the person of James I, their grandson.[2] On 6 August 1603 it was granted to Ludovick Stuart, Duke of Lennox, together with the manors of Settrington and Temple Newsam.[3] In Elizabeth's reign there had been disputes between the Crown and the

[1] *Victoria County History, North Riding*, i, 207. For a more recent account of the founding of the abbey, with the relevant documents, see *Early Yorkshire Charters*, vol. IV (The Honour of Richmond, Part I, ed. C. T. Clay), Yorkshire Archæological Society Record Series, Extra Series, i, 23–36.

[2] *V.C.H., N.R.*, i, 207. For the career of Matthew Earl of Lennox see the *Dictionary of National Biography*.

[3] *Calendar of State Papers Domestic*, 1603–10, p. 28; *D.N.B.*

tenants in 1570,[1] and between the Crown and the Countess of Lennox in 1573, over the title to the manor.[2] Now the Duke of Lennox found himself in conflict, not with the Crown, but with his new tenants.   This interesting conflict, which developed within three years of the grant of the manor to the Duke, can be unravelled from the Exchequer Depositions.[3] In the course of it the very existence of the manor was disputed, although Thomas Ascoughe, deputy steward, claimed that he knew the lands " on the Abbotside Called (as he hath sene and read in the book called Domesdaie) by the name of the manor or Lordship of Wensladale." Ascoughe appealed to Domesday Book with all the fervour that Parliamentarians were to appeal to Magna Carta forty years later, but with less justification, for the manor was not mentioned in the Book. The real cause of the conflict was the unfavourable terms upon which the tenants had taken their leases from their new landlord.   Under the late Countess of Lennox they had paid fines value 9–10 years' rent for leases of 21 years. Now, for leases of the same term of years, they were paying fines of 30 years' rent to the Duke. Apparently some 16–20 tenants, described by one deponent as " the duke's favourites," took leases on these conditions and paid the first instalment of their fines. They, and probably others, attended the court and acknowledged themselves to be tenants. Early in 1606, however, the tenants who had taken leases met at Hardrow and decided to ask Lennox to mitigate their fines. If he refused they would complain to the King. In the meantime they collected money for the necessary charges and put the matter in the hands of Peter Metcalfe (" Peter of the bowebrigge "). He, and apparently others, interviewed Lennox's commissioners and were sharply reproved as " but busy fellowes," who " came not in the business of their neighbours." This was the story Metcalfe brought back and told to a further meeting of tenants at Holehouses. The tenants thereupon assigned a letter of attorney to Peter Metcalfe and Edmond Pratt to solicit their cause.

There is no evidence of either Metcalfe or Pratt acting under the letter of attorney, for at this stage the movement among the tenants passed into the hands of Anthony Besson of Gray's Inn,

[1] Whaley, *Askrigg*, p. 63.
[2] Exchequer Depositions, 15 Eliz., East. no. 4.
[3] Exchequer Depositions, 5 Jas. I, Mich. no. 8.

the founder of Yorebridge Grammar School near Askrigg.[1] He, more than Metcalfe, was looked upon as the leader of the tenants against the Duke.[2] Ascoughe, for example, declared that the reasons for the discontent were the greatness of the fines and " Mr Besson's persuasion." At the third meeting of tenants, held at Askrigg Church, Besson declared that " they were about a Course which would be very Chargeable," and persuaded the tenants to bind themselves " for the Securitie of him or those that should prosecute the Cause." According to Tristam Janson, clerk of Aysgarth, Thomas Metcalfe and Richard Metcalfe, his father, had consulted him about becoming bound to Anthony Besson in £70. The condition was that they should contribute according to their tenement in support of the suit against the Duke. Janson urged caution as there was apparently no corresponding obligation on Besson's part; but others had already entered into such bonds. Anthony Besson himself spoke his mind freely on the whole subject to John Lambert of Marsett, yeoman, whom he met in London. The grant of land to the Duke, he said, " was nothing worth and merelie mistaken," and he, Besson, had said as much to the Duke himself. " If the tennants wolde be ruled and guided by him, they should not paié the dukes grace any rente or fines hereafter, or doe him any suite or service at his Courte," but for those who had taken up leases and paid fines " it was lost money." If the tenants would stand by him according to their agreement, Besson declared, he would discharge them at law against the Duke's title to the lands " for an Ascrigge shott."

In the spring, apparently of 1606, on a Sunday before the customary court was due to meet, Anthony Besson and a great part of the tenants of the land in variance met at Hawes Chapel " without the Lordship." There they attended a " preaching then and there made by Mr Leak," who was himself a tenant of Cotterdale. After the sermon Anthony Besson and the tenants held a long private discussion at which it was agreed that the tenants should not appear at the court. At this point Anthony Besson, who was not even a tenant, fell into the background

---

[1] In 1600 he gave two houses in York to maintain a master to teach in a free grammar school in Askrigg (*V.C.H. Yorks.*, i, 480).

[2] As early as 1585 he had been concerned in a case of a disputed lease of Cams House (Exch. Dep., 27 Eliz., East. no. 17—partly illegible; *ibid.*, 29 Eliz., East. no. 2).

and his place was taken by Richard Besson. There seems to be no evidence of the relationship between the two, though they may have been brothers. Richard appears to have been a man of some local importance. He had a farm at Litherskew and was, in 1606, charged with shooting two hares in the forest of Wensleydale with a gun.[1] At the end of Elizabeth's reign he apparently collected the rents for the manor of Wensleydale and in consequence became involved in a not unusual case concerning a certain discrepancy between the rents collected and the rents paid in.[2] In 1603 he was granted the bailiwick of Wensleydale for life,[3] and in the following year received a number of offices, including those of Forester of Kettlewell, Parker of Woodhall Park, Bow-bearer of Wensleydale and collector of rents of Bainbridge and Worton.[4] These grants did not go unchallenged.[5]

It was left for Richard Besson to challenge openly the Duke's authority. On the day following the meeting at Hawes Chapel he came into the room at Dale Grange, where Thomas Ascoughe was sitting as deputy steward to hold the court, and said, " verie contemptuouslie, without any reverence or regard, ' Howe nowe my maisters, for whome doe you kepe a Courte here ? ' " To this the deputy steward answered " For the Duke's grace," and Besson replied that the Duke had no authority to keep a court there " and they are fooles that doe appeare here at this tyme." As a result those who were indifferent withdrew, " so as there could not be a jurie had at that tyme," and " used verie hard speaches to the deputie steward and David Balie the duke's bailife, such as had bene sufficient to have drawne on further inconveniences."

There, for want of further evidence, the story ends; but it would appear that the tenants were unsuccessful, at least temporarily, in their struggle with their landlord. Whatever the issue, the conflict is not without interest, for it illustrates the impact of

---

[1] *North Riding Q.S. Records*, i, 45.

[2] Exch. Depositions, Special Commission, 11 Jas. I, 4861.

[3] *Cal.S.P.D.*, 1603–10, p. 21.

[4] *Ibid.*, p. 158.

[5] Exch. Dep., 6 Jas. I, Hilary, no. 3. This unfortunately contains only the list of questions, the actual depositions being missing. The grants were challenged by Thomas Lord Scrope, Sir Thomas Metcalfe, Christopher, John and Thomas Metcalfe, and George Dodsworth.

economic forces on a conservative community. The new commercial spirit that was abroad, and especially the general rise in prices of this period, led landlords to try to get more revenue out of their lands. A fine of 9–10 years' rent may have satisfied the 'late Countess', but apparently it did not satisfy the Duke. Hence the increase in fines which precipitated a conflict so characteristic of the agrarian problem of the seventeenth century.

In 1614 Lennox leased the manor for 21 years to Sir John Leedes, John Colby and Henry Goodreeke.[1] Little is known of these men. A Sir John Leedes was in constant trouble at this time for making disrespectful remarks about the King.[2] John Colby was probably the John Colby of Nappa who died in 1616[3] and whose widow, Mary, later acquired a share of the manor. Henry Goodreeke was perhaps the Henry Goodricke who was a Deputy Lieutenant of Yorkshire in 1638-9.[4] Later in the same year Lennox sold the entire manor to Sir Francis Baildon of Kippax, Thomas Roockwood of London and Edward Rolte of Gray's Inn for £10,000.[5] It then passed quickly through the hands of a number of men who were probably merely speculators. In May 1616 Baildon, Roockwood and Rolte sold one third of the manor for a " competent some " to Sir Thomas Smith of Kent and David Watkins of London, who in turn sold it for £4,750 to George and Thomas Cole. Another third part was sold by Baildon, Roockwood and Rolte to John Goodman and his son John, who in turn sold it to George Cole. The final third was acquired by Mary Colby,[6] who leased it to George Cole for ten years at a rent of £220 per annum.[7] Eight commissioners were appointed, four named by George and Thomas Cole and four by Mary Colby, to survey the manor and divide it into three equal parts, two of

---

[1] Survey, f. 1.

[2] *Cal.S.P.D.*, 1611–18, pp. 227–29, 344; *ibid.*, 1619–23, p. 276. His wife was apparently the chief offender.

[3] Dugdale, *Visitation of the County of York* (Surtees Soc.), xxxvi, 47.

[4] *Hist. MSS. Com. Cowper*, ii, 205, 208.

[5] Exch. Dep., Spec. Com., 16 Jas. I, no. 4894; Close, 16 Jas. I, pt. xii, no. 25. *Cf. V.C.H.*, *N.R.*, i, 208, where it is said that Lennox sold the manor in 1618 and where the various sales between 1614 and 1618 are completely ignored.

[6] Not, as Whaley says (*Askrigg*, p. 49), John Colby. John Colby, Mary's husband, died in 1616 (Dugdale, *Visitation*, Surtees Soc., xxxvi, 47).

[7] Exch. Dep., Spec. Com., 16 Jas. I, no. 4894; Close, 16 Jas. I, pt. xii, no. 25; pt. v, no. 35.

which were to go to the Coles and one to Mary Colby. George Cole was to get the schedule of Mary's share so that he could give leases to the undertenants. This survey was carried out by Robert Saxton, gentleman, aged 33, of Dunningley (?), Yorks. He was probably the Robert Saxton, son of the more famous Christopher, who was assisting his father in making surveys of property in the West Riding in 1601.[1] Robert Saxton made use of the plot or map which Samuel Peirse had drawn up for the survey of 1614.[2] He seems to have surveyed 3,003 acres of common, which may have been meant to represent a third of Stags Fell, but unfortunately the actual award is largely illegible.[3] From some later additions to the survey of 1614 it appears that the Colby share of the manor comprised Dale Grange, Helm, Skelgill, Yorescot, Brockillcote, and, except for one tenement, Shawcote and Holehouses.[4]

George Cole (for little more is heard of Thomas) was left in anything but quiet enjoyment of the manor. His position seems to have been challenged on the one side by those from whom he had bought part of the manor and on the other side by the tenants, who seem to have kept up a running fight with successive owners.[5] On 25 June 1623 provisional agreement was reached between Cole and his tenants. It was stated that for twenty years suits had been depending between the tenants of that part of Wensleydale north of the Ure and those that claimed from His Majesty, and between Sir Thomas Smith, Sir William Smith, John Goodman and John Colby on the one hand and George Cole on the other, concerning the conveyance of two thirds of the manor from the Smiths and Goodman. The suits had spent and wasted a great part of the tenants' estates, for they were " notable to contend in Law with the said George Cole fore redresse of theire wronges." The tenants petitioned the King on 9 June 1621, and they and Cole appeared before the Assizes at Lancaster, where it was decreed that they should quietly enjoy their houses and garths

[1] *Geographical Journal*, xciii (1939), 180.
[2] Survey, f. 2.
[3] Exch. Dep., Spec. Com., 16 Jas. I, no. 4894. *Cf.* Survey, f. 87d.
[4] Survey, f. 26d.
[5] See, *e.g.*, Exch. Spec. Com., 16 Jas. I, no. 4894, which shows that the tenants challenged the claims to ownership of the Smiths, John Goodman and Mary Colby.

and one third of their lands with rights of common, Cole keeping two thirds.[1]

Immediately after this decree Cole began to lease some of the land for 2,000 years for a capital sum and a nominal rent per annum. Thus on 1 November 1624 George Cole of the Inner Temple leased to Thomas Tinkard of Sedbusk, yeoman, for 2,000 years, for 20s. in cash and 1s. 6d. per annum, a dwelling-house, garths, a parcel of ground called Rush Dale and two cattlegates in the High Pasture, all in the occupation of Tinkard. The lessor retained all the mineral rights and the right of carriage of coal and turf through the premises. The lessee agreed to give two days mowing and two days haymaking per annum " in Mowing tyme and Haytime "; in default of a day's mowing he was to pay 12d. and of a day's haymaking 6d. He was also to give one day's labour with a horse to fetch coals from any place in the manor to Cole's mansion; on default he was to pay 8d. The lessee also agreed to pay the " Rateable contribution towards the Reparation of the Chappell of Hardrowe " and to grind his corn at Cole's mill in Hardrow, provided he was " used as well at the said Mill as . . . . at any other Mill or mills whatsoever." Finally he was to do suit and service at the court yearly, to procure the good and welfare of Cole, and not to be a party to plots and practices against him. Other houses, land and cattlegates in Sedbusk were leased on the same conditions.[2]

These conditions may have been considered too onerous or Cole may have refused to carry out the decree of 1623, for a final settlement between himself and his tenants was only reached in 1632. On 11 July 1632 it was stated that " whereas George Sadler, George Thwaites, Bartholomew Thwaites, George Wynne the elder, Thomas Tynkard, Charles Atkinson, Thomas Todd, George Wynne the younger, George Thwaites, Thomas Thompson, George Todd, Michael Metcalfe, John Metcalfe, Martin Thwaites, John Kettlewell, Michael and Henry Dent, John Wynne, Wilfred Moore, John Blencarne have exhibited their Bill of Complaint into his Maiesties Court of Whitehall against George Cole, esquire, defendant their Landlord for and concerning the better and more firm establishing of their houses and garthes and a third part

---

[1] MS. in my possession, unfortunately in very bad condition.
[2] MSS. in my possession.

of their tenements unto them and their heires," the Lord Privy Seal and the rest of His Majesty's Council decreed that the complainants " shall severally and respectively have hold and enioy their houses and garthes and such landes or tenements as were devided and sett out by the said defendant or his assignees with common of pasture proportionable thereunto, unto them . . . . for and during the whole and full Terme of two thousand years. Paying yearly at everie Martinmas hereafter the third part of their old rent which belonged to their whole farme when it was entire and one boone day yearly in hay time."[1] Although this judgment seems to have affected only a limited number of tenants, largely those of Sedbusk, it was favourable to those whom it did concern, which was a not unusual feature of judgments made by the central authorities during the years of the personal rule of Charles I.

After 1632 land in and around Sedbusk changed hands freely, being granted for the remainder of the term of 2,000 years on payment of capital sums together with a nominal rent to the " chief lord of the soil," who was Sir John Lowther of Lowther, although it is uncertain when he acquired an interest in the manor.[2] A small part of Cole's share of the manor also passed to Sir Robert Bindloss of Borwick, Lancashire.[3] This was the Cams House portion, for on 31 January 1652 Sir Robert sold to Bernard Smith of Cams House all the lands, messuages, etc., known by the name of Cams House. The whole comprised 333 acres, with two messuages, and the price was £1,125. The land was said to be late in the tenure of George Thwaite and now in the tenure of Bernard Smith.[4] Smith, who was chief constable of Hang West in 1665,[5] had married George Thwaite's widow sometime before 1635, and in that year he and his wife sold property in Sedbusk to Augustine Metcalfe and Henry, his son, for £135.[6]

In the second half of the seventeenth century a new dispute

---

[1] MS. in my possession.

[2] There are in my possession some twenty deeds relating to the transfe of land in and around Sedbusk in the seventeenth century.

[3] Survey, f. 27.

[4] There is a copy of this conveyance on a loose sheet in the survey.

[5] *North Riding Q.S. Records*, vi, 96.

[6] MS. in my possession.

arose, this time concerning the third part of the manor held by
Mary Colby. This was inherited by John Colby,[1] Mary's son, who
sold it in 1678 to Alexander Smith.[2]   The purchase price was
£4,300, of which £1,300 was paid and the remainder secured.
Anthony Fothergill[3] and Thomas Lambert were to have propor-
tions of Smith's purchase " on good consideration." After John
Colby's death his son and heir, Alexander, sued Smith, Lambert
and Fothergill in Chancery to have the purchase set aside. According to Alexander Colby's story the purchase, conveyance and fine
were obtained from his father by fraud.   The purchase money
was to be paid in instalments spread over seven years and was
therefore not really more than one third of the value of the
premises. The Court of Chancery agreed with Alexander Colby
and ordered the property to be re-conveyed to him. He took
possession and tendered £2,800 in repayment as decreed by the
Court, but Smith refused it.   According to the writer in the
Victoria County History, " Alexander Colby tried to set aside the
sale . . . . but apparently without success."[4] Actually the case
went to the House of Lords, which on 18 November 1685 dismissed
the appeal of Smith, Fothergill and Lambert and affirmed the
decree made in the Court of Chancery.[5]

After the seventeenth century the history of the manor is
uneventful. In 1717 the whole manor was in the hands of Lord
Lonsdale, who sold it in 1723 to Edward Wortley. As part of the
Wortley estates it appears under a new name, that of the manors
of High and Low Abbotside. It passed from Edward Wortley
to his descendants, the Earls of Wharncliffe. About 1885 part
of the estate which had belonged to John Colby was sold to the
Hon. William Lowther, and in 1913 the remainder was broken

---

[1] He is usually described as the builder of Colby Hall (Whaley, *Askrigg*,
p. 50), but the Hall was built in 1633 when he was only 19 (Dugdale, *Visitation*, Surtees Soc., xxxvi, 47). It seems more probable that it was built by
his mother.

[2] He may have been, as Whaley says (*Askrigg*, p. 50), of the family of
Smith of Cams House. An Alexander Smith of Cams House was one of the
Lords Trustees of the manor of Bainbridge in 1705 (*ibid.*, p. 83).

[3] Probably the Anthony Fothergill who was one of the original Lords
Trustees of the manor of Bainbridge (Whaley, *Askrigg*, p. 64).

[4] *N.R.*, i, 208.

[5] *Hist. MSS. Com.* xi (House of Lords, 1678–88), App. ii, p. 299; *Journals
of the House of Lords*, xiv, 75, 86. The final verdict, which has been over-
looked by the writer in the *V.C.H.*, is in the *Journals*.

up and disposed of in lots.[1] The lordship of the manor is now held jointly by S. H. Willan, esquire, and C. M. Fawcett, esquire.

(ii) THE LAND.

The survey of 1614 is written on paper and consists of 88 folios, $7\frac{1}{2}'' \times 9\frac{7}{10}''$, bound in contemporary vellum. The survey itself takes up ff. 1–80, the remaining folios being either blank or covered with notes and scribbles of a later date. Originally a map accompanied the survey, upon which the holdings were marked with letters or symbols, but unfortunately the map can no longer be traced. The whole was apparently the work of Samuel Peirse of Maidstone in Kent. The surveyor's county of origin has left its mark on the survey, for all the land measurements are given in acres, roods, day's works and perches. The day's work was " the smallest Kentish unit of superficial land measure "[2] and was equal to four perches.[3] Its appearance in the survey suggests that attention should be paid to the county of origin of surveyors before using land measures as evidence of a particular field system.[4] Peirse's arithmetic was not infallible, and a succession of minor errors in addition seems to justify the giving of two sets of figures, one obtained by adding particular items, the other comprising the surveyor's totals. The following two tables summarize the area and yearly value of the manor as revealed by the survey. The discrepancy between the value and the rent was probably covered by the fines, but there is no evidence in the survey itself of the value of such fines.

The manor was a well-defined area bounded on the east by Merbeck,[5] on the west by Hell Gill Beck, on the south by the Ure, and on the north, as a deponent[6] picturesquely described it, " as heaven water deales and divides the commons moores and waste from Swaledale," or more prosaically, by the watershed of

---

[1] *V.C.H.*, *N.R.*, i, 208. A schedule of the 1913 sale is in my possession.

[2] Gray, H. E., *English Field Systems*, Harvard Historical Studies, xxii, 301.

[3] Norden, J., *The Surveiors Dialogue*, ed. 1618, p. 148.

[4] Gray, for example, says (*op. cit.*) that the appearance outside Kent of the sulung, the iugum and the day's work " will suggest the Kentish system." He admits that this " is less true of the day's work," but pays no attention to the question of where the surveyor using the terms came from.

[5] Merbeck or Meer Beck—*i.e.* ' boundary beck '—is near the site of Fors abbey.

[6] John Lambert in 1607 (Exch. Dep., 5 Jas. I, Mich. no. 8).

Table I.

Place	Meadow and Pasture A[1]			Meadow and Pasture B[2]			Value per annum A[1]			Value per annum B[3]			Rent per annum A[1]			Rent per annum B[2]			Cowpasture		
	Acres	r.	p.	Acres	r.	p.	£	s.	d.	£	s.	d.	£	s.	d.	£	s.	d.	Acres	r.	p.
Dale Grange ..	220	0	8	220	0	9	121	3	1¼	121	9	9	8	16	9	8	16	8	61	1	24
Helm ..	159	2	18	163	2	18	40	4	8	40	4	9	5	10	2	5	10	2	124	0	20
Skelgill ..	79	2	17	79	1	37	38	7	9	37	8	7	3	7	7	3	7	7			
Yorescot ..	47	2	30	46	3	18	24	12	7	24	13	2	2	6	8	2	6	8			
Brockillcote	162	1	16	164	2	19	88	17	1½	89	3	3½	7	16	6	7	16	6			
Shawcote ..	101	1	30	100	3	30	44	15	0	45	5	1	5	6	8	5	6	8	522	0	20
Cams House ..	281	0	32	281	2	32	92	13	6½	92	13	5½	7	0	2	7	0	2	52	0	36
Litherskew ..	280	0	33	280	2	23½	50	5	11	51	16	11	4	18	4	4	18	4			
Sedbusk ..	163	1	6	163	2	17	88	1	8½	87	18	6	8	6	8	8	6	8	269	1	0
Simonstone ..	229	2	26	229	1	1½	93	1	7½	93	0	7	9	2	5	7	9	1	254	1	0
Hardrow ..	235	3	3	235	3	35	82	10	2	82	10	2	12	6	8	12	6	8	61	3	20
Fossdale ..	528	0	23	528	0	23	41	6	2	41	6	4	3	11	8	3	11	8			
Newhouses ..	114	1	8	114	1	8	26	0	8½	25	2	5	1	3	4	1	3	4			
Riggs Close ..	20	1	2	20	1	2	3	6	7	3	7	7		10	0		10	0			
Cotterdale ..	375	2	38[3]	375	3	38[3]	97	18	10[4]	98	0	9½[4]	9	7	2½	9	6	9½	468	3	0[5]
Cotterend ..	820	1	30	820	1	30	86	17	6	87	7	6	4	9	4	4	9	4			
Lunds ..	764	0	38	764	0	34	88	8	5	88	12	11	4	15	0	4	15	0	90	2	28
	4583	3	38	4590	0	15	1108	11	4¾	1110	1	9½	98	15	0½	97	1	3½	1904	2	28
Sargill Park ..	496	1	20	496	1	20	25	0	0	25	0	0	2	13	4	2	13	4			
Stags Fell ..	9422	0	0	9422	0	0	157	0	8	157	0	8	1	0	0	1	0	0			
Totals ..	14502	1	18	14508	1	35	1290	12	0¾	1292	2	5½	102	8	4½	100	14	7½	1904	2	28

[1] These are the figures obtained by the addition of particulars.   [2] These are the figures given by the surveyor.
[3] Including Cotterdale Banks.   [4] Including £5 for Cotterdale Banks.   [5] Excluding Cotterdale Banks.

Table II.

Summary.

				Acres	r.	p.
Houses and premises	..	..	..	25	1	1[1]
Meadow	..	..	..	228	3	31
Meadow and pasture	..	..	..	4329	3	6
Sargill Park	..	..	..	496	1	20
Cowpastures	..	..	..	1904	2	28
Stags Fell	..	..	..	9422		
Total		..		16407	0	6

Stags Fell. Outside these well-defined natural boundaries were the cottages in Askrigg, which were included in the survey but were " no parte of the landes of the Abby of Jarvax,"[2] and some land in Lunds, including part of the cowpasture.[3] The monks of Jervaulx had also had rights of pasture south of the Ure granted to them by Conan, duke of Britanny and earl of Richmond, in the twelfth century,[4] and confirmed by Ranulph son of Robert in 1218.[5] In the sixteenth century the abbot had paid £6 per annum and the tenants £10 for an agistment south of the river. Towards the £10 the tenants of Thwaite in Swaledale had paid 6s. 8d. " for the pasture of their cattell when they come on the Fell."[6] None of these rights of pasture is mentioned in the survey and it is possible that they lapsed in the course of the sixteenth century.

There is one preliminary problem concerning the manor and the survey which requires at least an attempted solution. It is the problem whether all the land within the boundaries given above was included in the survey. It can only be solved by comparing the area of land included in the survey with the total area of land within the rough rectangle formed by the boundaries.

[1] Including two gardens valued separately.
[2] Survey, f. 77.
[3] Ibid., ff. 67, 67d.
[4] Early Yorkshire Charters, IV (Honour of Richmond, Pt. I), p. 64.
[5] Feet of Fines, 1218–31, ed. J. Parker, Y.A.S. Record Series, lxii, 2–3. Ranulph, lord of Middleham, was hereditary forester of Wensleydale.
[6] Exch. Dep., 15 Eliz., East. no. 4.

This rough rectangle became later the townships of Low and High Abbotside, the former comprising Dale Grange, Helm, Skelgill, Brockillcote and Shawcote, the latter comprising the area from Cams House to Lunds. Low Abbotside had an area of 4,738 acres, of which 2,722 were unenclosed moor. Thus the enclosed portion comprised 2,016 acres, and this included Sargill Park.[1] The area of this enclosed portion which is included in the survey was 1,974 acres 3 roods 3 perches.[2] Thus as regards the eastern end of the manor, which later became the township of Low Abbotside, the survey comprises practically all the enclosed land. The township of High Abbotside had an area of 13,229 acres, of which 6,900 acres were open moor.[3] The enclosed land therefore comprised 6,329 acres, but the enclosed land, including the cowpastures, comprised within this area and given in the survey consisted of only 5,010 acres 1 rood 3 perches.[4] Thus some 1,319 acres of enclosed land in the area of the later township of High Abbotside were apparently not included in the survey. This discrepancy cannot be accounted for by a difference in the size between the acre of 1614 and the acre of the nineteenth century, for they seem to have comprised the same area. Nor can it be accounted for by a difference between the boundaries of the townships and the boundaries of the area within which the manor lay. These boundaries were the same on the east, south and west. The northern boundary is vaguer, but that is scarcely important, as it affects only the area of moorland and not of enclosed land. Nor can the discrepancy be accounted for by later enclosure of moorland, which would have helped to swell the nineteenth-century total of 6,329 acres.[5] It would seem, therefore, that some 1,300 acres of enclosed land in what was later the township of High Abbotside were not included in the survey. If they were

---

[1] Bulmer's *History and Directory of North Yorkshire* (1890), p. 336; Whaley, *Askrigg*, p. 43. The Broderick valuation gives the total as 4,708 acres 1r. 11p., of which 1,986a. 1r. 11p. were enclosed, and shows that the enclosed included Sargill Park, which had been divided into allotments.

[2] *I.e.* Sargill Park 496a. 1r. 20p., cowpastures 707a. 2r. 24p., land held in severalty 770a. 2r. 39p.

[3] Bulmer's *History and Directory of N.Y.* (1890), pp. 334–36. The Broderick valuation gives the total as 13,228a. 2r. 34p., of which 6,249a. 2r. 23p. were enclosed.

[4] *I.e.* cowpastures 1,197a. 4p., land held in severalty 3,813a. 39p.

[5] This is shown by the maps of the Broderick valuation, but there may have been some small enclosures of moorland between 1614 and 1872. The nineteenth-century total for moorland, 9,622 acres, compares fairly closely with the 9,422 acres (Stags Fell) of the survey.

part of the manor of Wensleydale they must have been held in freehold, which seems the most reasonable explanation.

The general lay-out of the manor and the type of agriculture employed are fairly clear from the survey. It was a pastoral manor with no arable land, and it was enclosed, only the moor and the cowpastures being held in common, and the latter were " for the most parte enclosed too."[1] Thus there is no question of open field cultivation, of scattered strips, or of two- or three-field systems. Thus, perhaps, there is no need for controversy. All the land outside the moor and the cowpastures was described as meadow and pasture. It is often impossible to distinguish the two, but the following table shows what were probably their relative values, the meadow being, as might be expected, much the more valuable of the two.

Table III.

Summary of values per annum (excluding Stags Fell).

Description	Area			Value			Value per a.	Highest	Lowest
	a.	r.	p.	£	s.	d.			
Meadow ..	228	3	31	105	9	7	9s. 2½d.	16s.	2s. 6d.
Meadow & pasture	4826	0	26	802	16	11¼	3s. 4d.	16s.	[2]4d.

There is little evidence of even former arable land. It is true that George Cole had his mill at Hardrow at which the tenants had to grind their corn, but the corn must have come from outside the manor, probably from lower down the dale. Only in a few field-names, ' Stubledayle ' and Reaper's close at Sedbusk and corn closes at Dale Grange, Sedbusk, Litherskew and Cams House, is there an echo of former arable cultivation.

In such a manor, rights of common were obviously important. On the Out Moor, which lay on Stags Fell, all tenants had " common of pasture as appurtenant to their Tenements without stinte or rate,"[3] and there, too, they had rights of common of turbary.[4] Before the dissolution the abbot had depasturage at ' Came ' (? Cams House) for " a great flocke of weathers " which were

[1] Survey, f. 79.

[2] Part of Cotterend, equal in value to Stags Fell.

[3] Survey, f. 68. The abbots of Jervaulx had had pasture for their sheep there (Exch. Dep., 15 Eliz., East. no. 4).

[4] Exch. Dep., 5 Jas. I, Mich. no. 8.

wintered at Simonstone. Cattle from the abbey had also mixed with those of the tenants in Sargill Park, Spen and Abbots Close, " wherein hay was gotten for the cattell and shepe of the Abbey."[1] By 1614 Abbots Close was no longer held in common.[2] The abbot had also had pasturage for a " stone horse and certen mares " in Cotterdale Bank and for " two stoned horses and certen amblinge mares " in " a place called Rigge under Cotterend," and here all the tenants' cattle had pasturage.[3] By the time of the survey the common pasturage for cattle was well defined in the stinted cowpastures. Various places had no cowpastures. This is true of Yorescot (which is rather surprisingly given as all meadow), of Litherskew, Abbots Close, Forsdale, Newhouses, Riggs Close and Thwaite. Yorescot, Abbots Close and Thwaite were single holdings, the last being very large with presumably enough pasture of its own. Newhouses, Riggs Close and Forsdale consisted of two holdings each. One tenant of Newhouses had six cattlegates in Simonstone pasture,[4] and Charles Atkinson of Forsdale had gates in Hardrow and Simonstone pastures.[5] At Litherskew it is possible that the cowpasture had been divided up even by 1614, for three tenants held parts of Litherskew Slights,[6] which may at one time have been a common pasture. Similarly at Shaw-cote the Little Cow Close, which had once been a cowpasture, was in 1614 divided into four parts, which were no longer held in common.[7] At Cams House, too, where the cowpasture was only 52 acres 39 perches in extent, earlier cowpastures appear to have been divided out.[8] The following table summarizes the number and value of the cattlegates. They seem to have varied in value not in accordance with the relation between the size of the pasture and the number of gates, but according to the fertility of the land.

The fact that the manor was enclosed by 1614 suggests some inquiry into when it was enclosed. Unfortunately there is not much evidence in the survey or elsewhere of recent enclosure. It seems fairly clear, however, that considerable enclosure was going on in the sixteenth century. In 1573 it was said that the late

[1] Exch. Dep., 15 Eliz., East. no. 4.
[2] Survey, f. 46d.
[3] Exch. Dep., 15 Eliz., East. no. 4.
[4] Survey, ff. 73d, 74d.   [5] Ibid., f. 74.
[6] Ibid , ff. 30d–31d.   [7] Ibid., ff. 25–29.
[8] Survey, ff. 28–30.

Table IV. Cattlegates.

Pasture	Number of cattlegates	@	Value £ s. d.			Area of pasture acres r. p.			Acres per gate[2]
Spen and Grange Gill	28¼ [28¹¹⁄₁₂ ?][1]	6/–	8	9	0	61	1	24	2.2
Helm Pasture	32¾	3/4	5	9	2	124	0	20	3.9
Cote Moor and Little Fell Meawes ..	218⅛ [218¼ ?]	2/4	25	8	11½	522	0	20	2.3
Cams House	21	1/6	1	11	6	52	0	36	2.5
Sedbusk Slights ..	70 [73⁷⁄₁₂ ?]	6/8	23	6	8	128	0	20	1.8
Sedbusk Upper Pasture	52 [48⅝ ?]	3/–	7	16	0	141	0	20	2.7
Simonstone	100 [100⅓ ?]	6/–	30	0	0	254	1	0	2.54
Hardrow Slights ..	35⅓ [34¹¹⁄₁₂?]	10/–	17	13	4	61	3	20	1.74
Cotterdale	82½	5/–	20	12	6	468	3	0	5.7
Lunds	28	4/–	5	12	0	90	2	28	3.2
	667⅞	4/4 Average	145	19	1½	1904	2	28	3.9

abbot had made some enclosures at Dale Grange, Litherskew, Sedbusk, Simonstone, and Hardrow. At Hardrow he had enclosed Broad Carr, which in the survey (f. 48) is given as containing 25 acres 2 roods 3 perches. A deponent, William Metcalfe, in the same year declared that Lord William Conyers, " called lame Conyers," Steward of Middleham, had appointed a parcel of common to be enclosed " for their (*i.e.* the tenants') commodities," and the abbot also appointed a parcel " about lviij yeres sinz for it was shortlie after Floden feild where the tennants had lost all their horses." The abbot had also taken off the common a piece of ground called " Rygge fote and Coterfosse," and by appointment of Conyers the tenants had taken a parcel of the said common " unto their commodities." The abbot had also begun to enclose a piece of ground called ' Jeprake ' (?), but the steward and tenants of certain of the grounds " would not suffer the same to procede, but cast downe that which was begun and so it was not inclosed." Metcalfe " being yonge was present at the castinge downe thereof," which was about 50 years since

[1] The queried figures are those obtained by an addition of particulars.
[2] It is possible that more gates were held by freeholders within the manor.

(*i.e.* about 1523).[1] Some thirty years later, in 1607, another deponent, John Lambert, declared that there had been improvements "taken of the commons and moores" and that divers houses had been built on the commons by the tenants of the late Countess.[2] There is little reflection of this in the survey, which does, however, record two houses in Cotterdale "lately erected upon the Out Moore."[3] Two other houses, one in Skelgill and one at Hardrow, were also "lately erected."[4] In two cases houses had been divided into two,[5] and in a third case a turfhouse had been converted into a dwelling-house.[6] These changes may mean little, and on the wider question of enclosure the survey is silent.

The holdings of which the manor was composed varied greatly in size, as the following table shows.

Table V. Summary of Holdings.[7]

Size of Holding	Number	Total Area of Class
		acres r. p.
Over 100 acres	6	2054 3 14
50 acres and over but under 100	14	943 1 35
40 ,, ,, ,, ,, 50	9	401 2 28
30 ,, ,, ,, ,, 40	9	300 2 5
20 ,, ,, ,, ,, 30	13 [? 14][8]	329 3 36 [? 353 1 3][8]
15 ,, ,, ,, ,, 20	6	105 2 0
10 ,, ,, ,, ,, 15	19 [? 17][8]	235 2 17 [? 212 1 10][8]
5 ,, ,, ,, ,, 10	21	152 1 8
1 acre ,, ,, ,, 5	7	19 3 39
Under 1 acre	15[9]	
Total	119 [? 118][8]	4543 3 22

[1] Exch. Dep., 15 Eliz., East. no. 4.
[2] Exch. Dep., 5 Jas. I, Mich. no. 8.
[3] Survey, ff. 57d, 60d.   [4] *Ibid.*, ff. 13, 51.
[5] *Ibid.*, ff. 41, 58d.   [6] *Ibid.*,f. 53.
[7] Not including Stags Fell or Sargill Park.
[8] The queries are due to the uncertainty whether "the widdowe of Edward Guy" of Dale Grange was the same person as Widow Guy of Brockillcote. The queried figures are based on the assumption that they were one and the same person.
[9] Includes 13 cottages in Askrigg.

Omitting holdings of under one acre, which were actually houses or cottages without land, simple division reveals that fictitious entity, the average farm, as comprising 43 acres. The range in size of the farms was very great—from just over one acre, if such can be dignified with the name of farm, to just over 800 acres. It is some indication of large-scale farming that 45% of the land (omitting Stags Fell, Sargill Park and the cowpastures) was occupied by only six farms. The farms themselves seem to have had an appearance similar to the present day, with the garths and closes round the house and the barns in the fields. Many had turf-houses for peat and the large number of gardens is rather noteworthy. Ten houses[1] had no gardens, sixty-two had one garden each, twenty-five had two gardens each, six had three each, four had ' several,' and one house had four gardens.

In the course of the next three centuries the land and its uses do not seem to have altered much. There is a continuity in agrarian history which is too often ignored. Parts of England may have experienced an agrarian revolution, but there seems to have been nothing revolutionary in the changes which took place on enclosed pastoral manors. Changes there were, in the case of the manor of Wensleydale, both in ownership and structure. The estate changed hands and was finally divided up, in this assisting in the emergence of the twentieth-century yeoman. In the nineteenth century the cowpastures were divided and allotted among the owners of cattlegates, but this occasioned no upheaval comparable to the enclosure of open arable field manors. Similarly the "several moors, commons and waste lands" over which the tenants had rights of common were converted into stinted pasture. Some 8,000 sheep-gates were created and distributed among the holdings. Communal shepherds are still kept to look after the ' gated ' sheep on the fells. Holdings have decayed and many of the farmhouses of the survey are in ruins or have become barns or have disappeared altogether. Such changes, spread over three hundred years, are as inevitable as they are evolutionary. The fields, and with them the field-names, remain—bound, as it were for ever, within their grey stone walls.

In May 1751 Dr. Richard Pococke travelled up Wensleydale, " generally esteem'd one of the most beautiful spots in the world."

---

[1] Not counting the Askrigg cottages.

He passed through Hardrow and climbed onto the fells above Cotterdale. " The prospect from the height of Cotter," he wrote, " is the most awful and grand I ever beheld. The mountain all around . . . . and the valley beneath, which tho' it is much narrower to the west of Ascrig, yet it is still a fine vale of good pasturage, and, what is uncommon, there are houses built in most of the fields, which is an unusual prospect, and at a distance make the appearance of scatter'd villages."[1] A hundred and fifty years earlier he would have seen much the same. A century and a half later he would have seen much the same, too.

II

Seventeenth-Century Surveys of the Lordships of Middleham and Richmond.

Edited by E. W. Crossley.

(A) The Lordship of Middleham.

At the date of the Survey of 1605 the lordship of Middleham was in the hands of the Crown. It had been granted by Edward IV in 1473 to his brother Richard, duke of Gloucester, on whose accession to the throne as Richard III in 1483 it again came to the Crown,[2] and so remained until Charles I in 1628 sold it, with certain reservations, to the citizens of London.[3] The lordship covered a large area in Wensleydale, including besides Middleham most of the extensive parish of Aysgarth, the parish of West Witton, and large parts of those of Coverham and East Witton, besides detached properties at Leyburn, par. Wensley, at Scotton, par. Catterick, and Crakehall and Rands in par. of Bedale, all in Richmondshire; and in addition the manor of Kettlewell, with Scale Park, par. Kettlewell, and some lands at Cold Coniston, par. Gargrave, in the West Riding.

The canons of Coverham were already endowed with lands in Coverham, but further lands in the parish passed out of the possession of the lords of Middleham when, in Feb. 1404-5, licence was obtained by Ralph, earl of Westmorland, the then lord, to grant in mortmain three messuages called Swineside,

---

[1] Pococke, *Travels* (Camden Society, N.S., xlii), pp. 187–190.
[2] *V.C.H., Yorks., N.R.*, i, 255.   [3] *Ibid.*, i, 255.

Hindlethwaite and Arkleside in Coverdale on the south side of
the river Cover in a place called Haucreygill, a messuage, etc., in
Scrafton in Coverdale, a close called Halleflatte in Carlton, with
houses in it, and common of pasture for 60 oxen, etc., held of the
King as of the castle and honour of Richmond, to the abbot and
convent of Coverham in exchange for a moiety of the manor of
Kettlewell in Craven, except the advowson of the church, and for
a messuage and common of pasture for 24 cows and 1 bull in
Coverham, not held of the King, and appropriated to them by
royal licence.[1] Further, on the 15 Dec. 1484 the feoffees of the
King of the lordship of Middleham granted to the abbot and
convent of Coverham a vaccary called Slapegill *als.* Coverhead,
late parcel of the said lordship, in exchange for 68 ac. of arable
land and a waste containing about 8 ac. now enclosed in the
King's park, called Cotiscugh by Middleham.[2] It was by the
first of these exchanges that Kettlewell came to be included in
the lordship of Middleham.   The King also, on 24 Feb. 1405,
granted to the said Ralph Nevill, earl of Westmorland, and his
heirs free warren in all their demesne lands in Kettlewell, and
licence to impark 300 acres of land in the same town, and hold
it as a park and fortify it with a wall of stone and mortar, and
crenellate the wall and make battlements on it.[3] To this was
added, on 10 Nov. 1409, a grant of free chase in all their demesne
lands in the town of Kettlewell.[4] This park was called Scale
Park, from the long and steep ascent within it from Craven into
Coverdale.

"A manor" in Aysgarth was held by the de Burghs in the
thirteenth century.   Thomas de Burgh died in 1322.   His sister
Elizabeth, who was the wife of Alexander de Mountford, obtained
"the manor" in 1324.   It descended with the Mountford lands
until Thomas Mountford conveyed his rights in Burton, Walden
and Aysgarth to Richard, duke of Gloucester, in 1480, and they
subsequently followed the descent of Middleham.[5]   There was a

---

[1] *C.P. Rolls*, 1401–5, pp. 495, 501. Such exchanges as this were of great
advantage to the canons, who naturally preferred to have property as near
to their monastic establishments as possible.

[2] *C.P. Rolls*, 1476–85, pp. 505–6.

[3] *Charter Rolls*, v, 427.

[4] *Charter Rolls*, v, 442.

[5] *V.C.H., Yorks.,* N.R., i, 205, 316; Feet of Fines, Yorks., 17 Edw. II,
No, 86, 20 Edw. IV, No. 23.

special grave for these lands mentioned in the list of fees, and a special keeper of these lands, with which was included the Heyning.[1]

(B) The Lordship of Richmond.

In 1605 this lordship included the parishes of Bowes and Arkengarthdale; Hope in the parish of Barningham; Crackpot, and certain tenements in Healaugh, Reeth and Harkerside in the parish of Grinton. Hope, although in the parish of Barningham, was in the New Forest and, forming part of the chase of the earls of Richmond, it followed the descent of the manor of Arkengarthdale.[2] The lordship of Richmond came to the Crown in the same way as Middleham and followed it in descent until Charles I sold it to the citizens of London in 1628.[3]

The Dispute with the Tenants.

In the Observations (p. 147) it is mentioned that the tenants of the two lordships had " long tyme before the 14th of Q. Elizabeth challenged a customary estate in the nature of Copiehold.... in all theyre severall Tenementes." There is a record of the consideration by the Privy Council on 28 Jan. 1551-2 of a letter to the chancellor, with a supplication exhibited by the tenants of the manor of Middleham, which he is willed to consider, and hereafter not to suffer any part of the same manor to be granted out by lease, but to let the tenants continue therewith as they have been accustomed.[4] On 8 June 1564 the Queen wrote to the earl of Northumberland that she had heard that as steward of her seigniories and lordships of Middleham and Richmond he did not conform to the order of the Court of Exchequer for her profit. She commanded him so to do, and to order his deputies so to proceed and keep their courts as the Exchequer officers desired.[5] On Sept. 15 following the Queen again wrote to the earl that she had authorized the Lord Treasurer, Sir Ric. Sackville, under Treasurer, to survey and let the castles, parks, farms, etc., belonging to his seigniory of Middleham. She required him to order his understeward, and other officers there, to attend upon her Commis-

---

[1] *Post*, p. 144.   [2] *V.C.H., Yorks., N.R.*, i, 41.   [3] *Ibid.*, i, 17.
[4] *Acts of the Privy Council*, N.S., iii, 465.
[5] *S.P. Dom., Add.*, 1547–65, p. 551.

sioners, to keep courts, and to enter all grants that should be made.[1] On the 23rd of the same month Lord Treasurer Winchester wrote the earl that the order of the Queen's lands in Middleham, whereof he was high steward, did not proceed, because he claimed for the tenants a tenant right whereof there is no record. The Queen had written to him to order his deputies to assist such commissioners as she had sent for doing thereof. If he suffered this to be done she had given order that it should be done agreeably to justice and the tenants' satisfaction, without touching his honour and office, for his understeward should keep the courts for the commissioners and make record. If he thought this prejudicial to his honour he would declare this to Her Highness and leave the matter to her own order.[1] The earl wrote to the Lord Treasurer on the 10 Oct. acknowledging the receipt of the Queen's and his letters, and added that when time shall serve he would be most willing in these affairs. Considering, however, how importunate he had been on the tenants' behalf for the establishment of their custom, he begged him to have in remembrance what good liking it had been to them, and commodity to Her Majesty, to have such custom established he well knew by report, and how much the former Councils respected its antiquity; now he, thinking to do good service by staying the suit of a multitude of the tenants to Her Majesty, took it upon himself, which he fancied the Lord Treasurer did not like, whilst they, the tenants, thought he had not done what they expected, and have lost what they could have secured, and this might impair his credit with them. If this may not persuade, and the contrary is to be used, rather than any delay of Her Majesty's profit shall be imputed to him, he would earnestly travail thereon.[1]

There is an abstract (24 June 1565) of the Commission to the Lord Treasurer, Chancellor and Understeward of the Exchequer for letting the Queen's lands—in the seigniories of Middleham and Richmond. In these seigniories, on account of the pretended title of tenants' rights, the lands may be let for 40 years after survey, two years' rent to be paid for a gressom,[2] repairs to be done and horse and armour found by the tenant; all lands of yearly value of 40s. and under may be let by copy of court roll,

---

[1] *Ibid.*, p. 551.

[2] A variant of " Gersum," a fine paid to a feudal superior on entering upon a holding (*N.E.D.*).

by the stewards and others, in commission and in open court, with certain provisos; widows to have their estate in the lands, eldest sons the preference in leases, etc., with rates of difference between this and the former Commission.[1]

There is an undated (? 1595) abstract of a decree as to the rights of the tenants of Middleham and Richmondshire, reciting that they held by tenant right until the 30th Eliz., when they had leases of 40 years, yielding their ancient rents and services, which services were inserted in their leases, *viz.*, that every tenant should furnish an able man for the service in the north, pay two years' rent as a fine at the death of the Prince, one year's rent upon every alienation, and two upon every renewal. At the end of every lease the eldest son of every tenant then living should have a new one like the former. To settle all questions and contentions upon these clauses all leases formerly or hereafter to be granted in reversion, but on expiration or surrender only. Also that the lease should revert to the heir, and not to the executor; and that the heir should pay the fine; and that the words " eldest son " should extend to the eldest daughter, and to the next of blood, in the male or female, in default of issue of the body.[2]

In regard to the fines in this abstract, they are the same as those mentioned in the Observations as being imposed in 14 Eliz., except that the fine of two years' rent on the death of a tenant is not included.[3]

On 17 Oct. 1608 a proposition was made to the Lord Treasurer for increasing the King's revenues by composition with the tenants of Richmond and Middleham. Apparently some arrangement was attempted on these lines, as there is a reference in the Observations[4] where it is stated that those who took leases of 40 years about the 8 James I, when they renewed their leases, paid four years' old rent fine for composition. On 30 June 1609 the King's tenants of Richmond and Middleham petitioned Salisbury, praying that a time might be appointed for them to attend and amend their defective titles.[5] In 1611, however, the tenants of

[1] *S.P. Dom., Add.*, 1547–65, p. 568.
[2] *S.P. Dom.*, 1595–7, p. 155.
[3] *S.P. Dom.*, 1603–10, p. 462.
[4] *Post*, p. 147.
[5] *S.P. Dom.*, 1603–10, p. 523.

Middleham and Richmond refused to pay the composition ordered to the steward, Sir Thomas Metcalfe.[1] From this time, at present, there is less evidence available in regard to the progress of the dispute.

The claim of the tenants was that they held their estates by custom in the nature of copyhold. A similar claim had been put forward by the tenants of Wensleydale and Barnard Castle. In the case of Wensleydale the Duke of Lennox and Richmond, to whom the King had granted that manor, overthrew the tenants in a suit in the Exchequer Court; and in the case of the King's tenants in the lordship of Barnard Castle they yielded themselves without suit.[2] The tenants of Middleham and Richmond, however, in spite of their having taken leases in 14 Eliz., persisted in their claim, partly on account of certain provisions contained in them. The Crown contended that the tenants could produce no documentary evidence of a custom in the nature of copyhold before the 14 Eliz.; that the tenants could not hold both by lease and custom; that the proviso in the lease that they should attend the warden of the Marches against Scotland, with horse and man furnished for war at their own expense, ceased with the coming of King James; that the covenant to renew their leases was vacated by the purchase made by the city; and that the fines due on the Prince's death could not be claimed by the city.[2]

The Grant to the City.

The grant of Charles I to the citizens of London, dated 25 Sept., 4 Chas. (1628),[3] begins by reciting "the divers large sums of money lent to our late most deare father the Lord James—of blessed memory—and also to us after our accession to the Crown," which with reasonable interest before 3 Jan. last came to the sum of £229,897; and then the King grants his reversion in the lordships of Middleham and Richmond, the castles, lordships, manors, comots,[4] parks, lands, etc., in Richmondshire, with many excep-

---

[1] *Ibid.*, 1611–18, p. 23.

[2] *Post*, p. 148.

[3] Y.A.S., MS. 666.

[4] Commot—(1) a territorial and administrative division, not unusual in Wales; (2) Sometimes identified with a seigniory, lordship or manor (*N.E.D.*). In this instance the word seems to denote a smaller division.

tions; amongst other things excluding " out of our present grant, to us, our heirs and successors altogether reserved " all and singular forests, chases and all parks now used and filled with deer, and all knights' fees, wards, marriages and all advowsons, donations, free dispositions and rights of patronage of all rectories, churches, vicarages, chapels and other ecclesiastical benefices within the premises, and also all mines of gold and silver; also 26s. 8d. yearly from the site of the castle of Middleham granted in fee farm to Sir Henry Lindley, Kt., and John Starkey; the West park of Middleham, granted in fee farm to Thomas Crompton, esq., at £22 0s. 8d. yearly; the East park of Middleham, the park of Wanlez (£6 13s. 4d.); and all those parks in fee farm called Cottescugh (£6 13s. 4d.), Sonscugh (£10), Capelbancke (£10); the water corn mill in Aiskarth (26s. 8d.); decayed rents (23s. 4d.); all liberties and jurisdiction of chases " as far as our chase of Bishopsdale extends " in the towns of Walden, Thoralby, New-bigging, Aikesgarth and Bishopsdale; the agistment of the park of Woodhall (£4); 20s. yearly for a parcel of pasture in fee farm at Middleham; all liberties and jurisdictions of a forest as far as the New Forest extends in the lordship or manor of Arkilgarth-dale; the manor of Crakehall (£34 9s. 3d.), the mill there (£3 13s. 4d.). The total fee farm rents reserved to the King were £778 3s. 8½d. Certain enclosures new approved in the two lord-ships (£121 11s. 1¼d.) were also excepted, and a number of other items.

The Manuscript.

The MS., which is beautifully written, consists of 46 pages, measuring 14½ by 10 inches. The pagination stops at p. 36, at the end of the general abstract of both lordships. Pages [37] and [38] are filled with " Some Observacions." A table of the divisions occupies page [39]. There is a second lot of " Observations " on page [40]. Pages [41] to [46] are blank. The MS. is bound in white vellum, with gold tooling on front and back covers, and has green silk ties. It contains a copy of the original surveys of 1605, which ends at the bottom of page 36. The two sets of Observations and the table are not part of the original surveys, which appear to have been made in the interests of the Crown, which was losing heavily owing to the greatly improved value of the lands. This view is supported by the statement in the survey of Middleham that the improvement in the value of the castle and demesnes might well be raised if his Majesty, by giving satisfaction to Sir Henry Lindley, would resume the grant (p. 83). There was also the additional inducement of finally settling the long-drawn-out dispute between the Crown and its tenants.

Two questions arise—(1) When was this copy made ? and (2) For what purpose ? Firstly, it is clear from numerous references in the margin of the MS. to the exclusion of certain properties from the grant by the King to the citizens of London in 1628, that the copy must have been made subsequent to that event. Secondly, as to its object. The grant did not include the whole of the lordships of Middleham and Richmond. There were numerous exceptions—*e.g.* forests, chases and parks, advowsons, fee farm rents, etc. The management of these properties and the collection of the rents and fees would necessitate the employment of an official, to whom the copy of the surveys would be of great assistance.

THREE YORKSHIRE SURVEYS

I. The Manor of Wensleydale.

f. 1.

This is the Booke of Survey mentioned in one paire of Indentures of Lease beareing Date the seave . . . .[1] Day of January Anno Domini 1613 made betweene the right honorable Lodowicke Duke of Lenox of the one party, And Sir John Leedes knight John Colby and Henry Goodreeke Esquire for the Terme of Twentie and one yeeres from the Feast Daie of The annunciation of our Lady the virgyn next (1614) of the Seigniory Dominion Lordshippe or Mannor of Wennesladale in the Countie of Yorke.

f. 1d.

[Blank except for memoranda in a different hand of later date and partly illegible.]

. . . . which was in the late occupation of one John Kettlewell and one Edward Pratt put in his horses presently after to drive him out of possession in the sight of Christopher Lawson Thomas B . . . . Edward Metton. rente concealed and not paide.

Imprimis Elmond Pratt of Shawcoate one close late in the occupation of one Owswould Kettlewell of the rente of 12s.

Christopher . . . . of Shawcoate paid for his rent for Mr Cole and payeth but now £4 13s 4d.

James Metcalfe of the Graunge his rent 40s and should be . . . .

John Guy his rent 32s and should be 40s.

f. 2.

A Booke or Tabliture of the particular Measures of all the inclosed Lands, and Tenements, Wastes, Fells and Moores, not inclosed, lyinge on the North side of the Ryver of Yore in Wennesladale in the countie of Yorke which sometymes were the landes and possessions of the right Honourable Mathew Earle of Lenox and Dame Margaret his wife mentioned in a plott and description thereof made and described by Samuell Peirse of Maidstone in the countie of Kente with the names of all the Tennants and occupiers of the said landes and their severall Rents. Together

---

[1] MS. torn.

A

also with the Totall measures and yearely values of all the landes belonging to every one of their severall Tenements which Tenements in the plott and description thereof are distinguished one from another with the severall Letters and Characters in this book upon their names appearing. And in the descriptions of the particular parcells of ground belonginge to every Tennante are in order placed divers Nombers whereunto the corresponding Numbers in the Tables of their severall Tenements hereafter mentioned are to be referred. Drawinge alwaies therewith the Measure and yearely value of that parcell wherein the nombers are equally agreeing as followeth.

f. 2d [*blank*].

f. 3.   Coleby[1]

TENAUNTS OF DALE GRAINGE

PETER METCALFE holdeth one Tenement or Dwelling ⎫ Val'
house att a place called Bowe brigge with a stable ⎬ per ann'
and Turfe house adioyninge. Val' per annu'   ⎭   xxs.

Whereunto is also belonging 11 Parcells of Meadow ground inclosed the descriptions whereof are noted with this character Ӿ and severally contain as followeth.

	[*ac. roo. da. pt.*]	
1. The crofte between the said house and the waterffall	1 - 1 - 8 - 0	xiiijs vjd.
2. Loky Hill	2 - 1 - 3 - 0	vs. xd.
3. Corne cloase.	7 - 0 - 1 - 2	iiij^{li} xiijs xd.
4.	2 - 0 - 2 - 2	xvjs. iijd.
5. Hardrow Bancke	5 - 0 - 8 - 0	lijs.
6. Myre closes	3 - 2 - 4 - 2	xviijs.
7. The ½ parte of Brakinbar	2 - 1 - 7 - 1	vjs jd.
8. The ½ of a close adioyninge to Crosse close & Brakinbar	2 - 1 - 5 - 0	xxijs. ixd.
9. Cowes Garthe	6 - 3 - 3 - 2	v^{li} ixs. vjd.
10. Abbye Heade	4 - 3 - 4 - 0	xxxijs. iiijd.
11. Abbye Holme	6 - 2 - 7 - 0	v^{li}
The Totall Measure of these 11 parcells of ground	44 - 3 - 4 - 1	

f. 3d.

There is also belonginge to the said Tenemente 5 cattlegats & an halfe in the comon pasture called the Spen & Grainger gill val' per ann'   xxxiijs

---

[1] In a different hand.

For all which landes & cattlegats he payeth the
yeerely rente of   xxxiijs. xjd.

Summa totius valoris inde per ann'   xxvj^{ll} vs. ijd.
[£26 5s. 1d.]¹

PETER HOLME holdeth two parcells of meddow ⎫ Val' p' ann'
ground adioyning to Stodallfflatt noted with ⎬ xls viijd.
this Character W conteininge togeather ⎭
                     5 - 0 - 3 - 2

Whereunto is belonginge one Cattlegate in the ⎫ vjs.
Spen and Grainger gill ⎭

For which landes & cattlegate he paieth the ⎫ vs.
yeerely Rente of ⎭

Summa totius valor' inde per Ann'   xlvjs viijd.

f. 4.

ROGER METCALFE² holdeth one dwellinge house ⎫
with a stable & Turfehouse and gardein plott ⎬ xiijs iiijd.
adioyninge val' per Annu' ⎭

Whereunto is belonginge 7 parcells of meadow
& pasture ground inclosed, the Description
whereof are noted with this Character —³ &
severally conteine as followeth

	[ac. roo. da. pt.]	
1.	3 - 3 - 0 - 2	lvjs iiijd.
2.	5 - 1 - 9 - 0	iiij^{ll} vjs.
3. The Flashe	4 - 3 - 6 - 0	xxxijs viijd.
4. In the Buttrees	5 - 3 - 1 - 3	lvijs xd.
5.	2 - 2 - 2 - 2	xxvs víjd.
6.	2 - 1 - 9 - 0	xvjs. vjd.
7.	9 - 3 - 3 - 2	xixs viijd.

The Totall Measure of theis
7 parcells   34 - 3 - 2 - 1

There is also belonginge to the said Tenemente ⎫
4 cattlegats & ¼ in the pasture called the Spen ⎬ xxvs vjd
and Grainger gill Val' ⎭

For which landes & cattlegats hee payeth the ⎫ xxvs iiijd.
yeerely Rente of ⎭

Summa totius valor' inde per Annu'   xvj^{ll} xiijs. vd.

---

¹ The figures in square brackets are totals obtained by the addition of
each item when such additions differ from those of the Survey.

² In 1607 he was charged with forestalling (*North Riding Q.S. Records*, i, 92).

³ To effect economies in printing, the remainder of these symbols have
been omitted. As the map to which they relate is lost, their reproduction
is not necessary for an understanding of the survey.

f. 4d.

THE WIDOWE of Symon Metcalfe holdeth **3** small parcells of meadow ground adioyninge to Stodall flatt noated with this Character — containinge togeather **5 - 0 - 6 - 3** } ljs viijd

Whereunto is also belonginge one cattlegate in the Spen & Grainger Gill } vjs.

For which land & cattlegate she payeth the yeerely Rente of } vs.

Summa valor' inde per Annu' lvijs viijd

RICHARD MATTOCK holdeth one Dwelling house with a meddow croft adioyninge noated with this character — containinge togeather **1 - 3 - 1 - 3** } xvijs xd

For which he payeth the yeerely Rente of ijs vjd

Summa valoris inde per Annu' xxiiijs vjd

[*17s. 10d.*]

There is noe comon belonging to this Tenemente.

f. 5.

ABRAHAM METCALFE houldeth one dwellinge house which seemeth to have beene a parte of the Decaied scite of the capitall Messuage called Dale Grainge with one gardein & the one ½ of a meddow crofte adioyninge noted with this charectèr — containing together **1 - 0 - 3 - 2** } xxiiijs vjd cum Scitu Domus

Whereunto is also belonginge **3** other parcells of ground noated with the said character containinge together

	[*ac. roo. da. pt.*]	
1.	1 - 1 - 5 - 0	xiijs xd.
2. The Flash	8 - 1 - 6 - 0	iijli vijs iiijd.
3. The ½ of Hunshaw	3 - 0 - 5 - 0	xxs xd
The Totall Measure	13 - 3 - 9 - 2	

There is also belonginge to the said Tenemente one cattlegate & ⅙ of a gate in the pasture called the Spen and Grainger Gill } vijs

For which landes & cattlegate he paieth the yeerely Rente of } vijs jd.

Summa valor' inde per annu' vjli xiijs iiijd.

f. 5d.

THE SAIDE Abraham Metcalfe holdeth also one smalle dwellinge house called the pantry which was sometyme parte of the said Capitall Messuage called Dale grainge with 3 little garden plotts & a smale crofte noated with this Character — & are lyinge together & betweene the said house & the River of Yore Containinge **0 2 - 3 - 0** xiiijs vjd cum Scitu Domus

One Fowerth parte of a Cattlegate in the Spen & Grainger Gill xviijd.

For which he paieth the yerely Rente of xxd.

Valor inde per Annu' xvjs.

This Tenemente was lately belonginge to one James Lobley

EDWARD NELSON holdeth one dwellinge house with a Turfhouse & a garden adioyninge val' per Annu' xs.

There is also belonginge to the said Tenemente 3 parcells of meddow ground noated with this Character — containinge as followeth

f. 6.   [ac. roo. da. pt.]

1.   2 - 3 - 3 - 2   xxxviijs viijd

2. Abby Head   3 - 1   2 - 0   xxijs.

3.   2 - 1 - 2 - 2   xvs vijd.

        The totall Measure   8 - 1 - 8 - 0

There is also belonginge to the said Tenemente one Cattlegate in the Spen & Grainger gill vjs.

For which land and Cattlegate he paieth the yerely Rente of vs xd.

Summa valor' inde per Annu' iiij^ll xijs iijd.

THE WIDOWE of Edward Guy holdeth one Dwellinge house with a Turfehouse, a garden plott & a meadow Crofte adioyninge noated with this Character — & containe togeather **2 - 0 - 1 - 0** xxvijs. Cu' xs pro Scitu Domus

Whereunto is also belonginge 2 other parcells of meddow ground noted with this Character — containinge as followeth

1.   2 - 0 - 4 - 2   xxjs jd ob

2. The Burtrees   6 - 0 - 3 - 1   iiij^ll xd ob

        The Totall Measure   10 - 0 - 8 - 3

f. 6d.

There is also belonginge to this Tenemente one⎫
Cattlegate and an halfe in the Spen & in Grainger ⎬ixs
Gill val' per Ann'   ⎭

For which Tenemente and Cattlegats she paieth⎫
the yeerely rente of   ⎭ xs

Summa valor' inde per Annu'   vj^{ll} vijs xjd
                                          [*£6 8s. od.*]

JAMES PEERSON holdeth one parcell of meadow
ground with a feild house upon the   xlixs
same noted with this Character —
containinge   3 - 1 - 1 - 0

Item halfe a Cattlegate in the Spen and Grainger⎫
Gill val' per annu'   ⎭ iijs.

For all which he paieth yeerely   iijs vjd
Summa valor' inde per Annu'   lijs.

f. 7.

ROBERT METCALFE houldeth one Dwellinge house⎫
with a gardein plott a Turfehouse and a smalle ⎬ xvs ixd.
crofte adioyninge noted with this⎫   ⎧cu' xs pro
Character — containinge 0 - 2 - 3 - 0 ⎭ ⎩ Scitu Domus

Whereunto is also belonginge 2 other parcells of ground noted
with the same Character severally containinge as followeth
                             [*ac. roo. da. pt.*]
1.   1 - 1 - 8 - 2 xiiijs vijd ob
2.   5 - 0 - 1 - 2 xls iijd ob
Summa Acrar'   7 - 0 - 3 - 0

Item halfe a Cattlegate in Spen & Grainger Gill⎫
val' per Annu'   ⎭ iijs.

For all which he paieth yeerely   iijs iiijd
Summa valor' inde per Annu'   iij^{ll} xiijs viijd
                                       [*£4 3s. 8d.*]

GEORGE METCALFE holdeth one dwellinge house⎫
val' per Annu'   ⎭ vjs viijd

Whereunto are belonging 6 parcells of ground noted with this
Character — conteininge as followeth

f. 7d.   [*ac. roo. da. pt.*]

1. One Crofte with a feilde house,⎫
   2 garden plotts, a meddow strake ⎪
   extended northward to the said ⎬ 2 - 1 - 4 - 0 xxxvs vjd
   Dwellinge house   ⎭

2.   5 - 1 - 4 - 0 iiij^{ll} iijd.
3. Abby Holme   3 - 1 - 5 - 0 ls vijd ob

4. Abby Head   3 - 0 - 3 - 0   xxiiijs vijd ob

5. The ½ of a close adioyninge to ⎱
   Crosse hill   ⎰ 2 - 1 - 5 - 0   xxiijs ixd

6. The Third parte of Brakinbarr   2 - 1 - 7 - 0   vjs jd.

The Totall Measure   18 - 3 - 8 - 1

                             [*18 - 3 - 8 - 0*]

For which Tenemente and Cattlegats and an halfe ⎱
in the Spen and Grainger Gill[1]   ⎰ xvs

For which Tenemente and Cattlegats he paieth ⎱
the yeerely Rente of   ⎰ xvs.

Summa valor' inde per annu'   xij[li] ijs vjd

ANTHONY PROTT[2] houldeth 8 parcells of meddow and pasture ground noted with this Character — severally containinge as followeth

f. 8.	[*ac. roo. da. pt.*]	
1.	4 - 3 - 8 - 2	xxxixs ixd
2.	4 - 3 - 0 - 0	xxxviijs qr
3.	1 - 3 - 3 - 0	xxiiijs iiijd
4. Hardrow Banke	7 - 0 - 4 - 2	iij[li] xjs jd ob
5. Paradice	4 - 3 - 2 - 2	xlviijs jd ob
6. The third parte of Brakinbarr	2 - 1 - 7 - 1	vjs jd.
7. Adioyninge to Brakinbarr	2 - 1 - 1 - 0	xxijs ixd.
8. Grainge feilde	9 - 0 - 2 - 0	iiij[li] xs vjd
The totall measure	37 - 0 - 8 - 3	

Item 3 cattlegats and ¾ in the Spen and Grainger ⎱
Gill val' per ann'   ⎰ xxijs vjd

For all which landes and cattlegats he paieth the ⎱
yeerely Rente of   ⎰ xxijs vjd

Summa valor' inde per Ann'   xviij[li] iijs ijd qr

         ☞ Looke more in Brockellcoat
              and Shawcoate.

---

[1] There were 2¼ cattlegates.

[2] In 1613 Anthony Pratt of Shawcote was charged with making a rescusse on James Metcalfe, Deputy Bailiff of Hang West, who had distrained ten sheep of which three at least belonged to Anthony, upon an execution out of H.M. Court of the Manor of Middleham. In the same year James Guy of Shawcote and Henry Metcalfe of Forsdale were charged with breaking into a cowshed, the door of which was locked, at High Cote and driving away a cow of Anthony Pratt's. Pratt was bound to appear to present a bill of indictment of felony, but he preferred an indictment of trespass, a preference which cost him a 10s. fine (*North Riding Q.S. Records*, ii, 11–13). In 1621 Anthony was charged with an assault on James Metcalfe, constable of Bainbridge, for serving a warrant on him, and " after he had assaulted him ran awaie from him " (*Ibid.*, ii, 251).

EDMUND METCALFE or his assignes holdeth one small Dwellinge ⎫
house & 5 parcells of ground thereto belonginge noted with this ⎬
Character — & severally containe as followeth ⎭

f. 8d.   [*ac. roo. da. pt.*]

1.   1 - 0 - 6 - 0   xvs iiijd

2. The halfe of a Crofte adioyninge
    to the grainge house   1 - 0 - 3 - 2   xiiijs vjd

3.   1 - 2 - 0 - 2   xvs jd ob

4.   3 - 1 - 8 - 2   xxxiiijs vijd ob

5. The ½ of Hunshaw   3 - 0 - 5 - 0   xxs xd

The totall measure   10 - 1 - 3 - 2

Item Two Beastgates in the Spen and Grainger ⎫
Gill val' per Annu'   ⎭ xijs.

For which landes and cattlegats he paieth the ⎫
yeerely rente of   ⎭ xijs ijd.

Summa valor' inde per Annu'   v^{ll} xixs jd
                     cu' vjs viijd pro Scitu Domus

EDEN MANSFEILD holdeth one parcell of ground ⎫
called Grainge Feild noated with   ⎬ iiij^{ll} xjs xd
this Character — containinge   9 - 0 - 7 - 0 ⎭

Item one Cattlegate in the Spen and Grainger ⎫
Gill   ⎭ vjs

For which he payeth the yeerely rente of   vjs viijd

f. 9.

Summa valor' inde per Annu'   iiij^{ll} xvijs ixd.

JAMES METCALFE or his assignes holdeth one ⎫
Dwellinge house & 4 parcells of meddow ground ⎪
inclosed noated with this Character — severally ⎬
containinge as followeth   ⎭

                           [*ac. roo. da. pt.*]

1.   0 - 2 - 6 - 0   viijs viijd

2.   1 - 0 - 5 - 0   xvs.

3.   2 - 0 - 8 - 0   xxijs.

4. Parcell of the Burtrees   5 - 0 - 4 - 0   ljs

    The Totall measure   9 - 0 - 3 - 0

Item 3 cattlegats in the Spen and Grainger
Gill val' per Annu'   xviijs

For which landes & cattlegats he payeth the ⎫
yeerely Rente of   ⎭ xvijs ijd

Summa valor' inde per Annu' cu' xs pro Annuo ⎫
valor' Domus praedictae   ⎭ vj^{ll} iiijs viijd

f. 9d.

MATH: METCALFE of the Helme holdeth two medow closes noted with this Character — called the Burtrees being parcell of Dalegrainge aforesaid, the measure and value whereof are mentioned in the Table of his Tenemente & landes att the Helme $\left.\right\}$ 3^{ll} 9s 4d

THE WIDOW of Luke Thwayte hath also 2 cloases of medow ground noted with this character — beinge parcell of Dalegrainge, the measure and value whereof are mentioned in the Table of her Tenemente & landes in Skellgill

The pasture before mentioned called the Spen & Grainger Gill wherein the Tennents of Dale Grainge aforesaid have their Cattlegats containeth $\left.\right\}$ 61 - 1 - 6 - 0

f. 10. Colebyes[1]

TENAUNTS OF THE HELME

MATHEW METCALFE houldeth one dwellinge house with a Turfhouse a garden plott a smalle meddow croft adioyninge noated with this character — containinge together $\left.\right\}$ 0 - 2 - 4 2 $\left.\right\}$ xxs Cu' Scitu Domus

Whereunto are belonging 14 parcells of land noted with this character — containinge as followeth

[ac. roo. da. pt.]

1. One crofte adioyninge to the laste with a Dwellinge house scituate upon the same containing $\left.\right\}$ 1 - 1 - 1 2 xixs vjd cum Scitu Domus

2. One garden plott adioyninge to the Spen $\left.\right\}$ 0 - 0 - 4 - 2 xviijd

3.   0 - 2 - 4 - 2 vs vjd ob

4. Forest Inge   48 - 2 - 9 - 0 iiij^{ll} js ijd

5.   3 - 1 - 9 - 0 xjs vijd

6.   2 - 2 - 1 - 2 xvjs xjd.

7.   3 - 1 - 9 - 0 xxiijs ijd

8. The ½ of one parcell of ground called the Banke $\left.\right\}$ 3 - 3 - 6 - 0 xixs vjd

9. Birke Rigg   2 - 3 - 5 - 2 xiijs vd.

10. East cloases   3 - 3 - 6 - 0 xxxjs iiijd

11. Foster Hill   1 - 2 - 5 - 0 xiijs ob.

12.   2 - 3 - 0 - 0 xxijs

[1] In a different hand.

f. 10d.

The 13 & 14 parcells here followinge are the two parcells which ⎱
are parte of Dale grainge as is before mentioned ⎰

Dale	⎰ 13.	4 - 1 - 9 - 2	xxxvjs
Graunge	⎱ 14.	4 - 0 - 6 - 2	xxxiijs iiijd
The totall measure		84 - 2 - 2 - 0	

There is also belonging to the said Tenemente ⎱
14 cattlegats and an halfe in the Helme pasture ⎬ xlvjs viijd
att iijs iiijd the gate ⎰

For all which landes and cattlegats he paieth the ⎱
yeerely rente of ⎰ xlviijs vjd ob

Summa valor' inde per Annu'   xix^{li} xvs vijd.

THE WIDDOW of ——[1] Blythe Thomas Blythe[2] ⎱
& Jeffrey Blythe doe ioyntly holde one Tene- ⎮
mente, whereupon are two dwelling houses with ⎬ xxiiijs
severall Turfhouses yardes & gardens Val' per ⎮
Annu' ⎰

Whereunto are also belonging 13 parcells of ground noted with ⎱
this Character ——[1] and severally containe as followeth ⎰

f. 11.	[ac. roo. da. pt.]	
1.	1 - 0 - 3 - 2	xs xd ob
2.	0 - 3 - 7 - 2	ixs iiijd ob
3. The halfe of one parcell called ⎱ the Banke	⎰ 3 - 3 - 6 - 0	xixs vjd
4.	2 - 3 - 2 - 2	xviijs ixd
5.	2 - 2 - 5 - 0	xvijs vjd
6.	2 - 1 - 9 - 2	xixs xd ob qr
7.	4 - 1 - 0 - 0	xvijs
8.	1 - 3 - 0 - 0	xjs viijd
9.	2 - 1 - 5 - 2	xvs xjd
10.	2 - 3 - 2 - 0	xviijs viijd.
11.	1 - 3 - 1 - 0	vs xjd
12.	3 - 1 - 7 - 0	viijs vjd ob qr
13. Forse Inge	22 - 0 - 5 - 0	xxxvjs xd ob
Summa Acrar'	52 - 1 - 4 - 2	

There is also belonginge to the said Tenement 14 ⎱
Cattlegats & ¾ in the Helme pasture ⎰ xliiijs ixd.

---

[1] Blank.

[2] On Oct. 6, 1612, Thomas Blyth of Helm, John Guy of West Grange, and James Guy of Brockillcote, appeared at Richmond charged with " riotously breaking into the house of William Nicholson at Askrigg, and damaging the doors and windows of the same " (*North Riding Q.S. Records*, ii, 5).

For all which lands & Cattlegats he payeth the
yeerely rente of   xlixs ijd ob
Summa valor' inde per Annu'   xiij^{ll} xixs iiijd.

[£*13 19s. 3d.*]

f. 11d.

GANDIAN BYWELL holdeth 3 parcells of ground called Collyer Holme noated with this Character — containinge as followeth

[*ac. roo. da. pt.*]

1.		1 - 3 - 8 - 0	xvs viijd
2.	Collyer Holme	3 - 0 - 2 - 0	xs ijd
3.		1 - 2 - 3 - 0	iijs xjd
	Summa Acrar'	6 - 2 - 3 - 0	

For which he paieth the yeerely rente of   viijd
Summa valor' inde per Annu'   xxixs ixd

☞ Looke more in Skellgill

JAMES PROTTE houldeth one Dwellinge house with two gardeins adioyninge val' per ann'   xs
Whereunto are belonging & adioyninge 2 parcells of land noated with this character — containing as followeth

[*ac. roo. da. pt.*]

1.	5 - 1 - 5 - 0	xxvjs xd ob
2.	5 - 1 - 5 - 0	xxvjs xd ob
Summa Acrar'	10 - 3 - 0 - 0	

f. 12.

There is also belonging one cattlegate & ¾ in the Helme Pasture val' per Annu'   vs xd
For which Tenemente and cattlegats he paieth the yeerely rente of   vs xd
Summa valor' inde per Ann'   iij^{ll} ixs vijd

☞ Looke more in Brockillcoate

THOMAS PROTTE holdeth two parcells of ground noated with this Character — containinge as followeth

1. Birke Rigge	3 - 0 - 5 - 0	xxs xd
2. Forse Inge	2 - 1 - 0 - 0	iijs xd
Summa Acrar'	5 - 1 - 5 - 0	

Item one Cattlegate & ¾ in the Helme pasture   vs xd
For which land & cattlegats hee payeth the yeerely rente of   vs xd
Summa valor' inde per Annu'   xxxs vjd

f. 12d.

The parcell of ground called the Helme Pasture wherein all the Tenannts of the Helme have their Cattlegats as aforesaid containeth	124 - 0 - 5 - 0

f. 13. Colebyes[1]

TENAUNTS OF SKELLGILL

THE WIDDOW of Luke Thwaite holdeth one Dwellinge house lately erected with a barne a stable a Turfehouse and garden adioyning val' per Ann'	xxs
Whereunto are belonginge & adioyninge 4 parcells of meddow ground lyinge together noted with this Character — containing as followeth	

	[ac. roo. da. pt.]	
1.	5 - 3 - 8 - 0	lixs vjd
2.	4 - 1 - 9 - 2	xxixs xjd
3.	2 - 3 - 0 - 0	xiijs ixd
4.	2 - 2 - 7 - 0	xiijs iiijd ob
Summa Acraru'	15 - 3 - 4 - 2	

There is also belonginge to the said Tenemente 8 cattlegats att ijs vjd the gate in the pasture called the Coate Moore val' per Ann'	xxs
Item 2 Cattlegats in the pasture called the little Fell Meawes att xviijd the gate	iijs
For all which lands tenements & cattlegats she paieth the yeerely rente of	xijs xd
Summa valor' inde per Annu'	vij^{li} xixs vjd ob

☞ Looke more in Lidderskewe

f. 13d.

GANDIAN BYWELL holdeth one dwellinge house with a garden adioyninge noated with this Character —— val' per Ann'	xs
Whereunto are belonginge 4 parcells of ground noated with the same — Character severally containing as followeth	

	[ac. roo. da. pt.]	
1.	2 - 2 - 0 - 2	xxvs jd ob
2.	4 - 1 - 9 - 3	xxxvjs ob
3.	6 - 3 - 8 - 0	xiiijs
4.	2 - 1 - 1 - 0	xjs iiijd ob
Summa Acrar'	16 - 0 - 9 - 1	

[1] In a different hand.

There is also belonginge to the said Tenemente⎫
6 Cattlegats & ⅔ of a gate in the Coate Moore ⎬xvjs viiijd
val' per Annu'   ⎭

Item one Cattlegate & ⅔ in the little Fell Meawes ijs vjd

For all which landes and cattlegats he paieth⎫
the yeerely rente of   ⎬ xjs jd

Summa valor' inde per Annu'   iiij^{li} xvjs vjd ob
                                     [£5 *15s.* 8½*d.*]

☞ Looke more in the Helme

f. 14.

SYMON KAYGILL holdeth one Dwellinge house⎫
with a gardein, and Turfhouse adioyninge val' ⎬xvjs viiijd
per Annu'   ⎭

Whereunto are belonginge 3 parcells of land⎫
noated with this Character — conteininge as ⎬
followeth   ⎭

                              [*ac. roo. da. pt.*]
1.   4 - 0 - 5 - 0   xljs iijd
2.   8 - 2 - 8 - 0   xvijs vijd
3.   1 - 3 - 1 - 0   xxjs iiijd
        Summa Acraru'   14 - 2 - 1 - 0
                            [*14 - 2 - 4 - 0*]

There is also belonginge to the said Tenemente⎫
4 cattlegats & ¾ of a gate in the Coate Moore ⎬xjs xjd
val' per Annu'   ⎭

Item one cattlegate and a ⅓ of a gate in the⎫
little Fell Meawes   ⎬xxijd

For which Tenemente and Cattlegats he payeth⎫
the yeerely Rente of   ⎬viijs

Summa valor' inde per Annu'   v^{li} xs vijd.

f. 14d.

THE WIDDOWE of Edmond Coats holdeth one⎫
Dwellinge house with a garden & a smalle |
meddow Crofte adioyninge noated⎫   ⎬xvs
with this ———^{1} containinge ⎬0 - 2 - 1 - 0|
together   ⎭   ⎭

Whereunto is also belonginge sixe other parcells⎫
of land noated with the same ———^{1} Character⎬
severally conteininge as followeth   ⎭

                              [*ac. roo. da. pt.*]
1.   1 - 1 - 5 - 2   ixs iijd.
2.   2 - 0 - 0 - 0   xiijs iiijd
3.   3 - 3 - 7 - 2   lijs vjd
                    ^{1} Blank.

4.	5 - 1 - 5 - 0	xliijs ob
5.	1 - 2 - 6 - 0	xjs.
6.	3 - 0 - 8 - 0	xxvs viijd
Summa Acrar'	18 - 0 - 3 - 0	

There is also belonginge to the said Tenemente ⎤
11 cattlegats & ⅓ of a gate in the Coate Moore ⎬ xxviijs iiijd
val' per Annu' ⎦

Item 3 Cattlegats in the little Fell Meawes ⎤ iiijs
val' per Annu ⎦

For which Landes & Cattlegats she payeth the ⎱ xixs
yeerely Rente ⎰

f. 15.

Summa valor' inde per Annu'   x^{ll} ijs jd
     [*£10 2s. 1½d.*]

ABRAHAM PROTT holdeth one Dwellinge house ⎤
with a garden & a smalle Crofte adioyninge ⎱ xiijs iiijd
noted with this Character —[1] ⎱
conteininge togeather   0 - 1 - 3 - 0 ⎦

Whereunto is also belonginge 5 parcells of land ⎤
noated with the same Character —[1] conteininge ⎬
as followeth ⎦

       [*ac. roo. da. pt.*]

1.	2 - 1 - 6 - 0	xvjs.
2.	1 - 1 - 3 - 2	vjs viijd
3.	1 - 1 - 7 - 0	xvijs ob
4.	7 - 1 - 2 - 0	iij^{ll} xiijs
5.	2 - 0 - 2 - 0	xvjs vd
Summa Acraru'	14 - 3 - 3 - 2	

There is also belonginge to the said Tenemente ⎤
9 cattlegats & ¾ of a gate in the Coate Moore ⎬ xxiiijs iiijd
val' per Annu' ⎦

Item 2 Cattlegats in the little Fell Meawes   iijs

For which Tenemente and cattlegats hee payeth ⎱ xvs xd
the yeerely rente of ⎰

f. 15d.

Summa valor' inde per Annu'   viij^{ll} ixs ixd ob qr
     [*£8 9s. 9½d.*]

THOMAS KETTLEWELL or his assignes holdeth ⎤
one Dwellinge house with a gardein plotte ad- ⎱
ioyninge & one other gardein plott adioyninge to ⎬ xd
the Coate Moore being both noated with this Char- ⎱
acter — for which house & gardein he paieth yeerely ⎦

[1] Blank.

Valor' inde per Annu'   xs

CHRISTOPHER DINSDALE of Brockellcoate
holdeth 4 parcells of ground noated with this
Character — which are parcell of Skellgill
The measures and values whereof are mentioned
in the Table of his tenemente and lands in
Brockellcoate

f. 16.   Colebyes[1]

YORESCOTE

GEORGE METCALFE holdeth one mansion house a
Barne and a Turfehouse called by the name of
Yorescote with a yarde, a garden & a Forestall }xxiiijs
adioyninge noated with this Char-
acter — containinge togeather   0 - 3 3 - 0

Whereunto is also belonginge 10 parcells of land lying together
by the Ryver of Yore noated with this Character — severally
containinge as followeth

	[ac. roo. da. pt.]	
1.	1 - 1 - 8 - 0	
2.	3 - 1 - 5 - 0	
3.	4 - 2 - 5 - 0	
4.	2 - 3 - 2 - 2	
5.	3 - 1 - 8 - 2	xxiij^ll
6.	17 - 1 - 0 - 0	'viijs vijd
7.	3 - 0 - 0 - 0	
8.	2 - 2 - 7 - 0	
9.	3 - 1 - 2 - 0	
10.	4 - 3 - 6 - 2	
Summa Acrar'	46 - 3 - 4 - 2	

[47 - 2 7 - 2—*including the
land valued with the house*]

f. 16d.

For which Tenemente and landes hee payeth the
yeerely Rente of   xlvjs viijd

Summa valor' inde per Annu'   xxiiij^ll xiijs ijd

Memorandum there are noe Cattlegats in any of
the pastures belonginge to this Tenemente

The pasture called the Coate
Moore wherein the Tenannts of
Skellgill Brockellcoate Shawcoate
& Jeffrey Prott & Franncis Prott   458 - 0 - 5 - 0
of the Hole House have their
Cattlegats Containeth

---

[1] In a different hand.

And the pasture called little Fell ⎫
Meawes wherein the said Tenannts │
of Skellgill Brockellcoate Shawcoate ⎬
& Jeffrey & Franncis Prott have │
their Cattlegats containeth[1] ⎭

f. 17.   Colebyes[2]

TENAUNTS OF BROCKILLCOATE

MICHAELL PROTT holdeth one Dwellinge house ⎫
with a gardein, and Turfehouse adioyninge ⎬ xs
Val' per Annu' ⎭

Whereunto are belonginge 8 parcells of meadow ⎫
ground noted with this character — severally ⎬
containinge as followeth ⎭

	[ac. roo. da. pt.]	
1.	2 - 0 - 0 - 0	xxs
2.	2 - 0 - 6 - 0	xxjs vjd
3.	4 - 3 - 7 - 2	xxxijs xjd
4.	3 - 2 - 4 - 0	xxxvjs
5.	5 - 2 - 4 - 2	xxxvijs vd

6. ⎫   ⎧ 5 - 1 - 6 - 0   xxxvjs
7. ⎬ Ingleby Leazes   ⎨ 3 - 0 - 8 - 2   xxjs vd
8. ⎭   ⎩ 2 - 2 - 0 - 0   xvjs viijd

The said Michaell Prott holdeth also one Dwel- ⎫
linge house with a yarde & garden adioyninge │ xs
in Shawcoate noated with this Character — ⎬
val' per Annu' ⎭

Whereunto is also belonginge 9 ⎫
parcells of ground in Shawcoate │
noted with the same Character — ⎬ 5 - 0 - 0 - 0   xvjs viijd
contayninge ⎭

f. 17d.

The Totall Measure of theis 9 ⎫
parcells of ground before men- ⎬ 34 1 - 1 - 2
tioned ⎭ [34 - 1 - 6 - 2]

There is also belonginge to the said Tenemente ⎫
in Brockillcoate and to the 5 first parcells of │
ground before mentioned 11 Cattlegats & ¾ of a ⎬ xxixs iiijd
gate in the Coate Moore val' per Annu' ⎭

Item 2 Cattlegats & ¾ in the Little Fell Meawes ⎫
val' per Annu' ⎬ iiijs ijd

For which two Tenements and Cattlegate he ⎫
payeth the yeerely Rente of ⎬ xxxvs viijd

[1] No area given here: it was 64 acres.
[2] In a different hand.

Whereof the yeerely rente of xiijs ⎫
iiijd is payable for the 3 parcells ⎪
of ground before mentioned called ⎰
Ingleby Leazes   ⎱
and iijs iiijd is payable for the ⎪
parcell of ground lying in Shawcoate ⎭

Whereunto are belonginge noe comon of pasture ⎫
in the Coate Moore or little Fell Meawes as to ⎪
the Tenements & the rest of the landes in Brockell- ⎰
coate   ⎭

f. 18.

Memorandum that one parcell of ground called ⎫
Cogill cloase lying at a place called Cogill Noted ⎪
with this Character — att the East ende of the ⎪
Out Moore containing   2 - 2 - 9 - 0 ⎪
being parte of the Tenemente and rente afore- ⎪
said was promised to Richard Allen of Bainbrigge ⎰
Togeather with the rest of the Lande at Cogill in ⎱
the occupation of Mathew Metcalfe of the Holme ⎪
noated with this Character — containing ⎪
                                  5 - 0 - 1 - 0 ⎪
which is not mentioned in the Table of his ⎪
Tenemente & lands att Holme ⎭

Summa Valor' terrarum et
Tentoriorum praedictorum   xiiij^ll xijs jd

JENKIN INGRAM holdeth one Dwelling house ⎫
with a gardein plott noated with this Character ⎬xs
— val' per Ann' ⎭

Whereunto is also belonging 2 parcells of meadow ⎫
ground with the same Character — conteininge ⎬
as followeth ⎭

                              [ac. roo. da. pt.]
1.   1 - 1 - 8 - 0   ixs viijd
2.   4 - 3 - 2 - 0   xlviijs

f. 18d.
        Summa Acrar'   6 - 1 - 0 - 0
There is also belonginge to the said Tenemente ⎫
9 Cattlegats in the comon pasture called the ⎬xxijs vjd
Coate Moore   val' per Annu' ⎭
Item 2 Cattlegats & ¼ of a gate in the little Fell ⎱
Meawes   ⎰iijs iiijd
For which landes and cattlegats he paieth the ⎱
yeerely rente of   ⎰xvs
Summa valor' per Annu'   iiij^ll xiijs vjd

B

FRANCIS PROTT holdeth 2 parcells of meddow ⎫
ground noated with this Character — conteininge ⎬
as followeth   ⎭

                                    [*ac. roo. da. pt.*]
1. parte of Huntgill Inge   2 - 3 - 2 - 2   xxvijs xd ob
2.   3 - 0 - 6 - 0   xxxjs vjd
           Summa Acrar'   5 - 3 - 8 - 2

Whereunto is belonging 2 cattlegats in the coate ⎫
Moore and a ½ of a Cattlegate in little Fell Meawes ⎬ vs ixd
val' per Annu'   ⎭

f. 19.

For which lande & Cattlegats he paieth the ⎱
yeerely rente of   ⎰ iijs iiijd

Summa valor' inde per annu'   iij^ll vs jd ob

           ☞ Looke for more in Shawcoate
                  and the Hole house.

EDMOND PROTT holdeth one mansion house ⎫ xliijs iiijd cum
with a gardein plott & 3 small Crofts adioyn- ⎰ xiijs iiijd pro
inge noated with this character ⎱   ⎰ Scit' Dom'
— containing together   ⎰ 2 - 3 - 5 - 0 ⎭

Whereunto are also belonginge 8 other parcells ⎫
of ground noated with the same Character — ⎬
conteininge as followeth   ⎭

                                    [*ac. roo. da. pt.*]
2.   3 - 1 - 6 - 0   xxxiiijs
3.   2 - 1 - 2 - 0   xxiijs
4.   4 - 1 - 1 - 0   xxxiiijs ijd ob
5.   6 - 2 - 0 - 0   iij^ll vs
6.   2 - 3 - 0 - 2   xviijs vd
7.   1 - 1 - 8 - 0   vijs iijd
8.   2 - 2 - 6 - 0   xxjs iijd
9.¹
           Summa Acrar'   28 - 2 - 6 - 2
                                    [*26 - 0 - 8 - 2*]
f. 19d.

There is also belonginge to the said Tenemente ⎫
14 Cattlegats & ⅛ of a gate in the Coate Moore ⎬ xxxvs iiijd
val' per Annu'   ⎭

Item 3 Cattlegats and ⅔ of a gate in little Fell ⎱
Meawes   ⎰ vs vjd

           ¹ No area or value given.

For all which landes and Cattlegats he paieth the yeerely rente of } xxiiijs vjd

Summa totius valor' inde per Annu'   xv^ll vjs vjd ob
[£15 os. 7½d.]

CHRISTOPHER DINSDALE holdeth one Dwellinge house with a gardein thereto belonging: val' per Ann' } xs

Whereunto is also belonginge 9 parcells of ground noated with this Character — whereof the 4 last parcels numbred 6–7–8–9 are lying in Skellgill as is before mentioned the severall measures of which 9 parcells hereafter followeth }

	[ac. roo. da. pt.]	
1.	2 - 2 - 2 - 0	xxs vd
2.	3 - 0 - 7 - 0	xxvs vd ob
3.	2 - 1 - 6 - 2	xxiijs xd ob
4.	1 - 0 - 3 - 0	vijs ijd
5.	3 - 3 - 8 - 0	xxxixs vjd

f. 20.

6.		1 - 0 - 6 - 0	vs ixd
7.		4 - 3 - 5 - 2	xxxijs vijd
8.	In Skellgill	2 - 3 - 8 - 2	xixs ixd
9.		2 - 2 - 2 - 0	xs ijd
	Summa Acraru'	24 - 2 - 8 - 2	

There is also belonginge to the said Tenemente & lands 9 Cattlegats in the Coate Moore val' per Annu' } xxijs vjd

Item 2 Cattlegats and ¼ in little Fell Meawes   iijs iiijd

For which landes and cattlegats he paieth the yeerely rente of } xvs

Summa valor' inde per Annu'   xj^ll vjd

JAMES BLAYDES holdeth one Dwellinge house with a garden adioyninge noated with this Character — val' per Annu' } xs

Whereunto is belonginge one parcell of ground called noble Farme noted with the same Character — conteininge } 4 - 3 - 4 - 0   xlvijs vijd

f. 20d.

There is also belonginge to the said Tenemente 2 cattlegats in the Coate Moore & ½ of a cattlegate in the little Fell Meawes val' per Annu' } vs ixd

For which Tenemente and cattlegats hee paieth ⎱
the yeerely rente of   ⎰ iijs iiijd
Summa valor' inde per Annu'   iij^ll iijs iiijd

EDMUND METCALFE or his assignes holdeth one ⎫
Dwellinge house with a garden adioyninge & two ⎪
other gardeins severally remote from the same ⎱ xvjs viijd
noted with this character — val' per Annu'   ⎭
Whereunto is also belonginge 3 parcells of meadow ⎫
ground noated with the same Character — con- ⎬
taininge as followeth   ⎭

	[*ac. roo. da. pt.*]	
1.	2 - 3 - 9 - 0	xxixs ixd
2.	3 - 3 - 1 - 2	xxxvijs xd ob
3. Huntgill Inge	5 - 2 - 8 - 0	iij^ll xvjs
Summa Acrar'	12 - 1 - 8 - 2	

f. 21.

There is also belonginge to the said Tenemente ⎱
8 cattlegats in the Coate Moore   val' per Annu' ⎰ xxs
Item 2 cattlegats in little Fell Meawes   iijs
For which lands & cattlegats he paieth the ⎱
yeerely rente of   ⎰ xiijs iiijd.
Summa valor' inde per Annu'   ix^ll iijs iijd ob

ANTHONY PROTT holdeth one Dwellinge house ⎱
with a garden   val' per Annu'   ⎰ xs
Whereunto is also belonginge 3 parcells of ground ⎫
noated with this Character — containinge as ⎬
followeth   ⎭

	[*ac. roo. da. pt.*]	
1.	2 - 2 - 7 - 2	xxjs vjd ob
2.	2 - 1 - 6 - 0	xxiiijs
3.	2 - 3 - 7 - 2	xixs vijd
Summa Acrar'	8 - 0 - 1 - 0	

There is also belonginge to this Tenemente 5 ⎱
cattlegats & an halfe in the Coate Moore   ⎰ xiijs ixd

f. 21d.

Item one Cattlegate & ¾ in the little Fell Meawes ijs vijd
Summa valor' inde per Annu'   iiij^ll xjs vd ob
For which Tenemente and cattlegats hee paieth ⎱
the yeerely rente of   ⎰ ixs ijd

☞ Looke moore in the Grainge
and in Shawcoate.

WIDDOW GUY houldeth one Dwellinge house with
a gardein adioyninge noated with this Charecter }xs
— Valo' per Annu'

Whereunto is belonginge 4 parcells of ground
noated with this same Character — containinge
as followeth

	[ac. roo. da. pt.]	
1.	0 - 1 - 7 - 2	iijs vd ob
2.	3 - 2 - 8 - 0	xxxvijs
3.	3 - 2 - 3 - 0	xxxvs ixd
4.	5 - 1 - 4 - 2	liijs vijd ob
Summa Acrar'	13 - 0 - 3 - 0	

f. 22.

There is also belonginge to the said Tenemente
7 cattlegats in the Coate Moore val' per Annu' }xvijs vjd

Item one cattlegate and ¾ in little Fell Meawes ijs vijd ob

For which Tenemente and cattlegats she paieth
the yeerely rente of }xjs viijd

Summa valor' inde per Annu'   vij^{li} xixs xjd ob

Querie whether this widow Guy and the
widow Guy of Dale grainge be all one }

THE WIDDOW of Gregorie Prott holdeth one
Dwelling house with a gardein adioyninge noted }vjs viijd
with this Character — val' per Annu'

Whereunto is also belonginge 2 parcells of ground noated with
the same Character whereof the parcell nombred 2 is parte of
Shawcoate severally conteinynge as followeth

	[ac. roo. da. pt.]	
1.	3 - 0 0 - 0	xxxs
2. In Shawcoate	3 - 2 - 9 - 0	xviijs vijd ob
Summa Acrar'	6 - 2 - 9 - 0	

f. 22d.

There is also belonginge to the said Tenemente 6
cattlegats in the Coate Moore val' per Annu' }xvs

Item one cattlegate and ½ in little Fell Meawes ijs iijd

For which Tenemente and cattlegats she payeth
the yeerely rente of }ixs viijd

Summa valor' inde per Annu'   iij^{li} xijs vjd ob

JAMES PROTTE holdeth one Dwellinge house with
a stable a Turfhouse a garden & a Crofte adioyninge with 3 other garden plotts severally remote }xxxs
from the same noated with this Character —
Val' per Annu'

Whereunto is also belonginge 5 parcells of land ⎫
noated with this Character — containing as ⎬
followeth ⎭

	[ac. roo. da. pt.]	
1.	0 - 1 - 9 - 0	iijs xd ob
2.	3 - 1 - 9 - 0	xxxiiijs ixd
3. New cloases	5 - 3 - 4 - 0	lviijs vjd
4. Harte Haw	6 - 3 - 6 - 0	lvs iijd
5.	2 - 3 - 8 - 2	xxiijs ixd
Summa Acraru'	19 - 2 - 6 - 2	

f. 23.

There is also belonginge to this Tenemente 9 ⎫
cattlegats & ¾ of a gate in the Coate Moare val' ⎬ xxiiijs iiijd
per Ann' ⎭

Item 2 cattlegats & ¼ in little Fell Meawes   iijs iiijd

For which Tenemente & cattlegats he paieth ⎫
the yeerely rente of ⎰ xvs xd

Summa valor' inde per Annu'   xj^{li} xiijs ixd ob

☞ Looke more in the Helme

JOHN PROTTE thelder of Shawcoate hath 2 Cloases ⎫
of meddow noated with this character — being ⎪
parcell of Brockellcoat the measure and values ⎬
whereof are mentioned in the Table of his Tene- ⎪
mente and landes in Shawcoate ⎭

f. 23d.   Colebyes[1]

TENAUNTS OF SHAWCOATE
and the Hole Houses

CHRISTOPHER PROTTE holdeth one Dwellinge ⎫
house with 2 gardeins adioyninge in Shawcoate ⎬ xiijs iiijd
val' per Annu' ⎭

Whereunto is belonginge 3 parcells of ground lying togeather
adioyninge to the said Tenemente noated with this Character —
containinge as followeth

	[ac. roo. da. pt.]	
1.	1 - 3 - 5 - 0	xviijs ixd
2.	1 - 3 - 7 - 0	xijs xd
3.	1 - 3 - 4 - 2	xviijs vijd ob
Summa Acraru'	5 - 2 - 6 - 2	

There is also belonginge to the said Tenemente ⎫
6 Cattlegats in the Coate Moare val' per Annu' ⎰ xvs

Item one cattlegate and an halfe in little Fell ⎫
Meawes val' per Annu' ⎰ ijs iiijd

---

[1] In a different hand.

For which Tenemente lands and cattlegats he ⎱
payeth the yeerely rente of ⎰ xs
Summa valor' inde per Annu' iiij^{li} ixd ob

f. 24.

JOHN PROTTE the elder holdeth one Dwellinge ⎫
house with a yarde and gardein adioyninge ⎬ xs
noated with this Character — val' per Annu' ⎭

Whereunto are belonginge 8 parcells of land noated with this
Character — whereof the first and second parcells are parte of
Brockillcoate containinge as followeth

		[ac. roo. da. pt.]	
1. ⎱ In Brockellcoate		⎰ 0 - 2 - 3 - 0	ijs xd ob
2. ⎰		⎱ 1 - 1 - 3 - 0	xs viijd ob
3. Grainger Inge		10 - 1 - 1 - 0	xvijs ijd
4.		3 - 3 - 9 - 0	xiijs iiijd
5.		1 - 3 - 8 - 2	xvs ixd
6.		8 - 0 - 2 - 0	xxvjs ixd
7.		3 - 2 - 7 - 2	xxxvjs xd ob
8.		1 - 3 - 0 - 0	xvijs vjd
	Summa Acrar'	31 - 2 - 4 - 0	

There is also belonging to the said Tenemente ⎱
14 cattlegats in the Coate Moore val' per Annu' ⎰ xxxvs
Item 3 cattlegats and ½ in little Fell Meawes vs iijd
For which Tenemente landes & Cattlegats he ⎱
paieth the yeerely rente of ⎰ xxxiijs iiijd

f. 24d.

Of which 33s 4d vjs viijd is yeerely payable for ⎫
the third parcell above mentioned & iijs iiijd is ⎮
yeerely paieable for the parcell nombred 4., and ⎬
there is no cattlegats belonginge to either of the ⎮
two parcells ⎭
Summa totius valor' inde per Annu' ix^{li} xjs ob

ANTHONY PROTTE of Brockillcoate holdeth one ⎫
parcell of land noted with this ⎬ xxxvs iiijd
character — containing ⎰ 3 - 2 - 1 - 2 ⎭

Whereunto is belonginge 4 cattlegats in the Coate ⎫
Moore & one cattlegate in little Fell Meawes ⎬ xjs vjd
Val' per Annu' ⎭

For which land and cattlegats he paieth the ⎱
yeerely Rente of ⎰ vjs viijd
Summa valor' inde per Annu' xlvjs xd

☞ Looke more in Brockellcoate
& in Dale Grainge.

f. 25.

Colebyes[1]   Holehouses[1]

JOHN PROTTE the younger holdeth one Dwellinge }
house with a gardein adioyninge   val' per Annu' } vjs viijd

JEFFREY PROTTE of the Hole houses houldeth }
one Dwellinge house with a Turfehouse a gardein
& a crofte adioyninge noated with }
this Character — conteininge } 0 - 3 - 0 - 0 } xxiiijs
together

Whereunto is also belonginge 6 parcells of ground }
noated with the same Character — containinge as }
followeth

	[ac. roo. da. pt.]	
1.	6 - 2 - 9 - 0	xliijs jd
2.	1 - 2 - 4 - 2	xvjs jd ob
3.	3 - 3 - 7 - 2	xxxixs iiijd ob
4.	3 - 0 - 2 - 0	xxxs vjd
5. In little Cow Close	7 - 0 - 1 - 2	xlvjs xjd
6. In the upper Camshouse slight	5 - 0 - 7 - 2	xxvs xjd
Summa Acrar'	28 - 0 - 2 - 0	
	[28 - 1 - 2 - 0]	

There is also belonging to the said Tememente }
12 cattlegats in the Coate Moore   val' per Annu' } xxxs
Item 3 cattlegats in the little Fell Meawes   iiijs vjd

f. 25d.

For all which landes, and cattlegats hee paieth }
the yeerely Rente of } xxs

Summa valor' inde per Annu'   xiij[11] vjd
                                          [£13 os. 5d.]

FRANCIS PROTTE of the Holehouses holdeth one }
Dwellinge house with a stable, & a Turfehouse } xiijs iiijd
adioyninge   val' per Annu' }

Whereunto is belonginge 6 parcells of ground }
noated with this Character — severally con- }
taininge as followeth

	[ac. roo. da. pt.]	
1.	2 - 0 - 1 - 0	xxs iiijd
2.	1 - 2 - 3 - 0	xs vjd
3. In little Cow cloase	7 - 0 - 1 - 2	xlvjs xjd
4.	3 - 1 - 1 - 0	xxxiijs ixd
5.	2 - 0 - 5 - 2	xiiijs iiijd
6.	3 - 3 - 7 - 2	xxijs vjd
Summa Acraru'	19 - 2 - 9 - 2	
	[19 - 3 - 9 - 2]	

[1] In a different hand,

There is also belonginge to the said Tenemente ⎱
14 cattlegats in the Coate Moore   val' per Ann' ⎰ xxxvs

f. 26.

Item 3 cattlegats & ½ in little Fell Meawes   vs iiijd

The said Francis Prott houldeth also one Dwel- ⎫
linge house in Shawcoat with 2 gardein plotts ⎬
adioyninge noated with this Character — val' ⎩ xiijs iiijd
per Annu'

For which Two Tenements, lands & cattlegats ⎱
he payeth the Yeerely rente of   ⎰ xxiijs iiijd

Summa valor' inde per Ann'   xj^li vs jd
                                          [£10 15s. 1d.]

☞   Looke more in Brockellcoate

Coles[1]

JOHN PROTTE of the Holehouses holdeth one ⎫
Dwelling house with a Turfhouse a yard and a ⎬ xiijs iiijd
gardein adioyninge noted with this Character — ⎭
Val' per Annu'

Whereunto are belonginge 3 parcells of ground ⎫
noated with the same Character — continginge ⎬
as followeth   ⎭

                            [ac. roo. da. pt.]
1.   1 - 1 - 9 - 0   xiiijs ixd
2.   3 3 - 3 - 2   xixs ijd
3. In the little Cow Cloase 7 - 0 - 1 - 2   xlvjs xjd

f. 26d.
         Summa Acrar'   12 - 1 - 4 - 0

For which Tenemente and landes he paieth the ⎱
yeerely rente of   ⎰ vjs viijd

Summa valor' inde per Annu'   iiij^li xiiijs ijd

Memorandum, there are noe Cattlegats belonging ⎫
to this Tenemente in the Coate Moore, nor in ⎬
little Fell Meawes.   ⎭

All those Tennannts in this Booke mentioned here before is Mr
Colbies Lande Excepte one Tennemente Lyinge in the Hole
housse of John Pratte.

There is more Belonginge to him Sargell Parke which you shall
finde in the hinder End of the booke and thre thowsand acres
of Common

And for the Rentall as yeete I Cannot gett[2]

---

[1] In a different hand.
[2] ' All those . . . . gett ' in a different hand

f. 27.

There belongeth unto the Feremes of Edward Pratt & James
Pratt of the Holehouses 14 Catle Gates in the Litle Cow Close
a Ground belonging to thei .r¹ of Sr Robert Binloss which have
not bine inioyed by my tenannts aboute 12 yeres²

[f. 27d *blank*.]

f. 28.   Coles²

TENAUNTS OF CAMSHOUSE
als Cannon house

RICHARD KETTLEWELL holdeth one Dwellinge
house with a Turfhouse, a yard a garden and two
small parocks adioyninge noated   xxs
with this Character — conteining 0 - 1 - 9 - 0
together

Whereunto is also belonging 8 parcells of land noated with the
same Character — containinge as followeth

	[ac. roo. da. pt.]	
1.	0 - 2 - 0 - 2	vjs xd.
2.	3 - 2 - 4 - 0	xxxvjs
3.	7 - 1 - 2 - 0	iiijˡˡ vijs vjd
4.	4 - 0 - 4 - 0	xljs
5.	4 - 2 - 9 - 2	iijˡˡ iijs ijd
6.	2 - 3 - 9 - 2	xxiijs xd.
7.	4 - 0 - 0 - 0	xxxijs
8. { In the upper Camshouse Slights ⅞ parte thereof }	36 - 1 - 2 - 2	ixˡˡ js vijd
Summa Acraru'	64 - 0 - 1 - 0	

For which Tenemente and lands with his cattlegats hereafter mentioned he payeth the yeerely   xxvs.
Rente of

Summa valor' inde per Annu   xxiiijˡˡ xvjs iiijd ob
[*£24 16s. 6½d.*
including cattlegates]

f. 28d.

JAMES KETTLEWELL AND OSWOLDE KETTLEWELL
Doe ioyntly occupie one Dwellinge house with a
Crofte adioyninge noted with this   xxs
Character — containinge 0 - 3 - 1 - 0

Whereunto is belonginge 5 parcells of ground noted with the
same Character — whereof the 4th parcell is parte of Shawcoate
& severally containe as followeth

---

¹ ' the heir ' ?   ² In a different hand.

[ac. roo. da. pt.]

1.	7 - 2 - 2 - 0	iij[ll] xvs vjd
2.	4 - 2 - 4 - 0	xxxvjs xd
3.	3 - 2 - 7 - 0	xxixs vd ob
4. In Shawcoate	1 - 3 - 3 - 0	xijs ijd
5. The lower Camshouse⎫ Slights ⎭	32 - 2 - 8 - 0	ix[ll] xvjs iijd
Summa Acraru'	51 - 0 - 5 - 0	

For the Moity of which Tenemente & lands the⎫
said James Kettlewell paieth the yeerely rente of⎭ xiiijs ijd

f. 29.

And the said Oswald Kettlewell payeth yeerely⎫
for the other Moity   ⎭ xiiijs iiijd

The totall yeerely value of which Tenemente &⎫
landes with the Cattlegats hereafter mentioned⎭ xviij[ll] xvjs vijd

THE WIDDOWE of Richard Nelson holdeth one⎫
Mansion house with a Turfehouse a yarde a ⎪
gardein & a small crofte adioyninge⎫   ⎬ xls
noted with this Character — con- ⎬0 - 2 - 5 - 0⎪
taininge togeether   ⎭   ⎭

Whereunto is belonging 12 parcells of land noted with the same
Character — containinge as followeth

[ac. roo. da. pt.]

1.	3 - 1 - 8 - 0	ljs ixd
2.	3 - 1 - 9 - 0	xlvjs iiijd
3.	3 - 1 - 3 - 0	xxvjs vjd ob
4.	4 - 3 - 0 - 0	xlvijs vjd
5.	2 - 2 - 2 - 0	xxs iiijd ob
6.	1 - 3 - 0 - 0	xiiijs
f. 29d.		
7.	1 - 3 - 2 - 0	xviijs iijd ob
8.	2 - 0 - 2 - 0	vjs vd
9.	1 - 3 - 6 - 0	xvs iiijd ob
10. ⅔ parte of the little Cow Cloase 31	2 - 7 - 0	x[ll] xjs ijd
11.	10 1 - 6 - 0	xxxiiijs viijd
12. ¼ of Camshouse pasture	19 - 0 - 2 - 2	xlvijs viijd
Summa Acraru'	87 - 1 - 3 - 0	
	[86 - 3 - 3 - 0]	

For which Tenemente & landes with her Cattle-⎫
gats heereafter mentioned she paieth the yeerely⎬ xlviijs iiijd
Rente of   ⎭

Summa valor' inde per Annu'   xxix[ll] xjs ob
                                      [£29 10s. 11½d.]

James Guye holdeth one Dwellinge house with a ⎫
Turfehouse & garden adioyninge noated with ⎬ xvjs
this Character — Val' per Annu' ⎭

Whereunto is belonging 5 parcells of land noted with the same
Character —

	[ac. roo. da. pt.]	
1.	4 - 1 - 9 - 0	xxxvs xd ob
2.	6 - 2 - 9 - 0	liijs xd ob
f. 30.		
3.	7 - 1 - 5 - 0	iiij^{ll} xviijs iiijd
4.	3 - 1 - 8 - 0	xxxiiijs vjd
5. ¾ of Camshouse pasture	57 - 0 - 8 - 0	vij^{ll} iijs
Summa Acrar'	79 - 0 - 9 - 0	

For which Tenemente and lands he paieth the ⎫
yeerely Rente of   ⎬ xxxviijs iiijd
Summa valor' inde per Annu'   xix^{ll} ixs vd ob

There is also belonginge to the ⎫
said Tennants of Camshouse one ⎪
pasture lyinge on the West side of ⎰ 52 - 0 - 9 - 0
the little Fell Meawes Containinge ⎱

Wherein the Tennants of Camshouse ⎫
aforesaid have theis cattlegats   ⎬
hereunder mentioned   ⎭

Richard Kettlewell	3 & ¾	iiijs vijd ob
James Kettlewell	2 & ⅛ parte ⎫	
	of a gate ⎬ vjs iiijd ob	
Oswold Kettlewell	2 & ⅛ parte ⎭	
The widdow of Richard Nellson	7 & ¼	xs xd ob
James Guy	5 & ¾	vijs xd ob

f. 30d.

Tenaunts of Lidderskew.

John Todd holdeth one Dwellinge house with a ⎱
garden plott adioyninge val' per Annu' ⎰ xs

Whereunto are belonging 5 parcells of ground ⎫
noated with this Character — containing as ⎬
followeth   ⎭

	[ac. roo. da. pt.]	
1.	2 - 1 - 8 - 0	xxiiijs vjd
2.	3 - 0 - 8 - 0	xs viijd
3.	2 - 1 - 5 - 0	ixs vjd
4. One quarter of Lidderskew	⎱	
Slighte containinge	⎰ 14 - 0 - 8 - 2	xxjs iiijd
5.	3 - 2 - 7 - 2	xiiijs viijd
Summa Acraru'	25 - 3 - 7 - 0	

For which Tenemente and lands he payeth the } viijs iiijd
yeerely Rente of

Summa valor' inde per Annu' iiij^{li} xixs
[*£4 10s. 8d.*]

JAMES TODD holdeth one dwellinge house with } xs
a garden plott adioyninge val' per Annu'

f. 31.

Whereunto are belonging 6 parcells of ground }
noated with this Character — containinge as }
followeth

[*ac. roo. da. pt.*]

1.	1 - 3 - 2 - 0	xijs
2.	1 - 1 - 1 - 2	vjs vd
3.	0 - 2 - 2 - 2	xxijd ob
4.	2 - 3 - 2 - 2	vijs
5.	3 - 2 - 1 - 0	xiiijs jd ob

6. One eight part of Lidder-Skew }
    Slights } 7 - 0 - 4 - 1 xs viijd

    Summa Acrar' 17 - 0 - 3 - 3

For which Tenemente and landes he paieth the } viijs iiijd
yeerely Rente of

Summa valor' inde per Annu' iiij^{li} xs vd
[*£3 2s. 1d.*]

GEORGE TODD holdeth one Dwellinge house with }
a garden and Crofte adioyninge noated with this } iijs iiijd
Character — conteininge togeather 0 - 2 - 0 - 0 }

Whereunto is also belonging 7 parcells of ground }
noated with the same Character severally con- }
taininge as followeth

f. 31d.

[*ac. roo. da. pt.*]

1. } 1. }	1 - 0 - 9 - 0 1 - 1 - 9 - 0	iiijs xd xiijs viijd
2.	0 - 2 - 1 - 0	iiijs viijd
3.	3 - 3 - 0 - 0	ixs vd
4.	4 - 0 - 0 - 0	xvjs
5. One halfe of Lidderskew Slights	28 - 1 - 7 - 1	xlijs viijd
6.	5 - 0 - 7 0	xxvs xd

    Summa Acrar' 45 - 1 - 0 - 3
    [*45 - 0 - 3 - 1*]

For which Tenemente & lands he paieth the } xvjs viijd
yeerely Rente of

Summa valoris inde per Annu' vij^{li} vijs jd
[*£6 0s. 5d.*]

RICHARD BESSON and his assignes hold one⎤
Dwellinge house with 2 garden plotts & a Croft ⎟
adioyninge noated with this Character — & also ⎟ xls cu' xiijs iiijd
one other gardein remote from the same noted ⎰ pro scit' Dom'
by like Character — containinge ⎱
togeather   2 - 1 - 5 - 3 ⎦

Whereunto is also belonging 11 parcells of Land⎤
noated with the same Character — severally ⎬
containinge as followeth ⎦

f. 32.	[ac. roo. da. pt.]	
1.	0 - 1 - 2 - 1	iijs
2.	3 - 0 - 8 - 0	viijs
3.	2 - 1 - 5 - 0	ixs vjd
4.	1 - 3 - 1 - 2	xvijs xd
5.	2 - 3 - 9 - 0	xxixs ixd
6.	3 - 1 - 3 - 0	xxxiijs iiijd
7.	3 - 3 - 7 - 2	xxxixs iiijd
8.	7 - 1 - 7 - 0	xviijs vijd
9.	9 - 2 - 5 - 0	iij^{11} iijs ijd
10.	4 - 2 - 6 - 3	xxxvijs ijd
11.	29 - 0 - 3 - 1	xxixs jd
Summa Acraru'	70 - 2 - 4 - 0	
	[71 - 0 - 4 - 0]	

For which Tenemente and lands is paid the⎤
yeerely Rente of   ⎰ xxvs

Summa valor' inde per Annu'   xvj^{11} ixs viijd
                           [£17 2s. 0d.]

MATHEW THWAITE holdeth one Dwellinge house⎤
with a yarde & garden adioyninge val' per Annu' ⎰ xiijs iiijd

Whereunto is also belonging 9 parcells of land noated with this
Character — the severall Measures whereof hereafter follow

f. 32d.	[ac. roo. da. pt.]	
1.	15 - 1 - 3 - 1	xxvs vjd
2.	1 - 1 - 3 - 0	iiijs vd
3.	3 - 1 - 7 - 0	xiijs viijd
4.	5 - 1 - 1 - 3	xxjs ijd
5.	0 - 1 - 5 - 0	xviijd
6.	7 - 0 - 7 - 0	xviijs
7.	1 - 0 - 4 - 0	viijs viijd
8.	0 - 3 - 8 - 2	vijs xd
9.	6 - 2 - 5 - 2	xxxiijs ijd
Summa Acraru'	41 - 2 - 5 - 0	

For which Tenemente & landes he paieth the } xiijs iiijd
yeerely Rente of

Summa Valor' inde per Ann' vij^{ll} vijs iijd

JOHN PROTTE holdeth one Dwelling house with a } xvjs viijd
garden plott & Turfehouse adioyninge noated
with this Character — val' per Annu'

Whereunto is belonging 10 parcells of land noated with the same
Character — severally containinge as followeth

f. 33.	[ac. roo. da. pt.]	
1.	5 - 2 - 8 - 3	xixs jd
2.	1 - 2 - 3 - 2	iiijs
3.	3 - 1 - 8 - 0	viijs vijd
4.	4 - 3 - 3 - 2	xijs jd
5.	4 - 3 - 5 - 2	xxxijs vijd
6.	2 - 0 - 5 - 0	viijs vjd
7.	3 - 3 - 8 - 0	xiijs ijd
8.	22 - 3 - 9 - 3	xxxviijs iiijd
9.	2 - 1 - 1 - 0	xiijs viijd
10.	0 - 1 - 8 - 0	xiiijd
Summa Acraru'	53 - 0 - 1 - 0	
	[52 - 1 - 1 - 0]	

For which Tenemente and lands he paieth the } xxs
yeerely Rente of

Summa Valor' inde per Annu' viij^{ll} vijs xd.

THE WIDDOW of Luke Thwaite holdeth one } vjs viijd
Dwelling howse with a yard & garden adioyninge
Noated with this Character — Val' per Ann'

Whereunto is belonging 6 parcells of ground
noated with the same Character — containinge
as followeth

f. 33d.	[ac. roo. da. pt.]	
1.	0 - 2 - 6 - 2	vjs vijd ob
2.	9 - 2 - 7 - 3	ixs ixd
3.	2 - 2 - 3 - 2	vs ijd
4.	3 - 0 - 6 - 0	vijs xd ob
5.	3 - 0 - 0 - 0	vijs vjd
6.	8 - 0 - 0 - 2	xxxijs jd
Summa Acrar'	27 - 0 - 4 - 1	

For which Tenemente & landes he paieth the } vjs viijd
yeerely Rente of

Summa valor' inde per Annu' iij^{ll} xvs viijd

☞ Looke more in Skellgill

f. 34.

TENAUNTS OF SEDBUSKE

FRANCIS WYNNE holdeth one Dwellinge house
& one garden with a Turfe house & a small
croft adioyning noted with theis   xvs
Lettres g g containinge togeather 0 - 1 - 3 - 0

Whereunto is also belonging 12 parcells of
Meddow ground noted with g g the measures
whereof hereafter follow

	[ac. roo. da. pt.]	
1.	1 - 1 - 6 - 0	xviijs viijd
2.	0 - 3 - 6 - 0	ixs
3.	2 - 1 - 7 - 2	viijs jd ob
4.	1 - 1 - 0 - 0	viijs jd ob
5.	0 - 3 - 2 - 0	viijs
6.	1 - 1 - 0 - 0	xijs vjd
7.	2 - 0 - 2 - 0	xiijs vd
8.	1 - 1 - 1 - 0	xijs ixd
9.	9 - 2 - 5 - 2	xxxijs jd ob
10.	1 - 1 - 6 - 0	xiiijs
11.	2 - 1 - 3 - 0	ixs iiijd ob
12.	1 - 1 - 6 - 0	xiiijs
Summa Acrar'	26 - 1 - 8 - 0	

f. 34d.

There is also belonging to the said Tenemente
10 cattlegats & ⅔ of a gate in the pasture called
Sedbuske Slights att vjs viijd the gate val' per   iij^{li} xjs jd
Annu'

Item sixe Cattlegats & ⅔ of a gate in the upper
pasture att iijs the gate   xxs

For which tenemente & Cattlegats he paieth the
yeerely rente of   xxiiijs ijd

Summa valor' inde per Annu'   xiij^{li} iiijs jd
          [£13 6s. 1d.]

THE CHILDREN of Thomas Thwaite holde one
Dwellinge house with a garden and a small crofte   xvjs viijd
adioyninge noated with this Letters
m m conteininge togeether 0 - 1 - 4 - 0

Whereunto is belonging 7 parcells of land noated
with the same Letters m m containinge as followeth

	[ac. roo. da. pt.]	
1.	1 - 0 - 5 - 2	xvs ijd
2.	0 - 1 - 3 - 0	ijs vijd ob
3.	2 - 0 - 3 - 0	xvjs vijd ob

f. 35.

4. { A garden plott remote from }
   { the house aforesaid   } 0 - 0 - 2 - 0   xijd

5.   1 - 1 - 3 - 3   xiijs vd.

6.   4 - 2 - 0 - 0   xvs

7.   3 - 2 - 6 - 0   xijs ijd

      Summa Acraru'   13 - 1 - 7 - 3

                             [*13 - 1 - 7 - 1*]

There is also belonginge to the said Tenemente }
& lands 6 cattlegats in the Slights val' per Annu' } xls

Item 4 cattlegats in the upper pasture val' per
Annu'   xijs

For which Tenemente lands & Cattlegats they }
pay the yeerely Rente of   } xiijs viijd

Summa valor' inde per Annu'   vij^{11} iiijs viijd

MARTYN THWAYTE & Thomas Thwayte holde }
one Dwellinge house with 2 severall gardein }
plotts neere adioyninge and Two Turfhouses } xvjs viijd
val' togeether per Annu'   }

f. 35d.

Whereunto is belonging 9 parcells of ground }
whereof Martyn Thwayte hath 4 parcells noated }
with kk and Thomas Thwayte hath 5 Noated }
with ll severally containinge as followeth }

                                   [*ac. roo. da. pt.*]

Martyn	{ 1 }		1 - 1 - 5 - 0	xviijs iiijd
Thwaite	{ 2. }	kk	2 - 1 - 3 - 0	ixs iijd
	{ 3 }		2 - 3 - 2 - 0	ixs iiijd
	{ 4. }		1 - 3 - 6 - 3	xixs ijd
	Summa Acrar'		8 - 1 - 6 - 3	

	{ 1. }		4 - 0 - 8 - 0	xs vjd
	{ 2. }		2 - 1 - 4 - 2	xviijs xjd
Thomas	{ 3. }	ll	2 - 2 - 2 - 2	xs iijd
Thwayte	{ 4. }		0 - 1 - 9 - 3	iijs iijd
	{ 5. }		1 - 1 - 2 - 0	viijs viijd
	Summa Acrar'		10 - 3 - 6 - 3	

There is also belonginge to the said Tenemente }
12 beastgats & ⅛ of a gate in the Slights val' } iiij^{11} js jd
per Annu'   }

Item 8 beastgats & ⅛ in the upper pasture
val' per Annu'   xxiiijs vjd

For which landes & Cattlegats they pay the }
yeerely rente of   } xxvijs viijd

  c

f. 36.

Summa valor' inde per Annu'   xj^ll ixs xjd ob
                                     [£11 9s. 11d.]

Whereof the said Martyn for halfe of the said⎫
Dwellinge house with his .4 parcells of land &⎬v^ll xvijs iijd
halfe the said Cattlegats   ⎭[£5 17s. 2½d.]

And the said Thomas for thother halfe of the⎫
said house with his 5 parcells of land & halfe⎬v^ll xijs viijd ob
the said Cattlegats   ⎭[£5 12s. 8½d.]

1. THOMAS SADLER houldeth one Dwelling house⎫
   with two garden plotts, and a smalle Crofte⎟
   adioyninge noated with thcis⎤   ⎬xvjs viijd
   Lettres cc lying neere the house⎬0 - 1 - 4 - 0⎭
   containing   ⎦

   Whereunto is also belonging 11 other parcells⎫
   of land noated with the said Lettres cc con-⎬
   taininge as followeth   ⎭

                         [ac. roo. da. pt.]
2.   1 - 0 - 3 - 0   xiiijs iiijd
3.   1 - 1 - 2 - 2   xiijs jd ob
4.   2 - 3 - 3 - 0   xxixs ixd
5.   4 - 1 - 5 - 0   xiiijs vijd
6.   3 - 3 - 5 - 0   xijs xjd

f. 36d.
7.   2 - 2 - 1 - 2   viijs vd ob
8.   1 - 0 - 5 - 0   iiijs vjd
9.   0 - 3 - 2 - 2   viijs jd ob
10.   0 - 3 - 1 - 0   vs ijd
11.   0 - 2 - 0 - 0   iiijs
12. In New Inge   1 - 1 - 2 - 0   viijs viijd
        Summa Acrar'   21 - 0 - 0 - 2
                         [20 - 3 - 4 - 2]

Whereunto is also belonging to the said Tenemente⎫
9 Cattlegats & ¾ in the Slights val' per Annu' ⎬iij^ll vs
Item 6 cattlegats & ½ in the upper pasture val'
per Ann'   xixs vjd
For which Tenemente lands & cattlegats he⎫
paieth the yeerely rente of   ⎬xxjs viijd
Summa valoris inde per Annu'   xj^ll iiijs ixd ob

THOMAS WYNNE holdeth one Dwellinge house⎫
with 2 gardens adioyninge & one other garden⎟
remote from the same, noated with theis Lettres⎬xvjs viijd
dd Val' per Annu'   ⎭

f. 37.

Whereunto is belonging 5 parcells of ground noted with the same lettres dd containinge as followeth

	[ac. roo. da. pt.]	
1.	0 - 3 - 8 - 2	ixs vijd ob
2.	0 - 1 - 9 - 2	ijs vjd
3.	1 - 1 - 9 - 0	xiiijs ixd
4.	1 - 1 - 8 - 2	ijs iijd
5.	2 - 2 - 7 - 0	xxvjs ixd
Summa Acrar'	6 - 3 - 5 - 2	
	[7 - 0 - 2 - 2]	

There is also belonging to the said Tenemente⎫
6 Cattlegats in the Slights val' per Annu' ⎰xls

Item 4 cattlegats in the upper pasture val' per⎱
Annu' ⎰xijs

For which Tenemente lands & Cattlegats he⎱
paieth the yeerely Rente of ⎰xiijs viiijd

Summa valor' inde per Ann' vjⁱⁱ iiijs vjd ob

JOHN WYNNE holdeth one Dwelling house with⎫
two small garden plotts remoate from the same⎬xiijs iiijd
Noated with theis Lettres bb val' per Annu' ⎭

f. 37d.

Whereunto is also belonginge 12 parcells of land noated with the said Lettres bb Containinge as followeth

	[ac. roo. da. pt.]	
1.	0 - 0 - 7 - 0	ijs iiijd
2.	0 - 1 - 1 - 2	ijs iijd
3.	1 - 3 - 0 - 2	ijs xjd
4.	3 - 0 - 8 - 0	xs viijd
5.	3 - 0 - 6 - 0	xs vjd
6.	1 - 1 - 2 - 2	xiijs jd ob
7.	1 - 2 - 9 - 0	xiijs xd ob
8.	1 - 2 - 2 - 0	xvs xd
9.	1 - 2 - 0 - 3	xvs ijd
10.	1 - 3 - 1 - 2	vs xjd ob
11.	0 - 3 - 9 - 0	vijs xd ob
12.	1 - 3 - 9 - 2	xxs xd ob
Summa Acraru'	19 - 1 - 7 - 1	

There is also belonging to the said Tenemente 7⎱
cattlegats in the Slights Val' per Annu' ⎰xlvjs viiijd

Item five Cattlegats in the upper pasture val'
per Annu' xvs

For which Tenemente lands & Cattlegats he ⎱
payeth the yeerely Rente of   ⎰ xvjs iiijd

Summa valor' inde per Annu'   ix[ll] xvs jd ob
                                      [*£9 16s. 4½d.*]

f. 38.

GEORGE THWAYTE[1] tholder holdeth one Dwellinge ⎱
house with a Turfehouse & a gardein adioyninge ⎰ xvs
noated with theis Lettres aa   Val per Annu' ⎰

Whereunto is belonging 11 parcells of ground noated with the
said Lettres aa Containinge as followeth

		[*ac. roo. da. pt.*]	
1.		0 - 1 - 4 - 1	iiijs ixd
2.		1 - 2 - 8 - 2	xxijs xd
3.		1 - 0 - 7 - 2	xjs xd ob
4.		2 - 2 - 8 - 3	xiijs vijd
5.		1 - 0 - 4 - 2	xjs jd ob
6.		3 - 1 - 3 - 2	vjs viijd
7.		1 - 3 - 7 - 3	vijs viijd
8.		4 - 1 - 3 - 2	xs xd
9.		1 - 2 - 5 - 2	xvjs iiijd
10.		0 - 1 - 7 - 2	ijs ijd
11.		2 - 3 - 7 - 2	xxiijs vjd
Summa Acrar'		21 - 2 - 8 - 3	

There is also belonginge to the said Tenemente ⎱
9 Cattlegats in the Slights   val' per Annu' ⎰ iij[ll]

Item 6 Cattlegats in the upper pasture Val' per ⎱
Annu'   ⎰ xviijs

f. 38d.

one Close called   For which lands Tenemente ⎱
Hilldale parcell of   & Cattlegats he paieth the ⎰ xixs viijd
Thomas Thwaits   yeerely Rente of ⎰
farme: Rent xvjd   Summa valor' inde per Annu'
let with this farme[2]   xj[ll] iiijs iiijd

GEORGE THWAITE the younger holdeth one Dwel- ⎱
linge house with a gardein plott adioyninge noated ⎰ xs
with theis Lettres ff, and one other small gardein ⎰
Distante from the same   Val' per Annu' ⎰

Whereunto is belonging Tenne parcells of land noted with ff
containinge as followeth

---

[1] His wife, Grace, was a recusant (*North Riding Q.S. Records*, ii, 186).
[2] In a different hand.

		[ac. roo. da. pt.]	
1.		0 - 3 - 5 - 1	viijs ixd ob
2.		0 - 0 - 4 - 0	viijd
3.		1 - 1 - 1 - 2	iijs ijd ob
4.		2 - 2 - 1 - 1	viijs vd
5.		1 - 1 - 7 - 1	xjs vjd
6.		1 - 2 - 2 - 2	xvs vijd ob
7.		0 - 2 - 3 - 2	iiijs viijd
8.		0 - 1 - 5 - 0	iijs ixd
9.		0 - 1 - 5 - 2	ijs vijd
10.		1 - 1 - 7 - 0	viijs viijd
	Summa Acraru'	10 - 1 - 7 - 3	
		[*10 - 2 - 2 - 3*]	

f. 39.

There is also belonginge to the said Tenemente ⎱
4 Cattlegats & ½ in the Slights val' per Annu' ⎰ xxxs

Item 3 Cattlegats in the upper pasture val' per
Annu'   ixs

For which Tenemente lands & cattlegats he ⎱
paieth the yeerely Rente of   ⎰ xs iiijd
Summa valoris inde per Annu'   v^ll xvjs xd ob

GEORGE TODDE for the sonnes of Barthollmew ⎤
Thwayte holdeth one dwellinge house with a |
stable a Turfehouse & two gardeins neere adioyn- ⎬ xxs
inge & one gardein Distante from the same |
noated with theis Lettres ee Val' per Annu' ⎦

Whereunto is belonginge 8 parcells of land Noated with the said
Lettres ee containinge as followeth

		[ac. roo. da. pt.]	
1.		0 - 1 - 1 0	iijs viijd
2.		1 - 1 - 1 - 2	iijs ijd ob
3.		2 - 2 - 1 - 1	viijs vd
4.		2 - 2 - 4 - 2	xxvjs jd ob
5.		2 - 3 - 6 - 2	ixs viijd ob

f. 39d.

6.		0 - 1 - 8 - 2	iijs ixd
7.		0 - 2 - 2 - 2	js xd ob
8.		1 - 2 - 7 - 0	xiijs vd ob
	Summa Acrar'	12 - 1 - 2 - 3	

There is also belonginge to the said Tenemente ⎱
4 cattlegats & ½ in the Slights val' per Annu' ⎰ xxxs

Item 3 Cattlegats in the Upper pasture val' per
Annu'   ixs

For which Tenemente lands and Cattlegats hee ⎫
payeth the yeerely Rente of ⎰ xs iiijd

Summa Valor' inde per Annu' vj^{li} ixs ijd ob

PERCIVALL THWAITE and his brothers sonne ⎫
holde one Dwellinge house with two gardeins ⎬ xs
neere adioyninge val' per Annu' ⎭

Item one small garth adioyning to the Tememente ⎫
of Martyn & Thomas Thwayte noated thus ⁞ ⎬ xviijd
containinge 0 - 0 - 4 - 2 val' per Annu' ⎭

f. 40.

Whereunto is also belonginge 11 parcells of ⎫
ground whereof the said Percivall hath 3 parcells ⎪
noated with theis Lettres hh and his Brothers ⎬
sonne hath 8 parcells noated with ij Containinge ⎪
as followeth ⎭

[ac. roo. da. pt.]

			ac. roo. da. pt.	
Percivall	1.	hh	1 - 3 - 0 - 3	iiijs vd
Thwayte	2.		1 - 1 - 0 - 3	xijs viijd
	3.		1 - 1 - 6 - 3	vijs ijd
Summa Acraru'			4 - 1 - 9 - 2	
			[4 - 1 - 8 - 1]	
	1.		1 - 3 - 4 - 2	iiijs viijd
	2.		2 - 1 - 2 - 0	ixs ijd ob
	3.		0 - 1 - 0 - 3	xiijd
His Brothers	4.	ij	0 - 0 - 4 - 0	vjd
Sonne	5.		1 - 0 - 1 - 2	vjs xjd
	6.		0 - 0 - 7 - 0	xiiijd
	7.		0 - 1 - 9 - 3	iijs iijd ob
	8.		1 - 1 - 2 - 0	viijs viijd
Summa Acraru'			7 - 2 - 3 - 0	
			[7 - 2 - 1 - 2]	

There is also belonginge to the said Tememente ⎫
4 cattlegats in the Slights   val' per Annu' ⎰ xxvjs viijd

f. 40d.

Item 2 cattlegats and ⅓ of a gate in the upper ⎫
pasture Val' per Annu' ⎰ vijs

For which Tenemente landes and cattlegats is ⎫
paide the yeerely Rente of ⎰ ixs ijd

Summa valoris inde per Annu' v^{li} iiijs xjd

Whereof the said Percivall for the said Dwellinge ⎫
house with his 3 parcells of ground & halfe the ⎬ xlvjs xd
said Cattlegats ⎭

And his said Brothers sonne for his 8 parcells of ⎫
ground, and halfe the said Cattlegats ⎰ lviijs jd

The pasture called Sedbuske
Slights wherein the said Tennants
of Sedbuske have their Cattlegats } 128 - 0 - 5 - 0
conteineth

And the pasture called the upper
pasture Containeth } 141 - 0 - 5 - 0

f. 41.

TENAUNTS OF SYMONSTONE

THE WIDDOW of Tryniam Metcalfe holdeth one
Dwellinge house, & a Kitchin Distant from the
same, which are now made two severall Dwellings
together with a barne, a Turfhouse severall } xxxs
gardeins & garthes adioyninge
noated with this Lettre d contein- } 1 - 0 - 2 - 2
inge togeather

Whereunto is belonging 7 parcells of Land noated
with the said Lettre d conteininge as followeth

[ac. roo. da. pt.]

1.	0 - 2 - 3 - 3	ijs xjd ob
2.	1 - 3 - 2 - 2	xviijs jd ob
3.	1 - 2 - 6 - 2	xiijs iiijd
4.	2 - 0 - 6 - 2	xiiijs vd
5.	1 - 1 - 2 - 0	viijs viijd
6.	1 - 3 - 3 - 0	xijs ijd
7.	0 - 1 - 6 - 3	vs vijd
Summa Acraru'	10 - 1 - 6 - 3	
	[10 - 3 - 3 - 2]	

There is also belonginge to the said Tenemente 9
cattlegats att vjs the gate in Symonstone pasture. } liiijs
4 gates to each noble rente val' per Ann'

f. 41d.

For which Tenemente lands & cattlegats she } xvs
paieth the yeerely Rente of

Summa valoris inde per Annu' viij^ll viijs viijd
[£7 19s. 3d.]

SIR THOMAS METCALFE[1] knight holdeth one Dwellinge house with a gardein plott adioyninge } xs
Noted with this Lettre c. Val' per Annu'

Whereunto is belonging 3 parcells of ground
Noated with the said Lettre c containinge as
followeth

---

[1] The son of James Metcalfe of Nappa and Joan, daughter of John Savile of Stanley. He married Elizabeth, daughter of Sir Henry Slingsby, and died July 1665 (Dugdale, *Visitation*, Surtees Soc., xxxvi, 47).

	[*ac. roo. da. pt.*]	
1.	4 - 1 - 4 - 0	xxvjs
2.	0 - 2 - 4 - 2	iijs
3.	1 - 0 - 1 - 0	viijs ijd ob
Summa Acraru'	5 - 3 - 9 - 2	

There is also belonginge to the said Tenemente 8⎫
cattlegats in Symonstone pasture. val' per Annu' ⎰ xlviijs

For which Tenemente & landes he paieth the⎫
yeerely Rente of ⎰ xiijs iiijd

Summa valor' inde per Annu'   iiij^{li} xvs ijd ob

f. 42.

JAMES METCALFE holdeth one Dwellinge house⎫
with a garden adioyninge Noated with this ⎬xs
Lettre h val' per Annu'⎭

Whereunto belonginge 11 parcells of ground noated with this
said Lettre h parte whereof was purchased of Adam Jaque containinge as followeth

	[*ac. roo. da. pt.*]	
1.	1 - 0 - 4 - 0	iiijs vd
2.	0 - 3 - 8 - 1	vjs iiijd ob
3.	1 - 1 - 5 - 0	xiijs ixd
4.	0 - 1 - 8 - 0	js xd
5.	1 - 0 - 4 - 3	vijs vd ob
6.	3 - 0 - 2 - 0	xxxs vjd
7.	2 - 3 - 2 - 0	xxviijs
8.	1 - 1 - 2 - 0	viijs viijd
9.	12 - 2 - 8 - 2	xxxjs ixd
10.	2 - 3 - 8 - 1	xjs xd
11.	9 - 0 - 4 - 2	xxijs ixd
Summa Acraru'	36 - 3 - 7 - 1	

There is also belonginge to the said Tenemente⎫
& landes 16 cattlegats in Symonstone pasture ⎬iiij^{li} xvjs
val' per Annu'⎭

f. 42d.

For which Tenemente, lands & cattlegats he⎫
paieth the yeerely Rente of ⎰ xxvjs viijd

Whereof vjs viijd is for the Tenemente and lands⎫
purchased of Adam Jaque ⎰

Summa valor' inde per Annu'   xiij^{li} xiijs iiijd

JAMES DENTE holdeth one Dwellinge house with⎫
a gardein and yard adioyninge val' per Annu' ⎰ xiijs iiijd

Whereunto are belonging 17 parcells of land Noated with this
Lettre c containe as followeth

[ac. roo. da. pt.]

1.	2 - 0 - 2 - 0	xxvijs iiijd
2.	0 - 3 - 8 - 1	vjs iiijd ob
3.	4 - 3 - 9 - 0	xjs vijd
4.	0 - 1 - 3 - 2	js viijd
5.	2 - 2 - 8 - 0	xvjs iiijd
6.	1 - 0˙- 1 - 2	iijs jd ob
7.	0 - 2 - 6 - 2	ijs viijd
8.	10 - 0 - 2 - 1	xls ijd
9.	1 - 2 - 1 - 2	iijs xd

f. 43.

10.	5 - 1 - 1 - 0	xxjs jd
11.	0 - 0 - 6 - 2	vjd ob
12.	0 - 1 - 4 - 2	js xd
13.	0 - 1 - 4 - 1	ijs iiijd
14.	1 - 2 - 2 - 0	vjs iiijd
15.	0 - 1 - 4 - 0	xiiijd
16.	0 - 0 - 3 - 3	vijd

17. ⎧ The halfe of one parcell of ground lying by ⎫
    ⎨ the Ryver of Yore, whereof Adam Jaque ⎬ xjs
    ⎩ hath thother halfe Containinge ⎭

    1 - 1 - 2 - 2

Summa Acraru' 33 - 3 - 1 - 0

There is also belonginge to the said Tenemente ⎫
13 cattlegats in Symonstone pasture val' per ⎬ iijli xviijs
Annu' ⎭

For which Tenemente landes & Cattlegats he ⎫
paieth the yeerely Rente of ⎭ xxjs vd

Summa valor' inde per Annu' xjli xixs jd ob
[£12 9s. 1½d.]

Querie also for another house & garden in Symon- ⎫
stone in the tenure of James Dent to which parte ⎪
of the lands of his Tenemente before mentioned ⎬
are belonginge, under the rente aforesaid val' ⎪
per Annu' [1] ⎭

f. 43d.

JOHN WYNNE the younger holdeth one Dwellinge ⎫
house with a gardein plott adioyning Noated with ⎬ xs
this Lettre f val' per Annu' ⎭

---

[1] No value given.

Whereunto is belonging 9 parcells of land noated with the said Lettre f [Val[1]] Conteininge as followeth

		[ac. roo. da. pt.]	
1.		0 - 3 - 0 - 2	vijs vijd ob
2.		0 3 - 4 - 2	viijs vijd ob
3.		2 - 0 - 3 - 2	xxijs viijd
4.		1 - 3 - 4 - 0	xijs iiijd
5.		0 - 1 - 7 - 1	ijs xd ob
6.	In the Shaw	4 - 1 - 7 - 2	xvijs viijd
7.		5 - 2 - 7 - 0	xiiijs ijd
8.		3 - 3 - 2 - 2	vijs vijd ob
9.		1 - 2 - 8 - 0	xiijs viijd
	Summa Acrar'	21 - 2 - 4 - 3	

There is also belonging to the said Tenemente⎱
8 cattlegats in Simonstone pasture val' per Annu' ⎰ xlviijs

For which Tenemente lands & cattlegats he⎱
payeth the yeerely Rente of   ⎰ xiijs iiijd

Summa valor' inde per Annu'   viij[li] vs iijd
                                                    [£8 5s. 2d.]

f. 44.

MICHAELL METCALFE[2] holdeth one Dwellinge⎫
house two garthes, 3 small gardein plotts a Turfe-⎪
house and a Crofte adioyninge called Cowes Myre ⎬ xliijs vjd
noted with this Lettre a   Contain-⎱   ⎪
inge togeather   ⎰ 3 - 2 - 1 - 0 ⎭

Whereunto is also belonging 20 other parcells of⎫
ground noated with the said Lettre a containinge ⎬
as followeth   ⎭

	[ac. roo. da. pt.]	
1.	0 - 3 - 3 - 0	iiijs jd ob
2.	3 - 0 - 3 - 0	xxs vjd
3.	1 - 0 - 5 - 0	vijs vjd
4.	2 - 0 - 9 - 0	xiijs viijd
5.	2 - 2 - 0 - 0	xxvs
6.	1 - 1 - 0 - 0	xijs vjd
6.	1 - 1 - 3 - 2	xiijs iiijd ob
7.	2 - 3 - 9 - 0	xxvijs vjd
8.	1 - 0 - 4 - 3	vijs vd
9.	13 - 3 - 9 - 0	xxxvs

[1] Crossed out.

[2] On July 5, 1628, Michael Metcalfe of Simonstone, yeoman, sold to William Steward (Stuart) of Simonstone, yeoman, his son-in-law, a third part of a tenement, the ancient rent of which was 42s. 6d., and three houses, various garths and closes and ten cattlegates in Simonstone pasture, for " a certaine Sum of Currant money " (MS. in my possession).

10.	2 - 2 - 3 - 0	viijs vijd
11.	0 - 2 - 5 - 0	ijs vjd
12.	0 - 3 - 1 - 0	vjs ijd ob
13.	0 - 3 - 9 - 2	ixs xd
14.	0 - 2 - 1 - 0	iiijs ijd ob
14. Simonstone Forse	7 - 2 - 7 - 0	xxxs viijd
15.	0 - 2 - 2 - 2	vijs vjd
16. In the Shawe	1 - 1 - 9 - 0	vs xd

f. 44d.

17.	7 - 1 - 4 - 0	xvijs ixd
18.	0 - 3 - 1 - 2	vs iijd
19.	0 - 2 - 1 - 2	iijs vijd
20.	6 - 2 - 4 - 1	xxijs
Summa Acrar'	64 - 0 - 8 - 0	
	[64 - 0 - 7 - 3]	

There is also belonginge to the said Tenemente ⎫
24 cattlegats & ⅓ of a gate in Simonstone pasture. ⎬ vij^{ll} vjs
val' per Annu' ⎭

For which Tenemente lands & cattlegats he paieth ⎫
the yeerely Rente of ⎬ xlijs vjd

Summa valor' inde per Annu' xxiij^{ll} xixs viijd

JOHN BATTERSBY holdeth one Dwelling house ⎫
with a yarde, a gardein a Turfe house and other ⎬ xxs
edifics Noated with this Lettre b val' per Annu' ⎭

Whereunto is belonging 7 parcells of ground ⎫
noated with the same Lettre b val' per Annu' ⎭

[ac. roo. da. pt.]

1.	1 - 2 - 5 - 0	xs xd
2.	2 - 0 - 8 - 2	xxijs jd ob

f. 45.

3.	0 - 1 - 5 - 2	js xjd
4.	0 - 2 - 0 - 0	ijs vjd
5.	2 - 2 - 4 - 2	xiijs
6.	4 - 1 - 7 - 2	xvjs viijd
7.	15 - 1 - 1 - 0	xxxviijs ijd
Summa Acrar'	27 - 0 - 2 - 0	

There is also belonginge to the said Tenemente ⎫
6 Cattlegats in Simonstone pasture. val' per Annu' ⎬ xxxvjs

For which Tenemente lands and cattlegats he ⎫
paieth the yeerely Rente of ⎬ xs vjd

Summa valor' inde per Annu' viij^{ll} js ijd ob

ADAM JACQUE holdeth the ½ of one parcell of
grounde noated with this Lettre M
adioyninge to the Ryver of Yore 1 - 1 - 2 - 2   } xjs
Containinge

Whereunto is belonging halfe a Cattlegate in
Simonstone pasture   } iijs

For which land & cattlegate he paieth the yeerely
Rente of   xd

f. 45d.

Summa valoris inde per Annu'   xiiijs

James Dente hath thother ½ of the said parcell
of ground mentioned in the Table of his Tenemente
aforesaid

WILLIAM THWAYTE holdeth one Dwelling house
with the halfe of a yarde and 2 gardeins neere } xs
adioyninge noated with gk.   val' per Annu'

Whereunto is belonging 11 parcells of ground
Noated with this Lettre k containing as followeth

	[ac. roo. da. pt.]	
1.	0 - 0 - 6 - 2	xiijd
2.	0 - 3 - 2 - 2	viijs jd ob
3.	0 - 0 - 9 - 0	xjd
4.	0 - 2 - 4 - 3	iijs
5.	1 - 0 - 9 - 0	vjs jd ob
6.	1 - 1 - 0 - 0	viijs iiijd
7.	0 - 3 - 5 - 1	vijs jd
8.	0 - 0 - 1 - 3	iijd ob
9.	0 - 1 - 4 - 2	ijs vd
10.	0 - 0 - 3 - 3	vijd ob
11.	3 - 1 - 2 - 0	xjs
Summa Acraru'	8 - 3 - 9 - 1	
	[8 - 3 - 9 - o]	

f. 46.

There is also belonginge to the said Tenemente
4 Cattlegats and ½ in Symonstone pasture, val' per } xxvijs
Annu'

For which Tenemente, lands and Cattlegats he
paieth the yeerely Rente of   } vijs vjd

Summa valor' inde per Annu'   iiij[11] vjs

ROWLAND AND Anthony Thwaite holde one Dwellinge house with the ½ of a yarde & two gardeins } xs
neere adioyninge Noated with theis Lettres g
val' per Annu'

Whereunto is belonging 11 parcells of ground noted with this
Lettre g containing as followeth

	[ac. roo. da. pt.]	
1.	0 - 0 - 6 - 2	xiijd
2.	1 - 0 - 3 - 0	xs ixd
3.	0 - 0 - 9 - 0	xjd
4.	2 - 3 - 3 - 0	ixs vd
5.	0 - 2 - 4 - 3	iijs
6.	1 - 0 - 3 - 1	vijs ijd
7.	0 - 3 - 5 - 1	vijs ijd
8.	0 - 0 - 1 - 3	iijd ob
9.	0 - 1 - 4 - 2	ijs vd

f. 46d.

10.	0 - 0 - 3 - 3	vijd ob
11.	3 - 1 - 2 - 0	xjs
Summa Acraru'	10 - 2 - 6 - 3	

There is also belonginge to the said Tenemente ⎫
4 cattlegats & ½ in Symonstone pasture   val' per ⎬ xxvijs
Annu' ⎭

For which Tenemente & Cattlegats he paieth the ⎫
yeerely Rente of   ⎭ vijs vjd

Summa valor inde per Annu'   iiij^{li} xs ixd ob
                                                               [£4 10s. 10d.]

PHILLIPP ALLEN of the Newhouses hath 6 Cattle- ⎫
gats in Symonstone pasture For which he paieth ⎬ vjd
the yeerely Rente of ⎭

Val' per Annu'   xxxvjs

f. 47.

☞ Looke more for his lands att New
   houses, & in Hardrow

ABBOTTES CLOASE

THE WIDDOW of John Wynne holdeth one ⎫
Dwellinge house with a gardein plott adioyninge ⎬ xiijs iiijd
val' per Annu' ⎭

Whereunto is belonging and adioyninge 3 parcells of ground lying
togeether with a feild house thereupon called Abbotts Cloase
Containinge as followeth

	[ac. roo. da. pt.]	
1.	1 - 2 - 6 - 0	xs
2.	2 - 1 - 6 - 2	xjs
3.	4 - 1 - 0 - 0	xvijs
Summa Acrar'	8 - 1 - 2 - 2	

For which Tenemente and landes she paieth the yeerely rente of } xxiijs iiijd

There are noe Cattlegats belonging to this Tene-ment }

f. 47d.

The pasture called Simonstone pasture wherein the Tennants of Simonstone, and Phillipp Allen of the Newhouses have their Cattlegats Containeth } 254 - 1 - 0 - 0

f. 48.

TENAUNTS OF HARDROWE

PHILLIPP ALLEN of the Newhouses holdeth one parcell of ground noated with this Lettre H which is parte of the lands called Broade Carr Conteininge } 4 - 3 - 1 - 3 } ijs vjd
For which he paieth the yeerely Rente of
Val' inde per Annu'   xs
Hee hath noe Common of pasture in Hardrow
Looke more for his Cattlegats in Symonstone and his lands att the Newhouses }

CHRISTOPHER METCALFE holdeth 2 parcells of ground Noated with this Lettre G which are parte of the Landes called Broade Carr Containinge as followeth

	[ac. roo. da. pt.]	
1.	10 - 0 - 9 - 2	xxvs viijd
2.	5 - 3 - 0 - 2	xixs ijd ob
Summa Acraru'	16 - 0 - 0 - 0	

f. 48d.

For which he payeth the yeerely Rente of   xs
Val' inde per Annu'   xliiijs xd ob
He hath noe Common of pasture
Looke more for his lands att the Newhouses

RICHARD METCALFE holdeth one Dwellinge house with a stable, a yarde, 2 gardeins, and a smalle Crofte adioyninge Conteininge   0 - 2 - 8 - 0 } xxs

Whereunto is belonginge 11 parcells of lande Noated with this Lettre E conteininge as followeth

	[ac. roo. da. pt.]	
1.	9 - 0 - 1 - 2	xxxvjs ijd
2.	7 - 3 - 5 - 3	xxxixs vd

3.   1 - 2 - 6 - 0   xjs
4.   4 - 0 - 8 - 0   xlijs
5.   4 - 0 - 6 - 0   xljs vjd
6.   3 - 1 - 5 - 0   xxvijs ob
7.   1 - 3 - 6 - 2   xvs iiijd

f. 49.
8. Browne Moore   11 - 3 - 4 - 2   xxixs viijd
9.   4 3 - 8 - 0   xvjs vjd
10.   1 - 1 - 1 - 2   iijs ijd ob
11.   0 - 1 - 5 - 1   iijs jd
      Summa Acraru'   51 - 1 - 7 - 0
                     [*51 - 1 - 6 - 0*]

There is also belonginge to the said Tenemente ⎱
9 Cattlegats at xs the gate in Hardrowe Slights ⎰iiij^{ll} xs
val' per Annu'

For which lands and cattlegats he paieth the ⎱
yeerely Rente of   ⎰iij^{ll} vjs

Summa Valoris inde per Annu'   xviij^{ll} xiiijs xjd

CHRISTOPHER WHALEYE holdeth one Dwelling ⎱
house with a garden adioyninge Noated with this ⎰xvs
Lettre D   Contayninge   0 - 0 - 8 - 2 ⎰

Whereunto are belonginge 9 parcells of Land Noated with the
said Lettre D containinge as followeth

                   [*ac. roo. da. pt.*]
1.   1 - 3 - 8 - 0   xvs viijd
2.   6 - 0 - 0 - 2   xxs ob

f. 49d.
3.   3 - 0 - 0 - 0   xxxs
4.   7 - 0 - 1 - 2   xlvjs xjd
5.   2 - 1 - 3 - 2   xxiijs iiijd ob
6.   4 - 0 - 1 - 0   xs jd
7.   0 - 3 - 2 - 2   vs vd
8.   13 - 0 - 7 - 0   iiij^{ll} vijs xd
9.   6 - 2 - 0 - 2   xvjs iiijd
      Summa Acraru'   45 - 0 - 3 - 0

There is also belonginge to the said Tenemente ⎱
8 Cattlegats and ⅔ of a gate in Hardrowe Slights ⎰iiij^{ll} vjs viijd
Val' per Annu'

For which Tenemente lands & cattlegats he ⎱
paieth the yeerely rente of   ⎰lvijs viijd

Summa valoris inde per Annu'   xvij^{ll} xvijs iijd

LEONARDE METCALFE holdeth one Dwelling house
with a gardein & a smalle Crofte
adioyninge noated with this Lettre c }0 - 2 - 1 - 3 }xxs
Containinge

Whereunto is also belonging 6 parcells of Lande
Noated with this Lettre c Conteininge as followeth

f. 50.

		[ac. roo. da. pt.]	
1.		3 - 0 - 0 - 1	xs
2.	Bellowes	4 - 0 - 8 - 0	xxviijs
3.		6 - 1 - 3 - 3	xlijs ijd
4.		2 - 0 - 5 - 5	vs vd
5.	Browne Moore	6 - 2 - 0 - 0	xiijs
6.		5 - 2 - 6 - 6	xxxiiijs
	Summa Acraru'	28 - 1 - 5 - 2	
		[28 - 1 - 7 - 0]	

There is also belonging to the said Tememente
4 cattlegats in Hardrow Slights val' per Annu' }xls

For which Tenement lands and cattlegats He
paieth the yeerely Rente of }xxvijs ijd

Summa valor' inde per Annu'   ix^{ll} xijs vijd

THE WIDDOWE of Peter Metcalfe holdeth one
Dwellinge house with a gardein adioyning Noated }xs
with this Lettre B   val' per Annu'

Whereunto are belonginge 12 parcells of land
Noted with this Lettre B conteining as followeth

f. 50d.

		[ac. roo. da. pt.]	
1.	parte of Broade Carr	4 - 2 - 9 - 0	xjs xjd
2.		5 - 1 - 2 - 0	xvijs viiijd
3.		2 - 2 - 1 - 2	xxvs iiijd
4.		1 - 2 - 7 - 2	xjs iijd
5.		2 - 1 - 7 - 0	xvjs ijd
6.		1 - 3 - 8 - 0	ixs ixd
7.		0 - 2 . 6 - 0	js viijd
8. }Birkehead 8.		{5 - 3 - 7 0 {0 - 1 5 - 2	xlijs jd
9.		8 - 0 2 - 0	xls iijd
10.		6 - 3 - 5 - 0	xljs iiijd
11.		0 - 2 - 9 0	vs xd ob
	Summa Acraru'	41 - 0 - 9 - 0	
		[41 - 0 - 9 - 2]	

There is also belonging to the said Tenemente ⎱
5 Cattlegats in Hardrow Slights   val' per Annu' ⎰ ls

For which Tenement lands and cattlegats he ⎱
paieth the yeerely Rente of   ⎰ xxxiiijs

Summa valor' inde per Annu'   xiiij^{li} iijs ijd ob

THE WIDDOW of Alexander Metcalfe holdeth one ⎫
Dwellinge house with a barne stable Turfhouse ⎬ xxiiijs
and gardein adioyninge noated with this Lettre A ⎭
val' per Annu'

f. 51.

Item one other Dwellinge house lately erected ⎫
neere unto the laste with a gardein adioyninge ⎬ xs
Noated with this Lettre A   val' per Annu' ⎭

Item one other Dwellinge house neere unto
Hardrow Chappell   val' per Annu'   vjs viijd

To which Dwellinge house first above mentioned are belonging
12 parcells of land Noated with the said Lettre A containing as
followeth

	[ac. roo. da. pt.]	
1.	1 - 3 - 8 - 2	xixs vijd ob
2.	3 - 1 - 4 - 2	xxvjs xjd
3.	1 - 0 - 1 - 2	vs ijd
4.	0 - 2 - 6 - 2	iiijs vd
5. with a feild house thereupon	0 - 3 - 0 - 0	vs
6.	0 - 3 - 8 - 1	vjs iiijd ob
7.	2 - 1 - 9 - 0	xvjs vjd
8.	1 - 2 - 8 - 0	vs viijd
9. Browne Moore	6 - 1 2 - 2	xijs viijd
10. with a feild house thereupon	4 - 0 - 3 - 0	xls ixd
11. The Strake	1 - 1 - 4 - 0	vjs ixd
12.	5 - 1 2 - 0	xvijs viijd
Summa Acraru'	29 - 3 - 7 - 3	

There is also belonging to the said tenemente ⎫
4 Cattlegats & ¾ of a gate in the Slights   val' per ⎬ xlvijs vjd
Annu' ⎭

f. 51d.

For which landes tenemente & Cattlegats he ⎱
paieth the yeerely Rente of   ⎰ xxxjs viijd

Summa valor' inde per Annu'   xij^{li} xvs viijd

CHARLES ATKINSON holdeth 4 parcells of land Noated with this
Lettre F containinge as followeth

D

	[ac. roo. da. pt.]	
1.	0 - 1 - 5 - 1	iijs jd
2. with a feildhouse thereupon	7 - 0 - 6 - 0	xlvijs viijd
3. Abbotts Dale	7 - 2 - 7 - 0	xxxs viijd
4.	3 - 2 - 7 - 2	xijs iijd
Summa Acraru'	18 - 3 - 5 - 3	

There is also belonginge to the said lands 3 cattle-⎫
gats & ½ in Hardrowe Slights val' per Annu' ⎰xxxvs

Item halfe a Cattlegate in Symonstone pasture   iijs

For which lands & cattlegats he payeth the ⎫
yeerely Rente   ⎰xxiijs ijd

Summa valoris inde per Annu'   vj^{li} xjs viijd

f. 52.

Looke more for his house & lands in Forsdaile
hereafter followinge

The pasture called Hardrow⎫
Slights, wherein the Tennants of ⎪
Hardrowe aforesaid have their ⎬
Cattlegats containeth[1]   ⎭

f. 52d.

TENAUNTS OF FORSDALE

CHARLES ATKINSON[2] holdeth one Dwellinge house⎫
with a gardein & Turfehouse adioyninge   val' ⎬xiijs iiijd
per Annu'   ⎭

Whereunto is belonginge 10 parcells of lande Noated with this
Lettre K conteininge as followeth

	[ac. roo. da. pt.]	
1.	0 - 1 - 2 - 2	ijs jd
2.	3 - 1 - 5 - 0	xxijs vjd
3. with a feildhouse thereupon	15 - 2 - 4 - 0	lijs
4.	18 - 3 - 6 - 2	xlvjs xd
5.	5 - 1 - 7 - 3	xxxvjs iijd
6.	3 2 - 3 - 0	xxiijs xd
7. with a feildhouse thereupon	2 - 3 - 6 - 0	xiiijs vjd
8. The halfe of Hutterill	4 - 3 - 9 - 0	ixs xd
9.	86 - 3 - 7 - 0	iiij^{li} vjs ixd
10.	51 - 0 - 2 - 0	xxxiiijs
Summa Acrar'	193 - 0 - 2 - 3	

---

[1] No area given here. The area was 61 - 3 - 5 - 0.

[2] Both he and his wife, Anne, were recusants in 1621 (*North Riding Q.S. Records*, ii, 252; iii, 124). A Charles Atkinson of Hardrow was charged with brewing without licence in 1610 (*ibid.*, i, 196); and a Charles Atkinson of Forsdale was one of the surveyors for Hardrow Bridge in 1604 (*ibid.*, i, 42).

For which Tenement and landes he paieth the ⎱
yeerely Rente of   ⎰ xxxvs xd
Summa valor' inde per Annu'   xvij^{ll} ijs
                                               [£17 1s. 11d.]

Looke more in Hardrowe

f. 53.

GEORGE STURDYE holdeth one Dwelling house ⎫
with a yarde, two gardein plotts, & a Turfhouse ⎬ xxs
which is now Converted into a Dwellinge house ⎪
noated with this Lettre L   Val' per Annu' ⎭

Whereunto is belonging 12 parcells of land Noated with this L
conteininge as followeth

		[ac. roo. da. pt.]	
1.		7 - 1 - 1 - 0	xxixs jd
2.		1 - 0 - 7 - 0	vijs xd
3.		1 - 1 - 2 - 0	viijs viijd
4.		4 - 2 - 5 - 0	xxxs xd
5.		15 - 0 - 3 - 0	xxxvijs viijd
6.		4 - 0 - 0 - 2	xxxijs jd
7.		44 - 3 - 2 - 2	iij^{ll} xiijs iijd
8.	Calfe parocke	2 - 2 - 7 - 2	xiijs vd
9.	The ½ of Hutterill	4 - 3 - 9 - 0	ixs xd
10.		27 - 2 - 3 - 2	iij^{ll} viijs xjd
11.	The Gill	10 - 0 - 6 - 0	xxvs iiijd
12.	The Moore	211 - 1 - 6 - 0	vj^{ll} vijs iiijd
	Summa Acrar'	335 - 0 - 3 - 0	

f. 53d.

For which Tenemente and lands he paieth the
yeerely Rente of   xxxvs xd
Summa valoris inde per Annu'   xxiiij^{ll} iiijs iiijd
                                               [£24 4s. 3d.]

TENAUNTS OF THE NEWHOUSES,

PHILLIPP ALLEN[1] holdeth one Dwelling house ⎫
with a yarde & gardein plott adioyning, & also ⎪
one Turfehouse with a gardein adioyninge to the ⎬ xvs
same being Distante from the house aforesaid ⎪
val' per Annu' ⎭

f. 54.

Whereunto is belonging 10 parcells of land Noated with this
Lettre H containinge as followeth

		[ac. roo. da. pt.]	
1.		7 - 2 - 5 - 0	xvijs xd
2.	with a barne adioyninge	4 - 2 - 8 - 0	xxxjs iiijd

[1] His wife, Mabel, was a recusant (*North Riding Q.S. Records*, ii, 186).

3.	0 - 3 - 7 - 2	vijs vd ob
4. with a feild house	4 - 2 - 7 - 0	xxxjs ijd
5.	18 - 1 - 8 - 0	xxxs ixd
6.	7 - 3 - 2 - 2	xxxixs
7.	1 - 2 - 3 - 2	xxd
8.	2 - 1 - 3 - 1	xvs vjd
9.	2 - 2 - 6 - 0	xxjs iijd
10.	5 - 1 - 5 - 2	ixs
Summa Acrar'	56 - 0 - 6 - 1	

For which Tenement and ·landes he payeth the } yeerely Rente of } xjs viijd

Summa valor' inde per Annu' xj^{ll}

[*£10 19s. 11½d.*]

☞ Looke more for his six Cattlegats in Symonstone pasture; his lands in Hardrow & in Riggs Cloase

CHRISTOPHER METCALFE holdeth one Dwelling } house with a yarde & garden adioyninge Noated } xvs with this Lettre G   val' per Annu' }

f. 54d.

Whereunto is belonginge 11 parcells of land Noated with the said Lettre G conteining as followeth

	[*ac. roo. da. pt.*]	
1.	2 - 1 - 4 - 2	xxiijs viijd
2.	7 - 2 - 5 - 0	xvijs xd
3.	2 - 1 - 7 2	xixs vijd
4. with a feildhouse	5 - 2 - 6 - 3	xxxvijs xd
5.	18 - 1 - 8 - 0	xxxs ixd
6.	7 - 3 - 2 - 2	xxxixs
7.	0 - 3 - 0 0	vs
8. with 2 feildhouses	4 - 2 - 2 - 3	xlvs ixd
9.	4 - 2 - 7 - 0	xxxvijs vjd
10.	2 - 0 - 8 - 1	viijs xd
11.	1 - 2 - 3 - 2	xxs
Summa Acraru'	58 - 0 - 5 - 3	

For which Tenemente and lands he paieth the yeerely Rente of xjs viijd

Summa valor' inde per Annu' xiiij^{ll} ijs vd

[*£15 0s. 9d.*]

☞ Looke more for his lands in Hardrowe

f. 55.

RIGGES CLOASE

PHILLIP ALLEN holdeth 2 parcells of ground noated } with this Lettre H which are parte of Riggs } Close conteininge as followeth }

[*ac. roo. da. pt.*]

1.	5 - 1 - 3 - 2	xvjs xd
2.	4 - 0 - 3 - 0	xiijs vijd
Summa Acrar'	9 - 1 - 6 - 2	
For which he payeth the yeerely Rente of		vs
Valor' inde per Annu'		xxxjs vd
		[*£1 10s. 5d.*]

☞ Looke more for his landes
att Newhouses

JOHN METCALFE holdeth one parcell of ground } being parte of Riggs Cloase Noated with this } xxxvjs ijd Lettre J Conteininge 10 - 3 - 4 - 0 }

For which he paieth the yeerely Rente of vs

f. 55d.

Valor' inde per Annu' xxxvjs ijd

TENAUNTS OF COTTERDALE[1]

PHILLIP LORD WHARTON holdeth two parcells of land Noated with this Lettre M conteininge as followeth

[*ac. roo. da. pt.*]

1.	0 - 1 - 9 - 1	ijs
2.	2 - 3 - 3 - 1	ixs vjd
Summa Acraru'	3 - 1 - 2 - 2	

f. 56.

Item 2 Cattlegats & ¾ in Cotterdale Cowe pasture   xiijs ixd
For which he paieth the yeerely Rente of   vs vjd
Valor' inde per Annu'   xxvs iijd

[1] It is not clear why small areas of land in Cotterdale should have been held by such distinguished tenants as Lords Wharton and Morley. The seclusion of the little dale suggests a suitable refuge for Roman Catholics; but that could hardly apply to Philip, Lord Wharton (1555–1625). He may, however, have had some local connexion, for the family were lords of the manors of Wharton and Nateby in Kirkby Stephen (*Complete Peerage*, ed. 1887–98, viii, 124–5). His second wife, whom he married in 1597, was a Dorothy Colby (E. R. Wharton, *The Whartons of Wharton Hall*, pp. 27–28), but it is uncertain whether she had any connexion with the local Colbys. Edward, Lord Morley (1551 ?–1618), came of a catholic family which was implicated in the Northern Rising of 1570, but he himself " appears to have conformed to the Protestant religion." He was a commissioner for the trials of Mary, Queen of Scots, of Philip, Earl of Arundel, and of Robert, Earl of Essex (*Complete Peerage*, ix, 226–27).

EDWARD LORD MORLEY holdeth 3 parcells of land Noated with this Lettre B Conteininge as followeth

	[ac. roo. da. pt.]	
1. with a feild house	0 - 2 - 8 - 3	viijs jd
2.	7 - 0 - 1 - 2	xxxvs ijd
3.	4 - 3 - 4 - 0	xixs vd
Summa Acraru'	12 - 2 - 4 - 1	

Item 5 Cattlegats & ¾ of a gate in Cotterdale Cowe pasture } xxviijs ixd

For which he paieth the yeerely Rente of   xijs ijd

Summa Valor' inde per Annu'   iiij^ll xjs vd

f. 56d.

SIR JAMES BELLINGHAM knight or his assignes holdeth one parcell of ground Noated with this
Lettre H Containinge   2 - 1 - 5 - 0

There is also belonginge to the said parcell of land 3 Cattlegats in Cotterdale Cowe pasture val' per Ann' } xvs

For which he paieth the yeerely Rente of   vjs viijd

Summa totius valor, inde per Ann' Omn' parcell' terre predict' } xxxviijs ixd

LEONARD LOWTHER Clarke holdeth one Dwelling house with a yarde, a garden, and Turfehouse adioyninge Noated with this Lettre D val' per Annu' } xxvjs viijd

Whereunto is belonginge 8 parcells of land Noated with the said Lettre D Containinge as followeth

	[ac. roo. da. pt.]	
1. with a feildhouse	10 - 2 - 4 - 2	v^ll vjs jd ob
2.	16 - 0 - 8 - 0	xls vjd
3.	119 - 1 - 8 - 0	ix^ll xviijs viijd
4.	13 - 2 - 6 - 0	iiij^ll xjs

f. 57.

5.	1 - 0 - 4 - 0	vs vjd
6.	0 - 0 - 4 - 2	vjd
7. Blacke Rashe	23 - 3 - 3 - 0	iiij^ll xjs vijd ob
8.	6 - 2 - 6 - 2	xvjs viijd
Summa Acrar'	191 - 2 - 4 - 2	

There is also belonginge to the said Tenement 28 cattlegats & ¾ of a gate in Cotterdale Cowe pasture Val' per Annu' } vij^ll iijs ixd

For which Tenement, landes & cattlegats he ⎱
paieth the yeerely Rente of ⎰ iij^{li} viijs vjd ob

Summa Valoris inde per Annu'   xxxvj^{li} ijs

THOMAS BARTON holdeth one parcell of ground ⎫
Noated with this Lettre N contain- ⎬ vjs vijd
inge   1 - 2 - 5 - 0 ⎭

Whereunto is belonginge one Cattlegate in the ⎱
Cowe pasture   Val' per Annu' ⎰ vs

For which land & Cattlegate he payeth the ⎱
yeerely Rente of ⎰ ijs ijd

f. 57d.

Valor' inde per Annu'   xjs vjd
                                  [*11s. 7d.*]

☞   Looke more for his Tenement & lands
att the Lundes

RICHARD LEAKE Clarke holdeth one dwelling ⎫
house lately erected upon the Out Moore   Val' ⎬ vs
per Annu' ⎭

Whereunto is belonginge one parcell of Land ⎫
Noated with this Lettre L Contain- ⎬ xs iijd
inge   3 - 0 - 3 - 0 ⎭

There is also belonginge to the said Tenement one ⎱
cattlegate & ½ in Cotterdale Cowe pasture ⎰ vijs vjd

For which lande & Cattlegats he paieth the ⎱
yeerely Rente of ⎰ iijs iiijd

Valor' inde per Annu'   xxijs ixd

MYLES TODDE holdeth one Dwelling house with ⎫
a Turfehouse & 2 gardeins adioyninge   Val' per ⎬ xxs
Annu' ⎭

f. 58.

Whereunto is belonginge 10 parcells of lande ⎫
Noated with this Lettre F   Containinge as ⎬
followeth ⎭

                     [*ac. roo. da. pt.*]

1.   0 - 1 - 4 - 0   iijs viijd

2.   2 - 0 - 6 - 2   xxviijs xd

3. with a feildhouse   2 - 0 - 0 - 0   xs

4.   1 - 0 - 5 - 2   vijs vijd

5. with a smale feild house   2   1 - 7 - 3   viijs ijd

6.   0 - 2 - 5 - 0   iijs jd ob

7.   0 - 1 - 6 - 0   js vijd

8,   2 - 0 - 2 - 0   xvjs vd

9.   1 - 0 - 6 - 2 iijs xjd
10.   3 1 - 4 - 0 xxs ijd
  Summa Acraru'   15 - 2 - 7 - 1

There is also belonginge to the said Tenemente ⎫
4 Cattlegats & ½ in the Cowe pasture   ⎰ xxijs vjd

For which Tenemente landes & Cattlegats he ⎫
payeth the yeerely Rente of   ⎰ xs

Summa Valor' inde per Annu'   vij^ll vijs
                                             [£7 5s. 11½d.]

f. 58d.

THOMAS MOORE and Christopher Moorc Doc holdc ⎫
one Dwellinge house now Divided into two   ⎱
Dwellings with two severall gardeins and Turfe- ⎰ xxs
houses adioyninge. Val' inde per Annu'   ⎰

Whereunto is belonging & ioyntly occupied by the said Thomas
and Christopher 15 parcells of ground Noated with this Lettre A.
Containinge as followeth

                          [ac. roo. da. pt.]
1.   4 - 2 - 9 - 0   xlvijs iijd
2.   1 - 0 - 8 - 0   iiijs xd
3.   6 - 1 - 0 - 0   xxvs
4.   6 - 0 - 0 - 3   xxiiijs jd
5. with a feildhouse   7 - 3 - 4 - 0   xxxixs iijd
6.   0 - 2 - 6 - 0   ijs viijd
7.   1 - 0 - 2 - 0   iijs ijd ob
8.   1 - 0 - 8 - 0   iiijs xd
9.   2 - 2 - 8 - 0   xiijs vjd
10.   3 - 0 - 0 - 0   xls
11.   2 - 2 - 6 - 0   xxvjs vjd
12.   1 - 2 - 5 - 0   viijs jd ob
13. with a feildhouse   3 - 1 - 0 - 0   xvjs iijd
14. with a feildhouse   1 - 3 - 7 - 2   xijs xjd
15.   0 - 1 - 0 - 1   xijd
  Summa Acraru'   44 - 1 - 4 - 2

f. 59.

There is also belonginge to the said Tenemente ⎫
12 Cattlegats in Cotterdale Cowe pasture   ⎰ iij^ll

For which Tenemente, lands and Cattlegats they ⎫
paie the yeerely Rente of   ⎰ xxvjs viijd

Summa Valor' inde per Annu'   xvij^ll xs vd
                                             [£17 9s. 5d.]

JOHN SHAWE holdeth one Dwellinge house with two gardeins and a smalle garthe adioyninge Val' per Annu' } xiijs iiijd

Whereunto is belonginge sixe parcells of lande Noated with this Lettre G conteininge as followeth

[ac. roo. da. pt.]

1. with a feildhouse	1 - 2 - 1 - 2	xxs vjd
2. with a feildhouse	6 - 3 - 1 - 3	xls viijd
3.	0 - 1 - 8 - 2	js xd
4.	0 - 2 - 7 - 0	ijs iijd
5. 6. }	{ 6 - 3 - 2 - 0	xxijs viijd
Summa Acraru'	16 - 1 - 0 - 3	

There is also belonginge to the said Tenemente 7 Cattlegats & ½ in the Cowe pasture Val' per Annu' } xxxvijs vjd

f. 59d.

For which Tenemente lands and Cattlegats he paieth the yeerely Rente of } xvjs xd

Summa Valor' inde per Annu'   vj^{ll} xviijs ixd

WIDDOWE HOGGE holdeth one Dwellinge house with a yarde, and gardein adioyninge Val' per Annu' } xs

Whereunto are belonginge 3 parcells of lande Noated with this Lettre K Containinge as followeth

[ac. roo. da. pt.]

1.	2 - 3 - 6 1	xjs vijd ob
2.	1 - 1 - 3 - 0	iiijs vd
3.	1 - 2 - 8 - 0	vjs xd
Summa Acraru'	5 - 3 - 7 - 1	

There is also belonginge to the said Tenemente 3 Cattlegats in the Cowe pasture Val' per Annu' } xvs

For which Tenemente lands & Cattlegats he paieth the yeerely Rente } vjs viijd

Summa Valor' inde per Annu'   xlvijs xd ob

f. 60.

THE WIDDOW of Henry Wilson holdeth one Dwellinge house with a garden adioyninge Noated with this Lettre I val' per Annu' } vjs viijd

Whereunto are belonginge 4 parcells of land Noated with the said Lettre I containinge as followeth

	[*ac. roo. da. pt.*]	
1. with a feildhouse	2 0 - 9 - 2	viijs xjd ob
2.	1 - 2 - 4 - 0	xixs iijd
3.	1 - 0 - 4 - 1	vjs viijd
4.	2 - 2 - 2 - 0	xijs ixd
Summa Acrar'	7 - 1 - 9 - 3	

There is also belonginge to the said Tenemente⎫
2 Cattlegats & ¼ in the Cowe pasture Val' per ⎬xjs iijd
Annu'　　　　　　　　　　　　　　　　　　　⎭

For which Tenemente lands and Cattlegats he⎫
paieth the yeerely Rente of　　　　　　　　⎰vs

Summa Valor' inde per Annu'　　　　　iij^ll vs vjd ob

THOMAS RAYNOLDSON houldeth one Dwellinge⎫
house with a Turfehouse & 2 gardein plotts ⎬xiijs iiijd
adioyninge val' per Annu'　　　　　　　　⎭

f. 60d.

Whereunto is belonginge 5 parcells of land Noated with this
Lettre C. Containinge as followeth

	[*ac. roo. da. pt.*]	
1. with 2 feildhouses	4 - 3 - 9 - 0	xxiiijs xd ob
2.	0 - 3 - 2 - 2	iiijs
3.	0 - 2 - 4 - 3	iijs jd
4. with a feildhouse	6 - 1 - 3 - 2	xxvs iiijd
5.	1 - 1 - 0 - 0	vjs iijd
Summa Acraru'	13 - 3 - 9 - 3	

There is also belonginge to the said Tenemente⎫
6 Cattlegats in the Cowe pasture. Val' per Annu'⎰xxxs

For which Tenemente lands and Cattlegats he⎫
paieth the yeerely Rente of　　　　　　　　⎰xiijs iiijd

Summa Valor' inde per Annu'　　　　　　v^ll vjs xd ob

WIDDOW BLAYDES holdeth one Dwelling house⎫
lately erected upon the out Moore with a small ⎬vs
garden plott adioyninge Val' per Annu'　　　⎭

Whereunto is belonginge & adioyninge one parcell⎫
of ground with a feild house thereon Noated with ⎬xxiijs vjd
this Lettre O Containing　　　　9 - 1 - 6 - 2⎭

f. 61.

Whereunto is belonginge one Cattlegate and an⎫
halfe in the Cowepasture. Val' per Annu'　　⎰vijs vjd

For which Tenemente & Cattlegats she paieth⎫
the yeerely Rente of　　　　　　　　　　⎰iijs viijd

Valor' inde per Annu'　　　　　　　　xxxvjs

RICHARD ROBINSON holdeth one Dwellinge house ⎱
with two garden plotts val' per Annu'　　　　⎰ vjs viijd

Whereunto are belonginge 2 parcells of land noated with this
Lettre E conteinynge as followeth

[ac. roo. da. pt.]

1. with a feildhouse　　　　　6 - 2 - 3 - 2　xxvjs iiijd
2.　　　　　　　　　　　　　1 - 1 - 2 - 0　viijs viijd

　　　Summa Acraru'　　　　7 - 3 - 5 - 2

There is also belonginge to the said Tenemente ⎱
3 Cattlegats in the Cowe pasture Val' per Annu' ⎰ xvs

For which lands and Cattlegats he paieth the ⎱
yeerely Rente of　　　　　　　　　　　　⎰ vjs viijd

Summa Valor' inde per Annu'　　　　　　　lvjs viijd

f. 61d.

Memorandum there is one parcell of ground called the Frith als
Cotterdale Bendes which is now wrongfully occupied by the
Tennants of Cotterdale aforesaid being noe parte of anie of their
Tenements neither is any Rente yeelded for the same but was
alwayes reserved for Hay & feedinge
for the Deere which Conteineth　　40 - 0 - 4 - 0

The parcell of ground called ⎤
Cotterdale Cowepasture wherein ⎟
all the Tennants of Cotterdale ⎬ 468 - 3 - 0 - 0
aforesaid have their Cattlegats ⎟
Conteineth　　　　　　　　　⎦

f. 62.　　　　STOODALE FLATTE & COTTEREND
　　　　　　　　　als Thwayte

FRANNCIS METCALFE gentleman holdeth by ⎤
Indenture of Lease Dated & made by the right ⎟ val' per Annu'
honorable Lodowicke Duke of Lenox for terme of ⎟
xxj yeeres 3 parcells of land noated with this ⎬
Character —- lyinge togeather adioyninge to Berk ⎟ xxll vs viijd
Brigge als Whytagill Becke neere unto Askrigge ⎟
being parte of Dale Grainge　　　⎱　　　　⎟
Containinge togeather　　　⎰ 27 - 1 - 5 - 2 ⎦

The saide Franncis Metcalfe holdeth also by the ⎤
said Indenture one Dwellinge house with a barne, ⎬ xxs
a Turfehouse, a yarde, and 2 gardeine plotts val' ⎟
per Annu'　　　　　　　　　　　　　　⎦

Whereunto is belonginge certein Lands called Cotterend als
Thwaite being 18 parcells of lande noated with this Character —
Containinge as followeth

		[ac. roo. da. pt.]	
1.	Thwaite Riggs	276 - 1 - 0 - 0	xiij^{li} xvjs iijd
2.	parte of the Thwayte Riggs	10 - 1 - 0 - 0	xs vd
3.	Collyer Holme	13 - 1 - 0 - 0	iiij^{li} viijs iiijd
4.		7 - 2 - 9 - 2	xlvjs vjd
5.		2 - 2 - 9 - 2	xiijs viijd

f. 62d.

6.		1 - 1 - 3 - 2	ijs viijd
7.		2 - 3 - 4 - 0	xiiijs iijd
8.		25 - 2 - 0 - 0	iij^{li} xvjs vjd
9.		6 - 0 - 2 - 2	xxxvjs iiijd
10.		4 - 0 - 9 - 0	xxjs jd
11.		32 - 2 - 9 - 0	v^{li} ixs jd
12.		7 - 3 - 1 - 0	xxjs jd
13.		11 - 3 - 0 - 0	xxxixs ijd
14.		21 - 3 - 5 - 0	iij^{li} xijs xjd
15.		65 - 2 - 8 - 0	v^{li} viijs iiijd
16.		51 - 1 - 0 - 0	xvijs ijd

17. { Two third parts of the banke / or Cliffe of Johnsons syde } 106 - 1 - 7 - 2   x^{li} xijs xd

18. { Two third parte of the Lower / pasture in Johnsons syde } 145 - 1 - 3 - 2   vij^{li} vs iijd

Summa Acraru'   820 - 1 - 7 - 2

For all which lands Stoodale Flatte & Cotterdale } als Thwayte he payeth the yeerely Rente of } iiij^{li} ixs iiijd

Summa totius Valor' inde per Annu'   lxxxvij^{li} vijs vjd
[£86 17s. 6d.]

f. 63.

TENAUNTS OF THE LUNDES

EDMUND BLAYDES holdeth one dwelling house } with a stable a Turfehouse and other edifics } xxs Distante from the same }

Whereunto is belonginge 14 parcells of Land Noated with this Lettre *A* the Measures whereof hereafter followe

		[ac. roo. da. pt.]	
1.	{ one third parte of the banke / or Cliffe of Johnsons side }	53 - 0 - 8 - 3	v^{li} vjs vjd
2.	{ One third parte of the lower / pasture in Johnsons side }	72 - 2 - 6 - 1	iij^{li} xijs viijd
3.		62 - 1 - 3 - 0	iij^{li} xvijs xd
4.		15 - 3 - 6 - 0	xixs xjd
5.		43 - 0 - 4 - 0	xxjs vijd

6.   85 - 1 - 6 - 0   viij^{li} xs vijd
7.   1 - 3 - 1 - 2   viijs xjd
8.   7 - 0 - 0 - 0   xxjs
9.   3 - 0 - 8 - 0   xs viijd
10.   9 - 0 - 5 - 2   liiijs ixd
11.   8 - 0 - 9 - 0   xljs jd ob
12.   4 - 3 - 1 - 1   viijs
13.   3 - 1 - 4 - 2   xiijs vd
14.   1 - 0 - 0 - 0   iijs iiijd

f. 63d.

       Summa Acrar'   371 - 0 - 3 - 3

For which Tenemente & lands he paieth the ⎫
yeerely Rente of   ⎬ xxxijs vjd

Summa Valor' inde per Annu'   xxxij^{li} xs iijd
                                       [*£32 10s. 3½d.*]

HENRY SHAWE holdeth one Dwellinge house with ⎫
a stakegarthe, a Turfehouse & 2 gardein plotts ⎬ xs
adioyninge   Val' per Ann'   ⎭

Whereunto are belonginge 7 parcells of land Noated with this Lettre *B* conteinynge as followeth
                         [*ac. roo. da. pt.*]

1.   0 - 0 - 8   0   js iiijd
2.   0 - 0   7 - 2   viijd
3.   6 - 3 - 1 - 1   xxijs vjd
4.   5 - 0 - 4 - 2   xijs ixd
5. with a feldhouse   5 - 0 - 0 - 0   xijs vjd
6.   2 - 3 - 6 - 0   vijs iiijd
7.   13 - 1 - 2 - 0   xjs jd

       Summa Acraru'   33 - 1 - 9 - 1

There is also belonginge to the said Tenemente ⎫
one Cattlegate in West Ende Inge   val' per Ann' ⎬ iiijs

f. 64.

For which Tenemente Landes and Cattlegate he ⎫
paieth the yeerely Rente of   ⎬ iiijs iiijd

Summa Valor' inde per Annu'   iiij^{li} ijs ijd

CUDBERTE SHAWE holdeth one Dwellinge house ⎫ Val' per Ann'
with a gardein plott neere thereunto   ⎬ vjs viijd

Whereunto are belonginge 6 parcells of lande noated with this Lettre *C* contayning as followeth
                         [*ac. roo. da. pt.*]

1.   0 - 0 - 5 - 0   xd
2.   6 - 3 - 1 - 1   xxijs vijd

3.   4 - 2 - 8 - 0   ixs vd
4.   4 - 1 - 9 - 0   xs vd
5.   2 - 3 - 2 - 0   vijs
6.   13 - 1 - 2 - 0   xjs jd
          Summa Acraru'   32 - 0 - 7 - 1

There is also belonginge to the said Tenemente ⎱
one Cattlegate in the West Ende Inge   Val' per ⎰ iiijs
Annu'

For which Tenemente lands and Cattlegate he ⎱
paieth the yeerely Rente of   ⎰ iiijs iiijd
Summa Valor' inde per Annu'   iij^{li} xijs

f. 64d.

THE CHILDREN or assignes of Rowland Shawe ⎱
hould one Dwellinge house with a yard a garden ⎰ xs
and a Turfhouse adioyning   val' per Ann'

Whereunto are belonging 4 parcells of lande Noated with this
Lettre *D.* containinge as followeth

                              [*ac. roo. da. pt.*]
1.   2 - 1 - 6 - 0   xijs
2.   1 - 0 - 7 - 0   vs xd ob
3. with 2 feildhouses   4 - 2 - 5 - 2   xxvijs xd
4.   6 - 2 - 6 - 0   vs vijd
          Summa Acrar'   14 - 3 - 4 - 2

There is also belonging to the Tenement 8 Cattle- ⎱
gats in the West Ende Inge   val' per Annu'   ⎰ xxxijs
For which Tenemente land & Cattlegats they pay ⎱
the yeerely Rente of   ⎰ vjs xjd
Summa valor' inde per Annu'   iiij^{li} xiijs iijd ob

WILLIAM PARKIN holdeth one Dwelling house with ⎱
a yarde a garden a Turfehouse, & a feildhouse with ⎰ xvjs viijd
a stake garth thereunto adioyninge neere unto the
Dwellinge house aforesaid val' per Ann'

f. 65.

Whereunto are also belonginge 9 parcells of land Noated with
this Lettre *E* containynge as followeth

                              [*ac. roo. da. pt.*]
1.   3 2 - 9 - 1   xxijs vd
2.   1 - 1 - 2 - 0   vs ijd ob
3.   0 - 2 - 6 - 2   js iijd
4. with a feildhouse   4 - 0 - 3 - 2   xxs vd
5.   0 - 2 - 9 - 1   js xd
6. with a feildhouse   3 - 1 - 3 - 0   xjs jd

7. with a feildhouse	8 - 1 - 3 - 1	xxs xd
8.	6 - 2 - 6 - 0	vs viijd
9.	4 - 0 - 4 - 2	viijs ijd
Summa Acrar'	32 - 3 - 7 - 1	

There is also belonging to the said Tenemente⎫
13 Cattlegats in the West end Inge Val' per Ann' ⎰ iijll vd

For which Tenement lands & Cattlegats he⎫
payeth the yeerely Rente of ⎰ ixs vijd

Whereof xxiijd is for a Tenemente & parte of the⎫
lands before mentioned which he purchased of ⎰ vjs viijd
widdow Wilson the Dwelling house of which Tene- ⎰ per ann'
mente is worth

And xvjd thereof is for a Dwelling house and parte⎫
of his lands before mentioned which he purchased ⎰ vs per ann'
of wyddow Parkin which Dwellinge house is worth

Summa valor' inde per Ann' ixll xs ijd ob
[£9 5s. 7½d.]

f. 65d.

JAMES PARKIN holdeth one Dwellinge house with⎫
a garden plott adioyninge val' per Annu' ⎰ xs

Whereunto are belonginge 3 parcells of land noated with theis
Lettres *ff* containynge as followeth

	[*ac. roo. da. pt.*]	
1.	1 - 3 - 4 - 2	vjs ijd ob
2. with a feildhouse	3 - 3 - 6 - 2	xxvjs jd
3.	1 - 1 - 7 - 1	vs ixd
Summa Acrar'	7 - 0 - 7 - 1	
	[*7 - 0 8 - 1*]	

There is also belonginge to the said Tenemente⎫
2 Cattlegats and an halfe in the West ende Inge ⎰ xs
Val' per Annu'

For which Tenemente landes & Cattlegats he⎫
paieth the yeerely Rente of ⎰ iiijs iijd

Summa Valor' inde per Annu' lviijs ob

CUDBERT BRAIDLYE holdeth one Dwellinge house⎫
with a gardein plott adioyning Val' per Ann' ⎰ xs

Whereunto are belonginge 3 parcells of land Noated with this
Lettre *G* containinge as followeth

f. 66.

	[*ac. roo. da. pt.*]	
1.	2 - 2 - 3 - 2	xijs xjd
2.	1 - 2 - 5 - 1	vs vd

3.　　　　　　　　　　　　　　　　3 - 1 - 4 - 0　xvjs ixd
　　　Summa Acrar'　　　　　　　7 - 2 - 2 - 3

For which Tenemente and lands he paieth the ⎱
yeerely Rente of　　　　　　　　　　　　⎰ iijs ixd
Summa Valor' inde per Annu'　　　　　　　　xlvs jd

ROBERT SHAWE holdeth one Dwellinge house with ⎱
a Turfehouse a yard & 2 garden plotts adioyning ⎬ xiijs iiijd
noated with this Lettre *H*　val' per Ann'　　　⎰

Whereunto are also belonginge 7 parcells of Land noated with
this Lettre *H* conteinynge as followeth

　　　　　　　　　　　　　　[*ac. roo. da. pt.*]
1.　　　　　　　　　　　　　　5 - 1 - 7 - 3　vjs viijd
2.　　　　　　　　　　　　　　13 - 2 - 4 - 0　xlvs iiijd
3.　　　　　　　　　　　　　　6 - 0 - 2 - 1　xxxs iijd
4.　　　　　　　　　　　　　　4 - 1 - 0 - 0　xvijs
5. with a feildhouse　　　　　　8 - 1 - 1 - 0　xxvijs vjd
6.　　　　　　　　　　　　　　23 - 0 - 1 - 0　xvs iiijd
7.　　　　　　　　　　　　　　5 - 1 - 2 - 3　xiijs iijd
　　　Summa Acrar'　　　　　　65 - 3 - 8 - 3

f. 66d.

For which Tenemente and lands he paieth the ⎱
yeerely Rente of　　　　　　　　　　　　⎰ iiijs iiijd
Summa Valor' inde per Annu'　　　　　　viij[li] viijs viijd

JOHN PARKIN holdeth one Dwelling house with ⎱
a stable a Turfehouse, a yard, & two gardeins ⎬ xvjs viijd
neere adioyninge Noated with this Lettre *K* val' ⎰
per Ann'

Whereunto are belonginge 7 parcells of lande Noated with this
Lettre *K* containynge as followeth

　　　　　　　　　　　　　　[*ac. roo. da. pt.*]
1.　　　　　　　　　　　　　　8　2　1 - 0　xs viijd
2.　　　　　　　　　　　　　　14　0 - 1 - 0　xxxvs jd
3.　　　　　　　　　　　　　　4 - 2 - 8 - 0　xjs ixd
4.　　　　　　　　　　　　　　30 - 3 - 6 - 0　xxxs xjd
5.　　　　　　　　　　　　　　4 - 0 - 8 - 0　xvjs xd
6.　　　　　　　　　　　　　　8 - 0 - 5 - 0　liiijs ijd
7. with a feildhouse　　　　　　5 - 1　7 - 2　xxxijs viijd
　　　Summa Acrar'　　　　　　75 - 3 - 6 - 2

There is also belonginge to the said Tenemente ⎱
2 Cattlegats and an halfe in the West ende Inge ⎬ xs
Val' per Ann'　　　　　　　　　　　　　⎰

f. 67.

For which Tenemente, Landes, & cattlegats he ⎫
paieth the yeerely Rente of ⎰ xs vjd

Summa Valor' inde per Annu' x^{ll} xviijs ixd

THOMAS BARTON holdeth one Dwellinge house ⎫
with a yarde, 2 garden plotts and a Turfehouse ⎬ xs
neere adioyning val' per Ann' ⎭

Whereunto are belonging 11 parcells of land Noated with this
Lettre L Containinge as followeth

		[ac. roo. da. pt.]	
1.		0 - 3 - 9 - 0	iijs iiijd
2.		20 - 3 - 3 - 2	xvijs vd
3.		69 - 1 - 5 - 0	iij^{ll} ixs iiijd ob
4.	with a Feildhouse	9 - 1 0 - 0	xxiijs jd ob
5.	with a feildhouse	3 - 2 - 8 - 0	xviijs vjd
6.		1 - 1 - 0 - 0	vjs iiijd
7.		2 - 0 - 3 - 0	ijs jd
8.		1 1 - 1 - 0	ijs ijd
9.		3 - 2 - 0 - 0	xiiijs
10.	⎧ Theis 2 parcells have been	1 - 2 4 - 2	xijs xjd
11.	⎨ alwaies lying on the south	9 - 0 - 7 - 1	xvs iiijd
	⎩ side of the Ryver of Yore		
	Summa Acrar'	123 - 0 - 1 - 1	

f. 67d.

For which Tenemente and lands he paieth the ⎫
yeerely Rente of ⎰ xiiijs vjd

Summa valor' inde per Annu' ix^{ll} xiiijs vjd

Looke more for a parcell of ground
in Cotterdale.

THE parcell of land called West Ende Inge, wherein Divers of
the Tennants of the Lunds aforesaid have their Cattlegats
Containeth 90 - 2 - 7 - 0 whereof 34 0 - 1 - 0 is and hath
alwaies beene on the south side of the River of Yore and the
residue being 56 - 2 - 5 - 0 on the north side.

f. 68.

Sayrgill Parke sometyme occupied by divers ⎫
personns for the yeerely Rente of ⎰ liijs iiijd

Containeth by Measure 496 - 1 - 5 - 0

Et Valor' inde per Ann' xxv^{ll}

Saggsfell for which is or hath beene paid by divers persons the
yeerely rente of xxs lyeth upon the Out Moore without mention
of any partition or Division from the said Moore so that the

E

Measure & value thereof is accompted with the measure & value of the Out Moore

The Out Moore wherein all the ⎫
Tennants in this book before ⎪
mentioned have taken common ⎪
of pasture as appurtenant to ⎬ 9422 - 0 - 0 - 0
their said Tenements without ⎪
stinte or rate containeth by ⎪
Measure ⎭

The yeerely value whereof att iiijd the acre ⎫ Clvij^{li} viijd
amounteth to ⎭

f. 68d [*blank*].

f. 69.

A Briefe Abstracte or Table of the Totall Measures, the yeerely Rente & yeerely value of every Tenemente in this book before mentioned with the nomber of cattlegats to eche Tenemente belonginge

TENAUNTS OF
Dale Grainge

Names of the Tenaunts	Measures [ac. roo. da. pt.]	Cattle-gats	yeerely Rents	yeerely values	Fynes
Peter Metcalfe	44 - 3 - 4 - 1^1	5½	xxxiijs xjd	xxvj^{li} vs ijd [£26 5s. 1d.]	
Peter Holme	5 - 0 - 3 - 2	1	vs	xlvjs viijd	
Roger Metcalfe	34 - 3 - 2 - 1	4¼	xxvs iiijd [£1 5s. 4d.]	xvj^{li} xiijs vd	
The widdowe of Symon Metcalfe	5 - 0 - 6 3	1	vs	lvijs viijd	
Richard Mattocke	1 - 3 - 1 - 3	0	ijs vjd	34s vjd [17s. 10d.]	
Abraham Metcalfe	13 - 3 - 9 - 2	1⅛	vijs ijd	vj^{li} xiijs iiijd	
the said Abraham for the tenemente late of James Lobley	0 - 2 - 9 - 0 [0 - 2 - 3 - 0]	¼	xxd	xvjs	
Edward Nelson	8 - 1 - 8 - 0	1	vs xd	iiij^{li} xijs iijd	

f. 69d.

The widdowe of Edward Guy	10 - 0 - 8 - 3	1½	xs	vj^{li} vijs xjd [£6 8s. 0d.]	

---

^{1} In the original the measures are recorded in two lines, *e.g.* 44 : 3
4 : 1

James Peerson	3 - 1 - 1 - 0	$\frac{1}{2}$	iijs vjd	lijs
Robert Metcalfe	7 - 0 - 3 - 0	$\frac{1}{2}$	iijs iiijd	iij^{li} xiijs viijd
George Metcalfe	18 - 3 - 8 - 1 [*18 - 3 - 8 - 0*]	2$\frac{1}{2}$	xvs	xij^{li} ijs vjd
Anthony Prott looke more in Brockellcoate and Shawcoate	37 - 0 - 8 - 3	3$\frac{1}{4}$ [*3$\frac{3}{4}$*]	xxijs vjd	18^{li} 3s 2d [*£18 3s. 2$\frac{1}{4}$d.*]
Edmond Metcalfe or his Assignes	10 - 1 - 3 - 2	2	xijs ijd	v^{li} xixs jd
Eden Mansfield	9 - 0 - 7 - 0	1	vjs viijd	4^{li} 17s 9d
James Metcalfe or his assignes	9 - 0 - 3 - 0	2$\frac{3}{4}$ [*3*]	xvijs ijd	6^{li} 4s 8d
The pasture called the Spen and Grainger gill	61 - 1 - 6 - 0			
Summa Totalis	281 - 1 - 8 - 1 [*281 - 1 - 8 - 0*]	28$\frac{1}{6}$ [*28$\frac{11}{12}$*]	8^{li} 16s 8d [*£8 16s. 9d.*]	121^{li} 9s 9d [*£121 3s. 1$\frac{1}{4}$d.*]

Tenaunts of the
Helme

Names of the Tenannts	ac: roo: da: pt	Cattle-gats	yeerely Rents	yeerely value	Fyne
f. 70.					
Mathew Metcalfe	84 - 2 - 2 - 0	14$\frac{1}{2}$	48s 7d ob	19^{li} 15s 7d	
The widdow of Blyth & c.	52 - 1 - 4 - 2	14$\frac{3}{4}$	49s 2d ob	13^{li} 19s 4d [*£13 19s. 3d.*]	
☛ Gandyn Bywell more in Skellgill	6 - 2 - 3 - 0	0	viijd	xxixs ixd	
☛ James Prott more in Brokellcoate	10 - 3 - 0 0	1$\frac{3}{4}$	vs xd	iij^{li} ixs vijd	
Thomas Prott	5 - 1 - 5 - 0	1$\frac{3}{4}$	vs xd	xxxs vjd	
The Helme pasture	124 - 0 - 5 - 0				
Summa Totalis	287 - 2 - 9 2 [*283 - 2 - 9 - 2*]	32$\frac{3}{4}$	v^{li} xs ijd	xl^{li} iiijs ixd [*£40 4s. 8d.*]	

Tenauntes of
Skellgill

Names of the Tennants	ac: roo: da: pt	Cattle-gats	yeerely Rents	yeerely values	Fyne
☛ The widdow of Luke Thwaite more in Lidderskew	15 - 3 - 4 - 2	10	xijs xd	7^{li} 19s 6d ob	

Gandyn Bywell more in the Helme	16 - 0 - 9 - 1	$8\frac{1}{3}$	xjs jd	4^{li} 16s 6d ob [*£5 15s. $8\frac{1}{2}$d.*]
Symon Kaygill	14 - 2 - 4 - 0	6 [*$5\frac{19}{20}$*]	viijs	v^{li} xs vijd
f. 70d.				
The widow of Edmond Coats	18 - 0 - 3 - 0	$4\frac{1}{3}$	xixs	x^{li} ijs jd [*£10 2s. $1\frac{1}{2}$d.*]
Abraham Prott	14 - 3 - 3 2	$11\frac{3}{4}$	xvs xd	8^{li} 9s 9d qr [*£8 9s. $9\frac{1}{2}$d.*]
Thomas Kettlewell or his assignes	one Dwelling house	0	xd	xs
Summa Totalis	79 - 1 - 9 - 1 [*79 - 2 4 - 1*]	$50\frac{1}{3}$ [*$50\frac{11}{30}$*]	iij^{li} vijs vijd	37^{li} 8s 7d [*£38 7s. 9d.*]
	Yorescoate			
George Metcalfe	46 - 3 4 2 [*47 - 2 - 7 2*]	0	xlvjs viijd	24^{li} 13s 2d [*£24 12s. 7d.*]

TENAUNTS OF
Brockellcoate

Names of the Tenannts	ac: roo: da: pt	Cattle-gats	yeerely Rents	yeerely value Fyne
Michaell Prott	34 - 1 1 - 2 [*34 - 1 6 - 2*]	$14\frac{1}{2}$	xxxvs viijd	14^{li} 12s 1d
Jenkin Ingram	6 - 1 - 0 - 0	$11\frac{1}{4}$	xvs	iiij^{li} xiijs vjd
f. 71.				
Franncis Prott more in the Holehouses	5 - 3 - 8 - 2	$2\frac{1}{2}$	iijs iiijd	iij^{li} vs jd ob
Edmond Prott	28 - 2 6 - 2 [*26 - 0 - 8 - 2*]	$17\frac{3}{4}$ [*$17\frac{5}{6}$*]	xxiiijs vjd	15^{li} 6s 11d ob [*£15 0s. $7\frac{1}{2}$d.*]
Christopher Dinsdale	24 2 8 2	$11\frac{1}{4}$	xvs	xj^{li} 0s vjd
James Blaydes	4 3 4 - 0	$2\frac{1}{2}$	iijs iiijd	iij^{li} iiijs iijd
Edmond Metcalfe or his assignes	12 - 1 8 2	10	xiijs iiijd	ix^{li} iijs iiijd [*£9 3s. $3\frac{1}{2}$d.*]
Anthony Prott more in Dale Grainge & in Shawcoate	8 0 - 1 - 0	$7\frac{1}{4}$	ixs ijd	iiij^{li} xjs vd ob
Widdow Guy query whether this be the widdow of Dale Grainge	13 - 0 - 0 - 3 [*13 - 0 - 3 - 0*]	$8\frac{3}{4}$	xjs viijd	7^{li} 19s 11d ob

	ac: roo: da: pt	cattle-gats	yeerely Rente	yeerely value Fynes
The widdow of Gregory Prott	6 - 2 - 9 - 0	7½	ixs viijd	3^{ll} 12s 6d ½
James Prott more in the Helme	19 - 2 - 6　2	12	xvs xd	xj^{ll} xiijs ixd ob
Summa Totalis	164 - 2 - 4 - 3　105¼ [162 - 1 - 4 - 0] [105⅓]	7^{ll}	xvjs vjd	89^{ll} 3s 3d ½ [£88 17s. 1½d.]

SHAWCOATE AND THE
Hole Houses

Names of the Tenannts	ac: roo: da: pt	cattle-gats	yeerely Rente	yeerely value Fynes
f. 71d.				
Christopher Prott	5 - 2 - 6 - 2	7½	xs	iiij^{ll} 0 9d ob
John Prott thelder 31	2 - 4 - 0	17½	xxxiijs iiijd	ix^{ll} xjs ob
☞ Anthony Prott more in Brockell-coate & in Dale Grainge	3 - 2 - 1 - 2	5	vjs viijd	ij^{ll} vjs xd
John Prott the younger	a dwelling house with a garden	0	vjs viijd	va' id' vjs viijd
Jeffry Pratt of the Holehouses	28 - 0 - 2 - 0 [28 - 1 - 2 - 0]	15	xxs	xiij^{ll} vjd [£13 0s. 5d.]
☞ Franncis Prott of the Holehouses more in Brockellcoate	19 - 2 - 9 - 2 [19　3 - 9 - 2]	17½	xxiijs iiijd	xj^{ll} vs jd [£10 15s. 1d.]
John Prott of the Holehouses	12 - 1 - 4 - 0	0	vj^{ll} viijd	iiij^{ll} xiiijs ijd
The Coate Moore & little Fell Meawes	522 - 0 - 5 - 0			
Summa totalis	623 - 0 - 2 - 2 [623 - 2 - 2 - 2]	62½	v^{ll} vjs viijd	xlv^{ll} vs jd [£44 15s. 0d.]

TENAUNTES OF
Camshouse

Names of the Tenannts	ac: roo: da: pt	Cattle-gats	yeerely Rente	yeerely value
Richard Kettlewell	64 - 0 - 1 - 0	3¾	xxvs	24^{ll} 16s 4½d [£24 16s. 6½d.]
f. 72.				
James Kettlewell & Oswald Kettlewell	51 - 0 - 5 - 0	4¼	xxviijs vjd	18^{ll} 16s 7d

Names	ac: roo: da: pt	cattle-gats	yeerely Rente	yeerely value Fyne
The widdow of Richard Nelson	87 - 1 3 - 0	7¼	xlviijs iiijd	29^{11} 11s 2d
	[86 - 3 - 3 - 0]			[£29 10s. 11½d.]
James Guy	79 - 0 - 9 - 0	5¾	xxxviijs iiijd	19^{11} 9s 5½d
The Cowepasture	52 - 0 - 9 - 0			
Summa Totalis	333 3 - 7 - 0	21	7^{11} 0 2d	92^{11} 13s 5½d
	[333 - 1 - 7 - 0]			[£92 13s. 6½d.]

TENAUNTES OF
Lidderskew

Here begynneth the Forreste[1]

Names of the Tennants	ac: roo: da: pt	Cattle-gats	yeerely Rente	yeerely value Fyne
John Todd	25 - 3 - 7 - ½	0	viijs iiijd	iiij^{11} xixs
	[25 - 3 - 7 - 0]			[£4 10s. 8d.]
James Todd	17 - 0 - 3 - 3	0	viijs iiijd	iij^{11} xs vd
				[£3 2s. 1d.]
George Todd	45 - 1 - 0 3	0	xvjs viijd	vij^{11} vijs jd
	[45 - 0 - 3 - 1]			[£6 0s. 5d.]
Richard Besson	70 2 - 4 - 0	0	xxvs	16^{11} 9s 8d
	[71 - 0 - 4 - 0]			[£17 2s. 0d.]
Mathew Thwayte	41 - 2 - 5 - 0	0	xiijs iiijd	vij^{11} vijs iijd

f. 72d.

John Pratt	53 - 0 - 1 - 0	0	xxs	viij^{11} vijs xd
	[52 - 1 - 1 - 0]			
☞ The widow of Luke Thwayte	27 - 0 4 - 1	0	vjs viijd	iij^{11} xvs viijd
more in Skellgill				
Summa Totalis	280 2 - 5 - 3½	0	4^{11} xviijs iiijd	51^{11} 16s 11d
	[280 - 0 - 8 - 1]			[£50 5s. 11d.]

TENAUNTES OF
Sedbuske

Names of the Tennants	ac: roo: da: pt	cattle-gats	yeerely Rente	yeerely Value Fyne
Franncis Wynne	26 - 1 - 8 0	17½	xxiiijs ijd	13^{11} 4s 1d
		[17⅓]		[£13 6s. 1d.]
The Children of Thomas Thwaite	13 - 1 - 7 - 3	10	xiijs viijd	7^{11} 4s 8d
	[13 - 1 7 - 1]			
Martyn Thwayte	8 - 1 6 - 3	10⅙	xiijs xd	5^{11} 17s 3d.
				[£5 17s. 2½d.]
Thomas Thwayte	10 - 3 - 6 - 3	10⅙	xiijs xd	5^{11} 12s 8½d
Thomas Sadler	21 - 0 - 0 - 2	16¼	xxjs viijd	11^{11} 4s 9½d
	[20 - 3 - 4 - 2]			

[1] In a different hand.

Names of the Tenannts	ac : roo : da : pt	cattle-gats	yeerely Rente	yeerely value	Fyne
Thomas Wynne	6 - 3 - 5 - 2 [7 0 - 2 - 2]	10	xiijs viijd	vj^{ll} iiijs vj½d	
John Wynne	19 - 1 - 7 - 1	12	xvjs iiijd	9^{ll} 15s 1½d [£9 16s. 4½d.]	

f. 73.

George Thwayte thelder	21 - 2 - 8 - 3	15	xixs viijd	xj^{ll} iiijs iiijd	
George Thwayte the younger	10 - 1 - 7 - 3 [10 - 2 - 2 - 3]	7½	xs iiijd	v^{ll} xvjs xd ob	
George Todd for the sonnes of Bartholomewe Thwaite	12 - 1 2 - 3	7½	xs iiijd	vj^{ll} ixs ijd ob	
Percivall Thwaite & his Brothers sonne several in the Booke	12 - 2 - 2 - 2 [12 - 0 - 4 - 1]	6⅓	ixs ijd	v^{ll} iiijs xjd	
Sedbuske Slights and their upper pasture	269 - 1 - 0 - 0				
Summa Totalis	432 - 3 - 4 - 1 [432 - 2 - 1 - 2]	122 [122¼]	8^{ll} 6s 8d	87^{ll} 18s 6d [£88 1s. 8½d.]	

TENAUNTES OF
Symonstone

Names of the Tenannts	ac : roo : da : pt	cattle-gats	yeerely Rente	yeerely value	Fyne
The widdow of Tryniam Metcalfe	10 - 1 - 6 - 3 [10 - 3 - 3 - 2]	9	xvs	8^{ll} 8s 8d [£7 19s. 3d.]	
Sir Thomas Metcalfe knight	5 - 3 - 9 - 2	8	xiijs iiijd	4^{ll} 15s 2½d	
James Metcalfe	36 - 3 - 7 - 1½ [36 - 3 7 - 1]	16	xxvjs viijd	13^{ll} 13s 4d	
James Dente	33 - 3 - 1 - 0	13	xxjs vd	xj^{ll} ixs jd ½d [£12 9s. 1½d.]	

f. 73d.

John Wynne Junior	21 - 2 - 4 - 3	8	xiijs iiijd	viij^{ll} vs iijd [£8 5s. 2d.]	
Michaell Metcalfe	64 - 0 - 8 - 0 [64 - 0 - 7 - 3]	24⅓	xlijs vjd	xxiij^{ll} xixs viijd	
John Battersby	27 - 0 - 2 - 0	6	xs vjd	viij^{ll} js ijd ½d	
Adam Jaque	1 1 - 2 - 2	½	xd	xiiijd [14s.]	

William Thwayte   8 - 3 - 9 - 1   4½   vijs vjd   iiij^ll vjs
                   [8 - 3 9 - o]

Rowland &
Anthony Thwaite   10 - 2 - 6 - 3   4½   vjs vjd   iiij^ll xs ixd ob
                   [7s. 6d.]   [£4 10s. 10d.]

☞ Phillip Allen   0 0 - 0 - 0   6   vjd   xxxvjs
  more att Newhouses

Symonstone
      pasture   254 - 1 - 0 - 0

The widdow of
John Wynne   8 - 1 - 2 - 2   0   xxiijs iiijd   ljs iiijd For
                                                     Abbotts
                                                     Cloase

Summa Totalis   483 - 2 - 0 - 1½ 100   vij^ll ixs jd   93^ll 0s 7d
                 [483 - 3 6 - 2] [100⅓]^1 [£9 2s. 5d.]   [£93 1s. 7½d.]

TENAUNTES OF
Hardrowe

Names of the Tennants	ac: roo: da: pt	cattle-gats	yeerely Rente	yeerely value	Fyne

f. 74.

Names of the Tennants	ac: roo: da: pt	cattle-gats	yeerely Rente	yeerely value	Fyne
Phillip Allen more in Symonstone and Newhouses	4 - 3 - 1 - 3	0	ijs vjd	xs	
Christopher Metcalfe more in Newhouse	16 - 0 0 - 0	0	xs	xliiijs xd ob	
Richard Metcalfe	51 - 1 - 7 - 0 [51 1 - 6 - o]	9	iiij^ll vjd	18^ll 14s 11d	
Christopher Whalay	45 - 0 - 3 - 0	8⅔	lvijs viijd	17^ll 17s 3d	
Leonard Metcalfe	28 - 1 - 5 - 2 [28 - 1 7 o]	4	xxvijs ijd	9^ll 12s 7d	
The widdowe of Peter Metcalfe	41 0 - 9 - 0 [41 - 0 - 9 - 2]	5	xxxiiijs	14^ll 3s 2½d	
The widdowe of Alexander Metcalfe	29 - 3 - 7 - 3	4¾	xxxjs viijd	12^ll 15s 8d	
Charles Atkinson more in Forsdale	18 - 3 - 5 - 3	3½ & ½^2	xxiijs ijd	6^ll xjs viijd	
Hardrow Slights	61 - 3 - 5 - 0				
Summa totalis	297 - 3 - 3 - 3 [297 2 5 - 3]	35⅓ [34¹¹⁄₁₂]	12^ll 6s 8d	82^ll 10s 2d	

¹ Including half a cattlegate held by Charles Atkinson of Hardrow.
² This half a cattlegate was in Simonstone pasture.

FORSDALE

Names of the Tennants	ac: roo: da: pt	0	yeerely Rente	yeerely Value
f. 74d.				
Charles Atkinson more in Hardrowe	193 - 0 - 2 - 3	0	xxxvs xd	xvij^{11} ijs [£17 1s. 11d.]
George Sturdy	335 - 0 - 3 - 0	0	xxxvs xd	24^{11} 4s 4d [£24 4s. 3d.]
Summa totalis	528 - 0 - 5 - 3	0	3^{11} 11s 8d	41^{11} 6s 4d [£41 6s. 2d.]

TENAUNTES OF THE Newhouses

Names of the Tennants	ac: roo: da: pt	cattle-gats	yeerely Rente	veerely Value
Phillip Allen ☞ more in Simonstone Hard-rowe & Riggs Cloase	56 - 0 - 6	1	0 xjs viijd	xj^{11} [£10 19s. 11½d.]
Christopher Metcalfe more in Hardrow	58 0 - 5 - 3	0	xjs viijd	xiiij^{11} ijs [£15 0s. 9d.]
Summa Totalis	114 - 1 - 2 - 0	0	xxiijs iiijd	25^{11} 2s 5d [£26 0s. 8½d.]

RIGGES CLOASE

Names of the Tennants	ac: da: roo: pt	0	yeerely rente	yeerely value Fyne
Phillip Allen more at Newhouses	9 - 1 - 6 - 2	0	vs	xxxjs vd [£1 10s. 5d.]
f. 75.				
John Metcalfe	10 - 3 - 4 - 0	0	vs	xxxvjs ijd
Summa Totalis	20 - 1 0 - 2	0	xs	3^{11} 7s 7d [£3 6s. 7d.]

COTTERDALE

Names of the Tenannts	ac: roo: da: pt	cattle-gats	yeerely Rente	yeerely value Fyne
Phillip Lord Wharton	3 - 1 - 2 - 2	2¾	vs vjd	xxvs iijd
Edward Lord Morley	12 - 2 - 4 1	5¾	xijs ijd	4^{11} xjs vd
Sir James Bellingham	2 - 2 - 5 - 0 [2 1 - 5 0]	3	vjs viijd	38s 9d

Leonard Lowther

	ac: roo: da: pt		yeerely rente	yeerely value	Fyne
Clarke	191 - 2 4 - 2	28¾	3ˡˡ 8s 6½d	36ˡˡ ijs	
Thomas Burton	1 - 2 - 5 0	1	ijs ijd	xjs vjd [*11s. 7d.*]	
☞ more at the Lundes					

Richard Leake

Clarke	3 - 0 - 3 - 0	1½	iiijs iiijd	xxijs ixd	
Myles Todd	15 - 2 - 7 - 1	4½	xs	vijˡˡ vijs [*£7 5s. 11½d.*]	
Thomas & Christo-pher Moore	44 - 1 - 4 - 2	12	xxvjs viijd	17ˡˡ 10s 5d [*£17 9s. 5d.*]	

f. 75d.

John Shawe	16 - 1 - 0 - 3	7½	xvjs vd [*16s. 10d.*]	6ˡˡ 18s 9d	
Widdow Hogge	5 - 3 - 7 - 1	3	vijs viijd [*6s. 8d.*]	47s 10d ½d	
The widdowe of Henry Wilson	79 - 1 - 9 - 3 [*7 - 1 9 - 3*]	2¼	vs	3ˡˡ vs 6d ½d	
Thomas Raynoldson	13 3 - 9 - 3	6	xiijs iiijd	5ˡˡ 6s 10d ½d	
Widdow Blaydes	9 - 1 - 6 - 2	1½	iiijs viijd	xxxvjs	
Richard Robinson	7 - 3 - 5 - 2	3	vjs viijd	lvjs viijd	
the parcell of ground called Cotterdale Bendes	40 - 0 - 4 - 0	0	0	vˡˡ	
Cotterdale Cowpasture	468 - 3 - 0 - 0				
Summa Totalis	844 - 2 9 2 [*844 - 1 - 9 - 2*]	82½	9ˡˡ 6s 9d ½d [*£9 7s. 2½d.*]	98ˡˡ 0s 9½d [*£97 18s. 10d.*]	

STOODALE FLATTE & COTTEREND als Thwayte

Names of the Tennants	ac: roo: da: pt		yeerely rente	yeerely value	Fyne
Franncis Metcalfe gentleman	820 - 1 - 7 - 2	0	4ˡˡ 9s 4d	87ˡˡ 7s 6d [*£86 17s. 6d.*]	

f. 76

TENAUNTS OF THE Lundes

Names of the Tennants	ac: roo: da: pt	Cattle-gats	yeerely Rente	yeerely value	Fyne
Edmond Blaydes	371 - 0 - 3 - 3	0	xxxijs vjd	32ˡˡ 10s 3d [*£32 10s. 3½d.*]	
Henry Shawe	33 - 1 - 9 - 1	1	iiijs iiijd	4ˡˡ 2s 2d	

Cutbert Shawe	32 - 0 - 7 - 1	1	iiijs iiijd	iij[li] xijs
The Children or assignes of Rowland Shawe	14 - 3 - 4 - 2	8	vjs xjd	4[li] xiijs 3d ½d
William Parkin	32 - 3 - 7 - 1	13	ixs vijd	9[li] 10s 2½d [£9 5s. 7½d.]
James Parkin	7 - 0 - 7 - 1 [7 - 0 - 8 - 1]	2½	iiijs iijd	58s ijd [£2 18s. ½d.]
Cutbert Braidly	7 - 2 - 2 - 3	0	iijs ixd	45s 1d
Roger Shawe	65 - 3 - 8 - 3	0	iiijs iijd [4s. 4d.]	8[li] 8s 8d
John Parkin	75 - 3 - 6 - 2	2½	xs vjd	x[li] xviijs ixd
Thomas Barton	123 - 0 - 1 - 1	0	xiiijs vjd	ix[li] xiiijs vjd

f. 76d.

West Ende Inge	90 - 2 - 7 = 0			
Summa Total'	854 - 3 - 5 - 2 [854 - 3 - 6 - 2]	28	4[li] 15s	88[li] 12s 11d [£88 8s. 5d.]
			rent	va'
Sayrgill Parke	496 - 1 - 5 - 0	0	liijs iiijd	xxv[li]
Stagges Fell				
Stagges Fell & the out Moore Containe	acres 9422	val' inde per Annu' att	iiijd the acre	157[li] 8d

COTTAGGES IN
Askrigge

The widdow of Jeffrey Metcalfe	A house & a garth or gardein
Martyn Wethered	A house & garth
George Metcalfe	A house & a little backside
John Metcalfe	A house & a garth

f. 77.

James Metcalfe	A house & a little garth
The said James Metcalfe	Another house & a little backside
[sold[1]] Thomas Atkinson	A house & garth
Thomas Grinswate	A house & garth
[sold[1]] George Atkinson	A house onely
Henry Foulthorp	A house & a little garth
	One housestead & garth lying waste late in the occupation of James Rawlinson for the yeerely rente of iijs iiijd
[sold[1]] John Atkinson	A house, a garth & a backside
[sold[1]] Michaell Smyth	A house and a little backside

[1] In a different hand in left margin.

For all which Cottags with their backsides & garthes, ⎱ xiijs iiijd & are
is paide the yeerely Rente of   ⎰ said to bee the
                                                           landes of Dame
                                    Margarett late Countesse of Lenox
                                    but no parte of the landes of the
                                    Abby of Jarvax Nor of the
                                    Cjˡˡ Rente Due to the same
f. 77d.

The totall yeerely value of all the said Cottags in ⎱
Askrigg aforesaid with their backsides   ⎰ vjˡˡ xiijs iiijd

And every of the Cottages
Doe also pay yeerely to the   ld by the name of a
Baylife   greene penny

                                                    [ac. roo. da. pt.]

THE Totall Measure of all the lands and Tenements ⎱
of Wennesladale in this booke before mentioned   ⎰ 16413 - 0 - 5 - 3

          ⎧ The Land inclosed   6991 - 0 - 5 - 3
          ⎪
Whereof ⎨
          ⎪ The out Moore with
          ⎩ Stagffell   9422 - 0 - 0 - 0

For all which lands & Tenements is paid the yeerely ⎱
Rente of   ⎰ Cjˡˡ 17s 11½d

     Cum 13s 14d pro Cotagij in Askrigge

The totall yeerely value of all Lands & Tenements ⎱
in this booke before mentioned   ⎰ 1298ˡˡ 15s 11½d

Cum vjˡˡ xiijs iiijd pro cotag' in Askrigge

f. 78.   Dale Grainge
                                        [ac. roo. da. pt.]
The meddow and pasture ground in Dale grainge ⎱ 220 - 0 - 2 - 1
besyde the Comon Cowe pasture   ⎰

The sayd Cowe pasture   61 - 1 - 6 - 0
                          The Helme
The meddow & pasture in the Helme besydes the ⎱
Common Cowe pasture   ⎰ 163 - 2 - 4 - 2

The Cowe pasture   124 - 0 - 5 - 0
                        Skellgill
The Meddow & pasture in Skellgill   79 - 1 - 9 - 1

                        Yorescoat
The Meddow ground in Yorescoat   46 - 3 - 4 - 2

                      Brockellcoate
The Meddow & pasture ground in ⎱
Brockellcoat   ⎰   164 - 2 - 4 - 3

Shawcoat & the
Hole houses

The Meddow & pasture ground there   100 - 3 7 - 2

Memorandum that the Tenaunts of Skellgill Brockellcoat with Shawcoat & the hole houses have their
Cattlegats in the two Common Cowe pastures Called }522 - 0 - 5 - 0
the Coat Moore, & little Fell Meawes, which Contayne
together

Camshouse

The Meddow & pasture ground in Camshouse besydes }
the Common Cowepasture   281 - 2 - 8 - 0

The sayd Cowpasture   52 - 0 - 9 - 0

Lidderskewe

The Meddow & pasture ground in Lidderskew }
haveinge noe Common Cowe pasture   280 - 2 - 5 - 3½

f. 78d.

Sedbuske

The Meddow & pasture ground in Sedbuske besydes }
the Common Cowe pasture   163 - 2 - 4 - 1

The Common Cowepasture   269 - 1 - 0 - 0

Symonstone

The Meddow and pasture ground in Symonstone }
besydes the Common Cowe pasture   229 - 1 - 0 - 1½

The sayd Common Cowe pasture   254 - 1 - 0 - 0

Hardrowe

The Meddow & pasture in Hardrowe besydes the }
Common Cowepasture   235 - 3 - 8 - 3

The Common Cowpasture   61 - 3 - 5 - 0

Forsdale
The Meddow & pasture in Forsdale 528 - 0 - 5 - 3
These have noe   The Newe houses
Common Cowe   The Meddow & pasture there   114 - 1 - 2 - 0
pasture   Riggs Cloase
    The Meddow ground there   20 - 1 - 0 - 2

Cotterdale

The meddow & pasture in Cotterdale besydes the }
Common Cowe pasture & besydes the parcel of grounde }335 - 3 - 5 - 2
called Cotterdale bends

The sayd Common Cowe pasture and }
Cotterdale Bends   508 - 3 - 4 - 0

Stodale Flatt & Cotterend
als Thwayte

The Meddow and pasture ground }
there   820 - 1 - 7 - 2

f. 79.

The Lundes

The Meddow & pasture grounds at the Lunds besydes the Common Cowe pasture	764 - 0 - 8 - 2
The Common Cowe pasture	90 - 2 - 7 - 0

The Totall Somme of all the Meddow and pasture ground aforesayd besydes the Common Cowepastures which are for the moste parte inclosed also   ac roo: da: pt: 4549 · 3 - 9 - 3

The Common Cowe pastures inclosed as aforesayde   1944 - 3 - 1 - 0

Sayrgill Parke being a Pasture inclosed   496 - 1 - 5 - 0

f. 79d.

A Noate of the number of Beastgates and their severall values In everye one of the common Cowe pastures belonginge to the severall villages before mentioned. Viz

Dale Grainge

In the Common pasture gates there called the Spen and 28 & ⅛ of a gate at vjs the gate Grainger gill   Summa   viij^ll ixs

The Helme

In the pasture called the gates Helme Pasture   32 & ¾ of a gate at iijs iiijd the gate   Summa   v^ll ixs ijd

Skellgill Brockellcoat and Shawcoat

In the Common pasture gates called Coat Moore & Little 218 & ⅛ of a gate at ijs iiijd the gate Fell meawes   Summa   xxv^ll viijs xjd ob

Camshouse

In the Common Pasture gates lynge on the west syde of 21 at   xviijd the gate Little Fell Meawes   Summa   xxxjs vjd

Sedbuske

In the pasture called Sed gates buske Slights, containing 70 at vjs viijd the gate 128 - 0 - 5 - 0   Summa   xxiij^ll vjs viijd

Also in the pasture called the upper pasture containing 52 gates at iijs the gate 141 - 0 - 5 - 0   Summa   vij^ll xvjs

Symonstone

In the Common pasture \
called Symonstone } gates
pasture / 100 at vjs the gate

Summa xxx^{ll}

f. 80.

Hardrowe
gates

In the pasture Called \ 35 & ⅓ of a gate at xs the gate
Hardrow Slights / Summa xvij^{ll} xiijs iiijd

Cotterdale
gates

In the pasture Called \ 82 & ½ at vs the gate
Cotterdale Cowe pasture / Summa xx^{ll} xijs vjd

The Lunds
gates

In the pasture called \ 28 at iiijs the gate
West end Inge / Summa v^{ll} xijs

The Totall Sum of all the \
Beastgates in the severall pastures } 668 & ⅞ parte of
before mentioned / a beastgate

Which at the severall rates aforesayd \
amounte to the yearly value of / Cxlv^{ll} xixs jd ob

ff. 80d—82d [blank].

f. 83.[1]

July 21 1679

Memorandum that the Boundery of Common lately belonging to
one Coleby and now belonging to Anthony Fothergill Alexander
Smith & Thomas Lambert was this day riden by the places and
severall Bounder marks as is herafter mentioned vizt

From Helme pasture vje [via ?] whytagill beck to Stony-gill
head, from thence towards the west (as heaven water fales) to
the great stone in or neare the Tarne from thence to Ogaram
Curack or Ogaram syde from thence to Cogill head Beakon, from
thence to Hygh-lovelysyde Beakon, from thence further towards
the west by a little rukle of stones that is on the West syde of
Lovely-syde to Bull Bogg in the Cliff head, and from thence
towards the South as a way or sheepe-raike goith lynially by a
pyke or Ruckle of stones in a little sheepe fou.. to the black-
second-Gill-pyke, from thence to the pyke-slack, and from thence
to the low-turne on the lower edge of Stagsfell, from thence
straight to gelding stone which is marked [f. 83d] with severall

---

[1] The rest of the MS. is in various hands, each different from the hand-
writing of the survey.

holes in it, and from thence lynially to the hyg west corner of Sedbuske pasture. there was present at the ryding of the Bounders as aforesaid

Thomas Metcalfe of Nappey Esq whoe was their Lord of Askrigg.

Edward Pratt of Shalcoate

Thomas Keygill
Matthew Keygill
James Pratt
Edmond Milner   } of Skelgill
Edmond Coats
George Keygill
Peter Keygill
James Winn
Richard Blayds   } of Low Coate
John Winterskell
James Metcalfe of Yoreskott
John Metcalfe of Gillyate
Peter Keygill of Grainge
Matthew Blyth senior   } of Bowbrigg
& Matthew Blyth junior
Anthony Fothergill
Alexander Smith
John Smith

f. 84.

Dec 1679

Mr Atkinson then steward to Sir John Lawder[1] . . . .

Aug: Metcalfe Sedbuske that the Bounders of Common went thus. vizt. vy. [*via* ?] whytagill beck to a hill on the west syde of Askrigg Common, from thence to hygh Angram from thence to a stone in Cogill head, from thence to Lovelysyde pyke, from thence to Bullbogg, from thence to a gray stone at the west end of the millstone & thence by the west syde of Symonstone peat-graft to a hill on the Eastsyde of the pyke slack thence to the low turne & soe on the edge.

Ed. Pratt information

That King Henry 8th gave The Abotsyde to Matthew duke of Linox and the Duke dying without issue it came to the Crowne againe, then in Queen Elizabeth: from her to K. James; King James gave it to Lodwick Duke of Linox, whoe sould it to Smith and others

f. 84d.

' A note of what moneys I have given to poor for this year 1692.' [*Followed by the names of the poor and the amounts given.*]

---

[1] Sir John Lowther of Lowther, first Viscount Lonsdale (1655–1700). For his career see *D.N.B.* and *Complete Peerage*, viii, 131–32.

f. 85 [*blank, except for two short columns of figures*].

f. 85d [*blank*].

f. 86.

A noate of those Tennauntes names that doe willingelie refer themselfes unto me

Richard Price

James Rallison

Roger Metcalfe.

f. 86d [*Jottings and scribbles*].

f. 87.

John Pratte Rent for Andrewtide last	1 - 12 - 0		
Edmond Coates	0	16	8
Edmond Prat	2	13	4
Edmond Pratt	1	5	0

John Blades saith he haith paide all his last Andrewtide Rent to Mi . . . .[1] Lodge

James Metcalfe haith paid his Andrewtide rent 7s.

f. 87d.

[*Rough draft, very illegible, of a statement concerning the survey of 3003 acres of common ' belonging to the manor or Lordshipp of Wensladale.' Mentions a Mary Colby, widow.*]

f. 88 [*scribbles*].

f. 88d [*blank*].

[1] MS. torn.

F

II.   A Survey of the Lordships of Middleham and Richmond in the County of Yorke, wth theyre severall Parts and Divisions taken in the Third Yeare of King James by Thomas Johnson and Aaron Rathborne Anno 1605.[1]

1. MIDLEHAM.

This Lordship consists of 7 principall parts or divisions, viz.

1 Midleham Towne.
2 Coverdale Chace.
3 West Witton.
4 Bishopsdale Chace.

5 Wensladale forest.
6 The Mannor of Cracall wth Rand, etc.
7 Certeyne tenementes in Carperby, Laborne, etc.

1. The Towneship of Middleham
is subdivided into 5 parts, viz.

1 The Castle and demeasnes.
2 The Township.
3 Westcote.

4 Brathwaite.
5 Ulshawe.

1. The Castle and demeasnes.

The Castle ꝑ Demeasnes were then part in fee ferme to S[r] Henry Linley[2] at the rent of 17[l] 7[s] 0[d] viz.

	acr. roods			*l.*	*s.*	*d.*
The Castle and scite therof conteyning	003	1	worth p' ann'	005	0	0
Sunscue[3] parke cont.	510	2	worth p' ann'	127	12	6
The West parke cont.	594	0	worth p' ann'	148	10	0
In all	1107	3	per an'	281	2	6

---

[1] The original MS. (M[s] 509) is in the possession of the Yorkshire Archæological Society.

[2] Sir Henry Linley lived in the castle. He was buried at Middleham 8 Nov. 1609 (Atthill, W., *Documents relating to the Collegiate Church of Middleham*, 22).

[3] Sometimes called " Sunskew," and also known as East Park. It lay to the south of the town, and together with the West Park was probably made by Ralph Nevile, who had a licence to impark his wood of Middleham in 1335 (*V.C.H., Yorks., N.R.*, i, 253-4).

The cleare yearly ymprovem^t is—263^l 15^s 6^d
W^{ch} improvem^t might well be raysed if his Matie would (by giving satisfaccon to Sr Henry Linley) resume the graunt, φ it would much tend to his Maties proffit, the good of the poore tenants there φ the Inhabitants, φ the beautifieing of the Mannor, wch is therby rent φ dismembred.

Memorand. that the Castle φ Scite is now rented at 1^l 6^s 8^d p' an' and the parkes are yet in lease for [blank] yeares to come during wch tyme the rent is 16^l 0^s 4^d φ after the expiracon therof (at wch tyme the grant in fee ferme commenseth) the rent therof is doubled wch will be —— 32^l 0^s 8^d

[p. 2

Note that these tables[1] throughout the whole Survey shew these particulars, viz.

1 The Tenants' Names.
2 What termes were then to come in the lands they held.
3 What houses φ outhouses φ lands of several qualities they held.
4 What fynes they had paid in 20 yeares before.
5 What yearly rent they paid to the King.
6 The yearly value of the things they held.
7 The Cleare yearly Improvement.[2]

[Editor's Note—

M.=Meadow. P.=Pasture. C.P.=Cowgate Pasture. P.G.= Pasture Gate. A.=Arable. When there is no term to run the second column is left blank.]

2. The Towneship of Midleham.

Chrofer. Sympson—(2) 7 years; (3) 1 house, no outhouse, M. 1 ac., P. 4 ac., A. nil; (4) 7^s 6^d; (5) 3^s 9^d; (6) 15^s 2^d.

Idem—(2) 7 years; (3) 1 house, 2 outhouses, M. 2 roods, P. 4 ac., A. 1 ac.; (4) 6^s 10^d; (5) 3^s 5^d; (6) 17^s 11^d.

Richard Loftus—(2) 6 years; (3) 1 house, 2 outhouses, M. 9 ac., P. 8 ac., A. 4 ac.; (4) 1^l 10^s 1^d; (5) 15^s 0½^d; (6) 3^l 17^s 5^d.

Idem—(2) 6 years; (3) 2 houses, no outhouse, M. 2 ac. 3 r., no P. or A.; (4) 8^s; (5) 4^s; (6) 13^s 9^d.

Chrofer. Best—(2) 6 years; (3) 2 houses, no outhouses, M. nil, P. 4 ac., A. nil; (4) 10^s; (5) 2^s 6^d; (6) 11^s 5^d.

Idem—(2) 6 years; (3) 1 house, 1 outhouse, M. 14 ac. 2 r., P. 4 ac., A. 3 roods; (4) 5^l; (5) 1^l 5^s; (6) 4^l 5^s 1½^d.

Idem—(2) 6 years; (3) 1 house, M. 5 ac., P. 8 ac., A. 1 ac. 2 r.; (4) 1^l 12^s; (5) 8^s; (6) 2^l 7^s 2^d.

[1] The tabular form in the original MS. has been abandoned in the transcript in order to avoid the heavy expense which would have been incurred by reproducing it in the text.

[2] The clear improvement is only given in the summary at the end of each sub-division.

Chrofer. Hobson—(2) 16 years; (3) no house or outhouse, M. 1 ac. 2 r., no P. or A.; (4) 8ˢ; (5) 4ˢ; (6) 7ˢ 6ᵈ.

    Idem—(2) 6 years; (3) 1 house, 1 outhouse, M. 1 ac. 3 r., P. 4 ac., A. 2 r.; (4) 13ˢ; (5) 6ˢ 6ᵈ; (6) 18ˢ 10ᵈ.

    Idem—(2) 6 years; (3) 1 house, 1 outhouse, M. 1 r., P. 4 ac.; (4) 9ˢ; (5) 3ˢ; (6) 9ˢ 4ᵈ.

Charles Tod—(2) 5 years; (3) 1 outhouse, M. 1 r.; (4) 5ˢ; (5) 1ˢ 8ᵈ; (6) 5ˢ.

John Tod—(2) 5 years; (3) 1 house, M. 1 r.; (4) 8ˢ; (5) 4ˢ; (6) 8ˢ.

Thomas Reynton—(2) 6 years; (3) 1 house, 1 outhouse, M. 5 ac. 1 r., P. 4 ac.; (4) 1ˡ 14ˢ 8ᵈ; (5) 8ˢ 8ᵈ; (6) 2ˡ 4ˢ 4ᵈ.

    Idem—(2) 7 years; (3) 1 house, P. 4 ac.; (4) 4ˢ 6ᵈ; (5) 1ˢ 6ᵈ; (6) 11ˢ 5ᵈ.

Tho. Holdsworth—(2) 18 years; (3) 1 house, 2 outhouses, M. 6 ac., P. 8 ac., A. 1 ac.; (4) 1ˡ 1ˢ; (5) 10ˢ 6ᵈ; (6) 2ˡ 15ˢ 11ᵈ.

    Idem—(2) 18 years; (3) 1 house, M. 1 ac., P. 4 ac., A. 1 ac.; (4) 1ˡ 4ˢ; (5) 6ˢ; (6) 1ˡ 0ˢ 6ᵈ.

Nicolas Gledstone—(2) 7 years; (3) 1 house, 2 outhouses, M. 10 ac. 3 r., P. 16 ac., A. 10 ac.; (4) 7ˡ 5ˢ 4ᵈ; (5) 1ˡ 16ˢ 3ᵈ; (6) 6ˡ 19ˢ 5ᵈ.

    Idem—(2) 17 years; (3) 1 house, 1 outhouse, M. 1 ac. 2 r., P. 8 ac., A. 2 r.; (4) 2ˡ; (5) 10ˢ; (6) 1ˡ 9ˢ.

    Idem—(2) 7 years; (3) no house or outhouse, M. 4 ac.; (4) 3ˡ 4ˢ; (5) 16ˢ; (6) 1ˡ.

Wᵐ Fosse—(2) 7 years; (3) 1 house, 1 outhouse, P. 4 ac.; (4) 6ˢ; (5) 3ˢ; (6) 11ˢ 5ᵈ.

    Idem—(2) 7 years; (3) 1 house, 1 outhouse, M. 2 ac. 3 r., P. 8 ac., A. 1 ac. 2 r.; (4) 2ˡ 0ˢ 6ᵈ; (5) 13ˢ 6ᵈ; (6) 1ˡ 19ˢ 11ᵈ.

    Idem—(2) 7 years; (3) M. 12 ac. 1 r.; (4) 3ˡ 12ˢ; (5) 1ˡ·4ˢ; (6) 3ˡ 2ˢ 6ᵈ.

    Idem—(2) 7 years; (3) 1 house, 2 outhouses, M. 4 ac. 2r., P. 4 ac.; (4) 1ˡ 7ˢ; (5) 9ˢ; (6) 1ˡ 10ˢ 7ᵈ.

Charles Michel—(2) 6 years; (3) 1 house, 3 outhouses, M. 8 ac. 1r., P. 16 ac., A. 2 ac. 3 r.; (4) 5ˡ 14ˢ; (5) 1ˡ 8ˢ 6ᵈ; (6) 4ˡ 17ˢ 11ᵈ.

John Waterson—(2) 16 years; (3) 1 house, 3 outhouses, M. 6 ac., P. 8 ac., A. 2 ac. 3 r.; (4) 2ˡ 11ˢ; (5) 17ˢ; (6) 3ˡ 5ˢ 2ᵈ.

John Loblow—(2) 7 years; (3) 1 house, 2 outhouses, M. 5 ac. 2 r., P. 8 ac., A. 1 ac. 1 r.; (4) 1ˡ 12ˢ 8ᵈ; (5) 16ˢ 4ᵈ; (6) 2ˡ 15ˢ 4ᵈ.

John Ingleton—(2) nil; (3) 1 house, M. 1 ac. 1 r., P. 4 ac., A. 1 ac.; (4) 1ˡ; (5) 5ˢ; (6) 1ˡ 1ˢ 8ᵈ.

Stephen Hobson—(2) 6 years; (3) 1 house, 1 outhouse, M. 1 ac. 2 r., P. 4 ac.; (4) 6ˢ; (5) 2ˢ; (6) 17ˢ 7ᵈ.

John Mason—(2) 7 years; (3) 1 house, M. 1 r., P. 4 ac.; (4) 6^s;
   (5) 2^s; (6) 10^s 1^d.
   Idem—(2) 7 years; (3) 1 house; (4) 5^s; (5) 1^s 8^d; (6) 5^s.
   Idem—(2) 7 years; (3) 1 house, 1 outhouse, M. 1 r., P. 8 ac.,
   A. 2 ac. 2 r.; (4) 2^l; (5) 10^s; (6) 1^l 12^s.
Robt Holdsworth—(2) 11 years; (3) 1 house, P. 4 ac.; (4) 11^s 3^d;
   (5) 3^s 9^d; (6) 11^s 5^d.
   Idem—(2) 11 years; (3) 1 outhouse; (4) 1^s 6^d; (5) 6^d; (6) 1^s.
   Idem—(2) 7 years; (3) 1 house, 2 outhouses, M. 2 ac., P. 4 ac.,
   A. 1 ac. 2 r.; (4) 18^s 4^d; (5) 9^s 2^d; (6) 1^l 10^s 8^d
   Idem—(2) 18 years; (3) 1 house, 2 outhouses, M. 8 ac.,
   P. 8 ac.; (4) 2^l 8^s; (5) 16^s; (6) 3^l 2^s 10^d.
John Wympe—(2) nil; (3) 1 house, 1 outhouse, P. 4 ac.; (4) 18^s;
   (5) 4^s 6^d; (6) 11^s 5^d.   [p. 3
George Spence—(2) 6 years; (3) 1 house, 4 outhouses, M. 3 ac.,
   P. 8 ac.; (4) 1^l 7^s; (5) 13^s 6^d; (6) 1^l 16^s 2^d.
   Idem—(2) nil; (3) 1 house, M. 2 ac.; (4) 2^s; (5) 1^s; (6) 12^s.
Rowland Atkinson—(2) 6 years; (3) 1 house, 1 outhouse, M. 2 r.,
   P. 8 ac.; (4) 3^l 12^s; (5) 12^s; (6) 1^l 2^s 10^d.
William Forest—(2) 6 years; (3) 1 house, 1 outhouse, M. 6 ac. 2 r.,
   P. 8 ac., A. 7 ac. 2 r.; (4) 4^l 12^s 8^d; (5) 1^l 3^s 2^d; (6)
   4^l 8^s 8^d.
Ralph Robinson—(2) 7 years; (3) 1 house, M. ½ r., P. 4 ac.;
   (4) 8^s; (5) 2^s; (6) 10^s 7^d.
Francis Midleton—(2) 6 years; (3) 1 house, 2 outhouses, M. 5 ac.
   1 r., P. 8 ac.; (4) 2^l 8^s; (5) 12^s; (6) 2^l 8^s 11^d.
   Idem—(2) 6 years; (3) M. 1 ac. 1 r., P. 4 ac.; (4) 16^s; (5) 4^s;
   (6) 14^s 3^d.
Symon Midleton—(2) 7 years; (3) 1 house, 1 outhouse, M. 1 ac.
   1 r., P. 4 ac.; (4) 12^s 6^d; (5) 4^s 2^d; (6) 17^s 8^d.
Francis Atkinson—(2) nil; (3) 1 house, P. 4 ac.; (4) 1^l 1^s; (5) 5^s 3^d;
   (6) 11^s 5^d.
Anne Collison—(2) nil; (3) 1 house; (4) 6^s; (5) 3^s; (6) 5^s.
Wm Robinson—(2) nil; (3) 1 house, 1 outhouse; (4) 4^s; (5) 2^s;
   (6) 4^s.
Francis Turner—(2) 6 years; (3) 1 house, 1 outhouse, M. 6 ac. 3 r.,
   P. 8 ac.; (4) 2^l 6^s 8^d; (5) 11^s 8^d; (6) 2^l 16^s 7^d.
Percival Langdale—(2) 7 years; (3) 1 house, 1 outhouse, M. 1 ac.
   1 r., P. 4 ac.; (4) 8^s; (5) 4^s; (6) 18^s 4^d.
John Spence—(2) 6 years; (3) 1 house, 2 outhouses, M. 3 ac. 3 r.,
   P. 8 ac.; (4) 2^l 16^s 3^d; (5) 11^s 3^d; (6) 2^l 4^s 11^d.
Willm. Nevile—(2) 7 years; (3) 1 house; (4) 2^s; (5) 1^s; (6) 3^s 4^d.
Symon Williamson—(2) 7 years; (3) 1 house; (4) 2^s; (5) 1^s; (6)
   3^s 4^d.

Charles Brewster—(2) 6 years; (3) 1 house; (4) 4ˢ; (5) 2ˢ; (6) 5ˢ.

Henry Dighton—(2) 7 years; (3) 1 house; (4) 1ˢ; (5) 6ᵈ; (6) 2ˢ 6ᵈ.

Adam Midleton, esq.—(2) nil; (3) 1 house; (4) 1ˢ; (5) 6ᵈ; (6) 2ˢ 6ᵈ.

Francis Foster—(2) 6 years; (3) 1 house, 1 outhouse, P. 8 ac.;
    (4) 1ˡ; (5) 6ˢ 8ᵈ; (6) 1ˡ 2ˢ 2ᵈ.

Thomas Ingleton—(2) nil; (3) 2 houses, 2 outhouses, P. 4 ac.;
    (4) 6ˢ; (5) 3ˢ; (6) 16ˢ 1ᵈ.

    Idem—(2) 7 years; (3) M. 1 ac. 2 r.; (4) 6ˢ; (5) 4ˢ; (6) 7ˢ 6ᵈ.

Wm Ploughwright, sen.—(3) 1 mill; (4) 13ˢ 4ᵈ; (5) 6ˢ 8ᵈ; (6) 1ˡ.

    Idem—(2) nil; (3) 1 house, 1 outhouse, M. 4 ac. 3 r., P. 8 ac.,
    A. 1 ac. 1 r.; (4) 6ˡ; (5) 1ˡ; (6) 2ˡ 11ˢ 7ᵈ.

Francis Mangie—(2) nil; (3) 1 house, 1 outhouse, M. 4 ac. 3 r.,
    P. 8 ac., A. 1 ac. 1 r.; (4) 6ˡ; (5) 1ˡ; (6) 2ˡ 11ˢ 7ᵈ.

Reynold Nelson—(2) nil; (3) 1 house, 1 outhouse, M. 1 r., P. 4 ac.,
    A. 1 r.; (4) 11ˢ 3ᵈ; (5) 3ˢ 9ᵈ; (6) 14ˢ 1ᵈ.

John Ibotson—(2) 7 years; (3) 1 house, P. 4 ac.; (4) 7ˢ 6ᵈ; (5)
    3ˢ 9ᵈ; (6) 13ˢ 2ᵈ.

George Cooke—(2) 6 years; (3) 1 house, 1 outhouse, M. 5 ac. 2 r.,
    P. 4 ac.; (4) 1ˡ 10ˢ; (5) 15ˢ; (6) 2ˡ 2ˢ 3ᵈ.

Chrofer. Bateman—(2) nil; (3) 1 house, P. 4 ac.; (4) 4ˢ; (5) 2ˢ;
    (6) 11ˢ 5ᵈ.

Francis Spence—(2) 7 yrs.; (3) 1 house, 1 outhouse, M. 4 ac. 2 r.,
    P. 8 ac., A. 1 ac. 3 r.; (4) 3ˡ 15ˢ 5ᵈ; (5) 15ˢ 1ᵈ; (6) 2ˡ 15ˢ 8ᵈ.

Robᵗ Hobson—(2) nil; (3) 1 house, 1 outhouse, M. 6 ac., P. 8 ac.;
    (4) 1ˡ 0ˢ 6ᵈ; (5) 10ˢ 3ᵈ; (6) 2ˡ 12ˢ 10ᵈ.

    Idem—(2) nil; (3) 1 house, 1 outhouse, M. 2 r., P. 4 ac.;
    (4) 9ˢ; (5) 4ˢ 6ᵈ; (6) 13ˢ 11ᵈ.

    Idem—(2) nil; (3) 1 house, M. 2 ac. 1 r., P. 4 ac.; (4) 11ˢ 3ᵈ;
    (5) 3ˢ 9ᵈ; (6) 1ˡ 1ˢ 10ᵈ.

    Idem—(2) 7 yrs.; (3) 1 house, 1 outhouse, M. 1 ac., P. 4 ac.;
    (4) 6ˢ; (5) 3ˢ; (6) 16ˢ 5ᵈ.

    Idem—(2) nil; (3) 1 house, 1 outhouse, M. 6 ac., P. 4 ac.;
    (4) 2ˡ 5ˢ 10ᵈ; (5) 9ˢ 2ᵈ; (6) 2ˡ 4ˢ 9ᵈ.

    Idem—(3) a shop; (4) 1ˢ 4ᵈ; (5) 8ᵈ; (6) 2ˢ.

    Idem—(2) nil; (3) M. 3 ac.; (4) 16ˢ; (5) 8ˢ; (6) 15ˢ.

    Idem—(2) nil; (3) 1 house, 2 outhouses, M. 17 ac. 1 r., P. 8 ac.,
    A. 8 ac. 1 r.; (4) 3ˡ 10ˢ; (5) 1ˡ 3ˢ 4ᵈ; (6) 7ˡ 0ˢ 5ᵈ.

Wᵐ Ploughwright, jun.—(2) 6 yrs.; (3) 1 house, 1 outhouse,
    M. 1 r., P. 4 ac.; (4) 15ˢ; (5) 3ˢ 9ᵈ; (6) 11ˢ 5ᵈ.

Henry Waterson—(2) 7 yrs.; (3) 1 house, 1 outhouse, M. 5 ac. 3 r.,
    P. 8 ac., A. 1 ac.; (4) 2ˡ 5ˢ; (5) 11ˢ 3ᵈ; (6) 2ˡ 12ˢ 11ᵈ.

    Idem—(2) 7 yrs.; (3) 1 house, 1 outhouse, M. 2 ac. 1 r.,
    P. 4 ac.; (4) 14ˢ 4ᵈ; (5) 3ˢ 7ᵈ; (6) 1ˡ 2ˢ 8ᵈ.

Percival Metcalfe—(2) 6 yrs.; (3) 1 house, 1 outhouse, M. 6 ac. 3 r.,
    P. 8 ac., A. 2 r.; (4) 2ˡ 5ˢ; (5) 11ˢ 3ᵈ; (6) 2ˡ 16ˢ 11ᵈ.

Charles Watson—(2) nil; (3) 1 house, 1 outhouse, P. 4 ac.; (4) 16^s;
  (5) 4^s; (6) 12^s 1^d.
Rich. Swyndebank—(2) 7 yrs.; (3) 1 house, 1 outhouse, M. 2 r.,
  P. 8 ac., A. 1 ac. 2 r.; (4) 1^l 12^s; (5) 8^s; (6) 1^l 8^s 8^d.
Wm Ploughwright, sen.—(2) 7 yrs.; (3) 1 house, 1 outhouse,
  M. 7 ac., P. 4 ac.; (4) 2^l 5^s; (5) 15^s; (6) 2^l 8^s 1^d.
  Idem—(2) nil; (3) 1 house, 1 outhouse, P. 4 ac., A. 3 r.;
  (4) 16^s; (5) 4^s; (6) 14^s 5^d.
James Gueldert—(2) 6 yrs.; (3) 1 house, 1 outhouse, M. 10 ac.,
  P. 8 ac.; (4) 2^l; (5) 1^l; (6) 3^l 12^s 10^d.
Widow Tenant—(2) 7 yrs.; (3) 1 house, M. 6 ac. 2 r., P. 8 ac.,
  A. 1 ac.; (4) 4^l 1^s 3^d; (5) 13^s 6$\frac{1}{2}$^{d}; (6) 2^l 17^s 8^d.

[p. 4

The Conclusion of the last table.		
The Number of Tenants—84		
The Quantity of Land—665 ac. 1 rood ℮ $\frac{1}{2}$		
Fynes paid within 20 years	117^l 17^s	3^d
The yearly rent	034^l 10^s	8^d
The yearly value	127^l 17^s	5$\frac{1}{4}$^{d}
The cleare Improvement	93^l 06^s	9$\frac{1}{2}$^{d}

3. Westcotes Demeasnes.

[1]Sir Henry Linley holdeth certayne lands called Westcotes at the
rent of £1 13^s 4^d; the quantity of meadow is 20 ac., pasture
8 ac., total 28 ac.; yearly value £5 16^s 2^d.
He also holdeth a parcell of Meadow called Kilne close at the
rent of 13^s 4^d; 7 ac. 3 r.; yearly value 1^l 18^s 9^d.
He also holdeth 3 closes called ye Wiseings, Guilpoole ℮ ye Mother
at the rent of 1^l 13^s 4^d; the quantity is 64 ac. 1 r.; yearly
value 16^l 1^s 3^d.

The conclusion of Westcote.		
The whole quantity of land is	100 ac.	
The yearly rent is	4^l 0^s	0^d
The yearly value is	23^l 16^s	2^d
The cleare improvement is	19^l 16^s	2^d

4. Brathwait.[2]

[3]Richard Ward[4] holdeth a Capitall Messuage or ferme called
Brathwayt ℮ payeth yearly rent for the same—10^l 16^s 8^d

[1] " Sold to Mrs Linley " in the margin.

[2] " In par. of East Witton " in the margin. This manor, since its first
mention in 1475, followed the descent of the manor of Middleham, of which
it was held (V.C.H., Yorks., N.R., i, 285).

[3] " Horner tenant " in the margin.

[4] Christopher, son of John Warde, had a grant of the site of the manor
of Brathwayte on 25 Aug. 1557 for 15 years from 1572 (C.P.R, Phil. and
Mary, iv, 33).

The house ꝑ scite contain 2 ac., meadow belonging to it 97 ac.
2 r., pasture 156 ac., total, 255 ac. 2 r.

The house ꝑ scite yearly worth 2^l; the meadow 24^l 7^s 6^d,
the pasture 31^l 4^s 0^d, total 57^l 11^s 6^d; the improvement is 46^l 14^s 10^d.

----

5. Ulshaw.[1]

Symon Beverley holds a Capital Messuage or ferme called Ulshaw
and payeth yearly rent for the same 6^l 13^s 4^d.

The house ꝑ scite contain 1 ac. 1 r.; Meadow belonging 63 ac.;
Pasture belonging 164 ac. 1 r.: Total 228 ac. 2 r.

The house ꝑ scite worth yearly 001^l 0^s 0^d; Meadow 015^l 15^s;
Pasture 27^l 7^s 6^d: total, 43^l 2^s 6^d (sic): the improvement is 37^l 9^s 2^d.

[p. 5

Demeasnes.

	£	s.	d.
[2]Chrofer. Crofts,[3] gent., holdeth Cottescue parke[4] and payeth yearly rent	03	06	8
It conteyneth 112 acres and is worth yearly	16	16	0
Md. that he held it from Q. Eliz. for 3 lives ꝑ afterwards in fee ferme at ye rent	06	13	4

James Ward holdeth the Toll of Midleham ꝑ 7 shops in the shambles and Market place at the yearly rent of	03	00	00
It is worth yearly	30	00	00

----

[5]Hee holdeth by lease of 14 years to come of all the Cole ꝑ Lead mynes wthin the lo^p of Midle-ham paying yearly	04	00	00
By these, formerly he rec^d small benefitt, but now nothing at all.			

----

[6]Mr. Aishe holdeth 2 watermills for corne ꝑ one fulling mill wthin this Township paying yearly	[blank]		
They are worth yearly	06	13	4

[1] In the par. of East Witton, but now in par. of Thornton Steward.

[2] " In fee farme before ye graunt to the City " in the margin.

[3] His son Christopher was Lord Mayor of York 1629 and 1641 and was knighted at York by the king on Sunday, 21 Nov. 1641, on which day he entertained His Majesty at dinner (*Skaife MS.*).

[4] In par. of Coverham. This park seems to have been formed in the middle of the fifteenth century (*V.C.H., Yks., N.R.,* i, 218).

[5] " Wharton held this since " in the margin.

[6] " Watson hath ye 2 Mills for 31 yeares, Blades has ye other " in the margin.

[1]The Deanry of Midleham.

This is in the guift of his Matie wherto is belonging
a fayre house wth Orcyards, gardens, etc.,
and is worth yearly   05 00 00
The Gleab consists of

Meadow 43 acr., yearly worth	10	15	00
Pasture 10 acr., yearly worth	02	00	00
The Tithes, Easter booke, etc., yearly worth	62	5	00

In all   80 00 00

The generall Conclusion
of the Towneship of
Midleham, being the
first division of the Lo^p
of Midleham

Tenement Land.
The number of Tennants [*blank*]

	l.	*s.*	*d.*
Quantity of Land 1149 acr.			
Fynes paid w^thin 20 yeares	187	17	03
The yearly rent	052	00	08
The yearly value	229	11	05½
The cleare improvement	177	10	09½

Demeasnes.

The Quantity of Land 1319 acr.			
The yearly rent	044	07	08
The yearly value	385	14	08
The cleare improvement	341	07	00

[p. 6

2. Coverdale Chace.[2]

This consists of seaven Parts, viz.

Carleton, Coverham, Gamersgill, Flemshope, Horsehouse, Bradley, Woodall.

1. Carleton.[3]

Vincent Metcalfe—(2) 3 lives; (3) 1 house, 2 outhouses, M. 19 ac.
3 r., A. 7 ac., Cowgate Pasture, 12; (4) 3^l 2^s 8^d; (5)
1^l 11^s 4^d; (6) 10^l 19^s 9^d.

John Horner—(2) 3 lives; (3) M. 4 ac. 1 r., A. 1 ac. 1 r., C.P. 2;
(4) 13^s 4^d; (5) 6^s 8^d; (6) 2^l 2^s 3^d.

Richard Gueldert—(2) 3 lives; (3) M. 3 ac.; (4) 4^s; (5) 2^s; (6) 15^s.

Vincent Metcalfe—(2) 3 lives; (3) a brewing house; (4) 10^s; (5) 5^s;
(6) 1^l.

Thomas Dawson—(2) —; (3) 1 house, 2 outhouses, M. 13 ac. 3 r.,
A. 1 ac. 2 r., C.P., 3; (4) 1^l 9^s 4½^d; (5) 9^s 9½^d; (6) 3^l 14^s 6^d.

Idem—(2) —; (3) 1 house, 2 outhouses, M. 8 ac. 2 r., A. 2 ac.
3 r., C.P. 3½; (4) 1^l 15^s; (5) 11^s 8^d; (6) 2^l 17^s 3^d.

[1] " Not the Cities " in the margin.
[2] The forest of Coverdale is mentioned in 1270 (*V.C.H.*, *Yks.*, *N.R.*, i, 218).
[3] In par. of Coverham.

Arthur Dawson, jun.—(2) —; (3) 1 house, 1 outhouse, M. 15 ac.
2 r., A. 1 ac. 1 r., C.P. 3; (4) 1^l 9^s $4\frac{1}{2}^d$; (5) 9^s $9\frac{1}{2}^d$; (6)
3^l 19^s 1^d.

Idem—(2) —; (3) 1 house, 2 outhouses, M. 8 ac. 2 r., A. 2 ac.
3 r., C.P. $3\frac{1}{2}$; (4) 1^l 15^s 0^d; (5) 11^s 8^d; (6) 2^l 17^s 3^d.

Antho. Dawson, jun.—(2) —; (3) 1 house, 1 outhouse, M. 15 ac.
2 r., A. 1 ac. 1 r., C.P. 3; (4) 1^l 9^s $4\frac{1}{2}^d$; (5) 9^s $9\frac{1}{2}^d$;
(6) 3^l 19^s 1^d.

Antho. Dawson, sen.—(2) —; (3) 1 house, 3 outhouses, M. 24 ac.
3 r., A. 10 ac., C.P. 8; (4) 5^l 6^s 10^d; (5) 1^l 6^s $8\frac{1}{2}^d$;
(6) 6^l 14^s 2^d.

John Dawson—(2) —; (3) 1 house, 1 outhouse, M. 25 ac. 1 r.,
A. 3 r., C.P. $5\frac{1}{2}$; (4) 1^l 16^s 10^d; (5) 18^s 5^d; (6) 5^l 10^s $4\frac{1}{2}^d$

John Foxgill—(2) —; (3) 1 house, 5 outhouses, M. 37 ac., C.P. 6;
(4) 2^l 11^d; (5) 1^l $5\frac{1}{2}^d$; (6) 7^l 1^s.

Thomas Gueldert—(2) —; (3) 1 house, 4 outhouses, M. 23 ac.
2 r., A. 4 ac. 1 r., C.P. 5; (4) 3^l 8^s; (5) 17^s; (6) 5^l 15^s 5^d.

James Gueldert—(2) —; (3) 1 house, 1 outhouse, M. 13 ac. 3 r.,
A. 1 ac. 3 r., C.P. 3; (4) 1^l 9^s 6^d; (5) 9^s 10^d; (6) 3^l 6^s 8^d.

Richard Gueldert—(2) —; (3) 1 house, 2 outhouses, M. 21 ac. 3 r.,
A. 3 ac., C.P. 3; (4) 1^l 19^s 4^d; (5) 9^s 10^d; (6) 4^l 14^s.

Idem—(2) —; (3) 6 outhouses, A. 3 r., C.P. 1; (4) 1^l 16^s;
(5) 9^s; (6) 1^l 14^s.

Idem—(2) —; (3) 1 house, 1 outhouse, M. 8 ac. 1 r., A. 1 ac.
1 r., C.P. $3\frac{1}{2}$; (4) 1^l 2^s 6^d; (5) 5^s $7\frac{1}{2}^d$; (6) 2^l 5^s 5^d.

Barthol. Gueldert—(2) —; (3) 1 house, 2 outhouses, M. 21 ac.
1 r., A. 5 ac., C.P. 5; (4) 1^l 14^s; (5) 17^s; (6) 5^l 4^s 2^d.

Henry Lambert—(2) —; (3) 1 house, 3 outhouses, M. 7 ac.,
A. 2 ac., C.P. 2; (4) 14^s; (5) 7^s; (6) 1^l 18^s 4^d.

Henry Dawson—(2) —; (3) 1 house, 1 outhouse, M. 13 ac. 2 r.,
A. 2 ac., C.P. $3\frac{1}{2}$; (4) 1^l 3^s 4^d; (5) 11^s 8^d; (6) 2^l 16^s 8^d.

Idem—(2) —; (3) 2 outhouses, M. 12 ac., C.P. 3; (4) 1^l;
(5) 10^s; (6) 2^l 18^s.

John Horner—(2) —; (3) 1 house, 1 outhouse, M. 5 ac. 3 r.,
C.P. 2; (4) 1^l; (5) 6^s 8^d; (6) 1^l 10^s 2^d.

William Watson—(2) —; (3) 1 house, 1 outhouse, M. 9 ac., A. 1 ac.,
C.P. 2; (4) 1^l 2^s 4^d; (5) 5^s $7\frac{1}{2}^d$; (6) 2^l 3^s.

George Foster—(2) —; (3) 1 house, 1 outhouse, M. 8 ac. 3 r.,
C.P. 1; (4) 12^s; (5) 4^s; (6) 1^l 15^s.

William Buckle—(2) —; (3) 1 house, 1 outhouse, M. 13 ac. 3 r.,
A. 1 ac., C.P. 5; (4) 2^l 9^s; (5) 16^s 4^d; (6) 3^l 10^s.

Anthony Becke—(2) —; (3) M. 6 ac., C.P. 2; (4) 1^l; (5) 6^s 8^d;
(6) 1^l 6^s 8^d.

Gawen Spence—(2) —; (3) 1 house, 1 outhouse, M. 6 ac. 1 r.,
A. 3 ac., C.P. 4; (4) 2^l; (5) 13^s 4^d; (6) 2^l 4^s 2^d.

John Pickering—(2) —; (3) 1 outhouse, M. 3 ac., A. 1 ac., C.P. 4; (4) 1^l 2^s; (5) 11^s; (6) 1^l 13^s 4^d.

Idem—(2) —; (3) 1 house, M. 3 r.; (4) 5^s; (5) 1^s 8^d; (6) 4^s.

Richard Dawson—(2) —; (3) an overshot mill[1]; (4) 2^l 13^s 4^d; (5) 1^l 6^s 8^d; (6) 5^l.

Chrofer. Lobley—(2) —; (3) 1 house, 1 outhouse, M. 17 ac. 2 r., A. 1 ac., C.P. 3½; (4) 2^l 7^s 4^d; (5) 11^s 10^d; (6) 3^l 17^s 6^d.

Idem—(2) —; (3) 1 house, M. 6 ac., C.P. 2; (4) 1^l 6^s 8^d; (5) 6^s 8^d; (6) 1^l 6^s 8^d.

John Holdsworth—(2) —; (3) 2 houses, 2 outhouses, M. 18 ac., A. 3 ac., C.P. 5; (4) 1^l 12^s 2^d; (5) 16^s 1^d; (6) 4^l 8^s 2^d.

Thomas Buckle—(2) 7 yrs.; (3) 1 house, 1 outhouse, M. 5 ac., C.P. 1½; (4) 1^l; (5) 5^s; (6) 1^l 3^s 8^d.

William Hammond—(2) —; (3) 1 house, 2 outhouses, M. 11 ac., A. 2 ac., C.P. 5; (4) 2^l 8^s 6^d; (5) 16^s 2^d; (6) 3^l 3^s 4^d.

Symon Dawson—(2) —; (3) 1 house, 3 outhouses, M. 13 ac., A. 1 ac. 2 r., C.P. 4; (4) 1^l 6^s 11^d; (5) 13^s 5½^d; (6) 3^l 4^s 6^d.

The Conclusion of Carleton	Tennants—34	£	s.	d.
	Lands—459 ac. 3 r.			
	Beastgates—115			
	Fynes p^d in 20 years	55	0	3
	The yearly rent	19	9	11½
	The yearly value	111	16	2½
	The cleare improvement	91	16	3

2. Coverham.

[p. 7

	£	s.	d.
Mr. Loftus[2] holdeth certeyne lands at the rent of	4	12	2
Medow—28 ac. 1 rood ⎫ worth yearly			
Pasture—48 ac. 2 roods ⎰ both of them	10	10	0
Fynes pd in 20 yeares for it	9	04	4
The cleare improvem^t is	5	17	10

3. Gamersgill.[3]

Leonard Ryder—(2) —; (3) 1 house, 5 outhouses, M. 28 ac., P.G. 11; (4) 3^l; (5) 1^l 10^s; (6) 7^l 8^s.

Chrofer. Ripley—(2) —; (3) 1 house, 3 outhouses, M. 12 ac., P.G. 5; (4) 2^l 5^s; (5) 15^s; (6) 3^l 9^s 8^d.

William Foster—(2) —; (3) 1 house, 3 outhouses, M. 26 ac., P.G. 11; (4) 3^l 6^s 8^d; (5) 1^l 13^s 4^d; (6) 6^l 10^s.

[1] Overshot, driven by water shot over from above; overshot mill, a mill to which the power is supplied by an overshot wheel (N.E.D.).

[2] In the Patent Roll 1628 the Coverham lands are described as lately in the hands of Adam Loftus and lately demised to Christopher Loftus, gent. Rent 4^l 12^s 2^d.

[3] A hamlet in tnshp. of Carlton-high-dale, par. Coverham.

Symon Topham—(2) —; (3) 1 house, 3 outhouses, M. 12 ac.,
  P.G. 5; (4) 3^l 6^s 8^d; (5) 13^s 4^d; (6) 3^l.
  Idem—(2) —; (3) 1 house, 2 outhouses, M. 13 ac., P.G. 4$\frac{1}{2}$;
  (4) 3^l 6^s 8^d; (5) 13^s 4^d; (6) 3^l 5^s 8^d.
George Foster—(2) —; (3) 1 house, 4 outhouses, M. 27 ac., P.G.
  11; (4) 8^l 6^s 8^d; (5) 1^l 13^s 4^d; (6) 6^l 11^s 8^d.
  Idem—(2) —; (3) 1 house, 1 outhouse, M. 6 ac., P.G. 2$\frac{1}{2}$;
  (4) 1^l; (5) 6^s 8^d; (6) 1^l 8^s 4^d.
Charles Watson—(2) —; (3) 1 house, 2 outhouses, M. 24 ac.,
  P.G. 11; (4) 9^l; (5) 1^l 10^s; (6) 6^l 1^s 8^d.
George Ripley—(2) —; (3) 1 house, 2 outhouses, M. 13 ac.,
  P.G. 5; (4) 2^l; (5) 13^s 4^d; (6) 3^l 3^s 4^d.
Robert Yeoman—(2) —; (3) 1 house, 2 outhouses, M. 12 ac.,
  P.G. 5; (4) 1^l 10^s; (5) 15^s; (6) 3^l 0^s 8^d.
Willm. Topham—(2) —; (3) 1 house, 2 outhouses, M. 7 ac.,
  P.G. 2$\frac{1}{2}$; (4) 1^l; (5) 6^s 8^d; (6) 1^l 14^s 2^d.
Henry Dawson—(2) —; (3) 1 house, 1 outhouse, M. 17 ac.,
  P.G. 5$\frac{1}{2}$; (4) 1^l 10^s; (5) 15^s; (6) 3^l 18^s 6^d.
  Idem—(2) —; (3) 1 house, 1 outhouse, M. 17 ac., P.G. 5$\frac{1}{2}$;
  (4) 3^l 15^s; (5) 15^s; (6) 3^l 18^s 4^d.

			l.	s.	d.
	The number of Tennants 13				
	Meadow ground	214 ac.			
The Conclusion	Pasture gates	84$\frac{1}{2}$			
of Gamersgill	The fynes in 20 yeares		43	6	8
	The yearly rent		12	0	0
	The yearly value		53	10	0
	The cleare improvem^t		41	10	0

4. Flemshope.[1]

Henry Hodgson—(3) 1 tenement, M. 14 ac. 3 r., P.G. 3; (4)
  4^l 10^s; (5) 1^l 10^s; (6) 2^l 13^s 4^d.
James Smith—(3) 1 tenement, M. 13 ac., P.G. 3; (4) 3^l; (5) 1^l
  10^s; (6) 3^l 8^s 8^d.
Michael Hammond—(3) 1 tenement, M. 13 ac., P.G. 3; (4) 3^l;
  (5) 1^l 10^s; (6) 3^l 8^s 8^d.
Widow Whitay—(3) 1 tenement, M. 14 ac., P.G. 3; (4) 6^l; (5) 1^l
  10^s; (6) 3^l 12^s 8^d.

			l.	s.	d.
	The Number of Tennants—4				
	Quantity of Meadow	54 ac.			
The Conclusion	Pasture gates	12			
of Flemshope	Fynes paid in 20 yeares		16	10	0
	The yearly rent		06	00	0
	The yearly value		13	03	4
	The cleare improvem^t		07	03	4

[1] Fleensop, hamlet in tnshp. of Carlton-high-dale, par. Coverham.

5. Horse house.[1] [p. 8

Raph Rider, senior—(2) —; (3) 1 house, 6 outhouses, M. 16 ac., P.G. $6\frac{3}{4}$; (4) 3^l 5^s; (5) 1^l 12^s 6^d; (6) 4^l 1^s 4^d.

Francis Rider—(2) —; (3) 1 house, 2 outhouses, M. 16 ac., P.G. $6\frac{3}{4}$; (4) 6^l 10^s; (5) 1^l 12^s 6^d; (6) 4^l 1^s 4^d.

James Topham—(2) —; (3) 1 house, 1 outhouse, M. 10 ac., P.G. 3; (4) 4^l 17^s 6^d; (5) 16^s 3^d; (6) 2^l.

Anthony Yeoman—(2) —; (3) 1 house, 4 outhouses, M. 14 ac., P.G. 6; (4) 5^l 15^s 8^d; (5) 1^l 8^s 11^d; (6) 3^l 11^s 8^d.

Otwell Rider—(2) —; (3) 1 house, 5 outhouses, M. 17 ac., P.G. 9; (4) 9^l 15^s; (5) 1^l 12^s 6^d; (6) 4^l 2^s 2^d.

John Hamond—(2) —; (3) 1 house, 2 outhouses, M. 9 ac., P.G. 4; (4) 2^l 8^s 4^d; (5) 16^s 3^d; (6) 3^l 3^s 4^d.

John Yeoman—(2) 33 yrs.; (3) 1 house, 2 outhouses, M. 8 ac., P.G. 15; (4) 1^l 6^s 8^d; (5) 6^s 8^d; (6) 3^l 4^s.

Idem—(2) 18 yrs.; (3) 1 house, 2 outhouses, M. 8 ac., P.G. 3; (4) 3^l 12^s 1^d; (5) 14^s 5^d; (6) 1^l 19^s 8^d.

The Conclusion of Horsehouse	The Number of Tennants	8			
	Quantity of Meadow	98 ac.			
	Pasture gates	$53\frac{1}{2}$	l.	s.	d.
	Fynes in 20 yeares		37	10	8
	Yearly rent		09	0	0
	Yearly value		26	3	6
	Cleare improvem^t		17	3	6

6. Bradley.[1]

Miles Gueldert—(2) —; (3) 1 house, 5 outhouses, M. 30 ac., P.G. 22; (4) 4^l; (5) 2^l; (6) 7^l 13^s 4^d.

Richard Gueldert—(2) —; (3) 1 house, 1 outhouse, M. 7 ac., P.G. $5\frac{1}{2}$; (4) 1^l; (5) 10^s; (6) 1^l 11^s.

Idem—(2) —; (3) M. 6 ac., P.G. $5\frac{1}{2}$; (4) 1^l; (5) 10^s; (6) 1^l 6^s.

Ralphe Hammond—(2) —; (3) 1 house, 4 outhouses, M. 12 ac., P.G. 11; (4) 2^l; (5) 1^l; (6) 3^l 10^s.

John Hamond—(2) —; (3) 1 house, 4 outhouses, M. 13 ac., P.G. 11; (4) 3^l; (5) 1^l; (6) 3^l 12^s 6^d.

Leonard Spence—(2) —; (3) 1 house, 4 outhouses, M. 30 ac., P.G. 22; (4) 8^l; (5) 2^l; (6) 7^l 6^s.

John Ripley—(2) —; (3) 1 house, 4 outhouses, M. 30 ac., P.G. 22; (4) 4^l; (5) 2^l; (6) 7^l 6^s.

Henry Garthforth—(2) —; (3) 1 house, 4 outhouses, M. 30 ac., P.G. 22; (4) 10^l; (5) 2^l; (6) 7^l 6^s.

Tho. Messenger—(2) —; (3) 1 house, 3 outhouses, M. 14 ac., P.G. 11; (4) 2^l; (5) 1^l; (6) 3^l 11^s 4^d.

[1] A hamlet in tnshp. of Carlton-high-dale, par. Coverham.

	The Number of Tennants	9			
	Quantity of Meadow	172 ac.			
The Conclusion	Pasture Gates	132	*l.*	*s.*	*d.*
of Bradley.	Fynes in 20 yeares		35	00	00
	Yearly rent		12	00	00
	Yearly value		43	02	02
	Cleare improvem^t		31	02	02

7. Woodall.[1] [p. 9

Otwell Rither—(2) —; (3) 1 house, 3 outhouses, M. 24 ac., P.G. 26; (4) 2ˡ 13ˢ 4ᵈ; (5) 1ˡ 6ˢ 8ᵈ; (6) 7ˡ 2ˢ.

George Ripley, sen.—(2) —; (3) 1 house, 1 outhouse, M. 24 ac., P.G. 26; (4) 2ˡ 13ˢ 4ᵈ; (5) 1ˡ 6ˢ 8ᵈ; (6) 7ˡ 2ˢ.

Francis Ripley—(2) —; (3) 1 house, 3 outhouses, M. 12 ac., P.G. 13; (4) 2ˡ 13ˢ 4ᵈ; (5) 13ˢ 4ᵈ; (6) 3ˡ 11ˢ.

George Ripley, jun.—(2) —; (3) 1 house, 3 outhouses, M. 18 ac., P.G. 13; (4) 1ˡ 13ˢ 4ᵈ; (5) 13ˢ 4ᵈ; (6) 4ˡ 7ˢ 4ᵈ.

John Spence—(2) —; (3) 1 house, 1 outhouse, M. 4 ac., P.G. 8; (4) 19ˢ; (5) 16ˢ 8ᵈ; (6) 1ˡ 16ˢ.

James Hamond—(2) —; (3) 1 house, 4 outhouses, M. 20 ac., P.G. 19½; (4) 3ˡ; (5) 1ˡ; (6) 5ˡ 11ˢ 10ᵈ.

Francis Wynne—(2) —; (3) 1 house, 5 outhouses, M. 20 ac., P.G. 26; (4) 2ˡ 13ˢ 4ᵈ; (5) 1ˡ 6ˢ 8ᵈ; (6) 6ˡ 12ˢ.

Percivall Hammond—(2) —; (3) 1 house, 8 outhouses, M. 20 ac., P.G. 26; (4) 3ˡ 6ˢ 8ᵈ; (5) 1ˡ 6ˢ 8ᵈ; (6) 6ˡ 12ˢ.

	The Number of Tennants	8			
The Conclusion	Quantity of Meadow	142 ac.			
of Woodall.	Pasture gates	157½	*l.*	*s.*	*d.*
	Fynes in 20 yeares		19	12	04
	Yearly rent		08	00	00
	Yearly value		42	14	02
	Cleare improvem^t		34	14	02

	The Number of Tennants in this division—77			
The Generall	Quantity of Meadow—1216 ac. 2 roods			
Conclusion of	Pasture Gates—554½	*l.*	*s.*	*d.*
Coverdale Chace	Fynes paid in 20 yeares	216	04	03
being the Second	Yearly Rent	071	12	01½
Division of	Yearly value	300	19	04½
Midleham	Cleare yearly improvement	229	07	03

---

[1] Woodale or Wood-dale, hamlet in tnshp. of Carlton-high-dale.

3. West Witton.[1]   [p. 10

The partes of this are

1. West Witton Towneship ꝑ 2. Swynninthwait.

---

1. Westwitton Township consists of

1. Demeasnes, vz. Caplebank park[2] ꝑ Wanlas Parke,[3] and the
Parsonage ꝑ Tenement Lands.

	l.	*s.*	*d.*
[4](1) The Lord Scroop[5] holdeth Caplebank parke at the rent of	05	00	00
The quantity of land is 390 acres, worth yearly	65	00	00
After a leasse in being he hath it in fee ferme from Q. El. at ye rent of	10	00	00

---

[6](2) Sr Thomas Metcalfe[7] holds Wanlas parke by leasse at ye rent of	06	13	04
The quantity of land is 280 acres—worth yearly	46	13	04
George Story is keeper of it by patent, his fee is	03	00	08

It is well stored with fallow deere ꝑ woods ꝑ underwoods.

---

	l.	*s.*	*d.*
(3) The Parsonage is an Impropriation in the kings guift ꝑ is held by leasse by Sir Tho. Metcalfe for [*blank*] yeares, the rent is	06	13	04
The scite of it conteynes 1 acr. ½ and it is worth yearly	00	13	04
The tithe corne, small tythes and other proffitts are worth yearly	40	00	00

It was leaseed to Sr Hen. Slingsby[8] ꝑ Sr Major
(*sic*) Vavasor[9] who assigned the leasse to S^r
Tho. Metcalfe.

---

[1] A parish town 5 m. from Middleham.

[2] In the east of the par. of West Witton (*V.C.H., Yks., N.R.,* i, 287).

[3] In the par. of West Witton, NE. of Swinithwaite, and known as the park of West Witton in the thirteenth century. By 1465 it had obtained its present name (*V.C.H., Yks., N.R.,* i, 286).

[4] " In fee farm " in the margin.

[5] Thomas, 10th Lord Scrope of Bolton, died 1609 (Clay, J. W., *Extinct and Dormant Peerages,* p. 201).

[6] " In fee farme, as is said. Q^ro " in the margin.

[7] Son of James Metcalfe of Nappa. He died 1655 (Clay, J. W., *Dugdale's Visitation of Yorkshire,* ii, 123).

[8] Vice-President of the Council of the North in 1629, died 1634. He mar. Frances, dau. of William Vavasor of Weston. His dau. Elizabeth mar. Sir Thomas Metcalfe of Nappa (Clay, J. W., *Dugdale's Visitation of Yorkshire,* ii, 69).

[9] Sir Mauger Vavasor of Weston mar. Joan, the widow of James Metcalfe of Nappa (Clay, J. W., *Dugdale's Visitation of Yorkshire,* ii, 123). Sir Mauger's will was proved in 1611 (Baildon, W. P., *Baildon and the Baildons,* i, 539–40).

The Conclusion of Westwitton demeasnes.		*l.*	*s.*	*d.*
	The quantity of land is 671 ac. ½			
	The yearly rent is	18	06	08
	The yearly value is	152	06	08
	The cleare yearly improvem^t is	134	00	00

Westwitton Tenement Lands.

Thomas Walker—(2) 6 yrs.; (3) 1 house, 2 outhouses, M. 10 ac., A. 10 ac., P.G. 4; (4) 4^l 2^s 6^d; (5) 13^s 9^d; (6) 3^l 13^s 4^d.

Willm. Spalton—(2) 9 yrs.; (3) 1 house, M. 2 ac.; (4) 16^s; (5) 5^s 4^d; (6) 14^s 8^d.

Otwell Spoughton—(2) 6 yrs.; (3) 1 house, 1 outhouse, M. 8 ac., A. 8 ac., P.G. 2; (4) 1^l 5^s; (5) 12^s 6^d; (6) 3^l 7^s 8^d.

Lancelot Hunter—(2) 6 yrs.; (3) 1 house, 1 outhouse, M. 4 ac., A. 8 ac.; (4) 16^s 9^d; (5) 8^s 4½^d; (6) 2^l 4^s.

James Goodyer—(2) 6 yrs.; (3) 1 house, 1 outhouse, M. 4 ac., A. 6 ac.; (4) 13^s 8^d; (5) 6^s 10^d; (6) 1^l 17^s 4^d.

Henry Buckle—(2) 6 yrs.; (3) 1 house, 1 outhouse, M. 6 ac., A. 3 ac.; (4) 1^l 7^s 4^d; (5) 6^s 10^d; (6) 1^l 16^s 4^d.

Otwell Johnson—(2) 6 yrs.; (3) 1 house, 2 outhouses, M. 16 ac., A. 5 ac., P.G. ½; (4) 2^l 13^s 6^d; (5) 13^s 4½^d; (6) 4^l 5^s 8^d.

Cutbert Metcalfe—(2) 28 yrs.; (3) 1 house, 1 outhouse, M. 20 ac., P.G. ½; (4) 4^l 16^s 8^d; (5) 1^l 4^s 2^d; (6) 4^l 11^s 8^d.

Idem—(2) 6 yrs.; (3) M. 3 ac.; (4) 8^s; (5) 4^s; (6) 12^s.

Francis Becke—(2) 6 yrs.; (3) 1 house, 1 outhouse, M. 6 ac., A. 7 ac., P.G. 1; (4) 17^s 10^d; (5) 8^s 11^d; (6) 2^l 16^s 8^d.

Richard Fothergill—(2) 6 yrs.; (3) 1 house, 1 outhouse, M. 6 ac., A. 4 ac., P.G. 1; (4) 17^s 10^d; (5) 8^s 11^d; (6) 2^l 2^s 8^d.

Willm. Bellerby—(2) 6 yrs.; (3) 1 house, 2 outhouses, M. 5 ac., A. 6 ac.; (4) 16^s 8^d; (5) 8^s 4^d; (6) 2^l 3^s.

Richard Morrow—(2) 6 yrs.; (3) 1 house, 1 outhouse, M. 9 ac., A. 6 ac., P.G. 2; (4) 2^l 10^s 5^d; (5) 10^s 1^d; (6) 3^l 5^s 8^d.

Leonard Butterfeild—(2) 6 yrs.; (3) 1 house, 1 outhouse, M. 6 ac., A. 9 ac., P.G. 2; (4) 1^l 15^s 6^d; (5) 11^s 10^d; (6) 3^l 1^s 8^d.

John Wray—(2) 6 yrs.; (3) 1 house, 1 outhouse, M. 12 ac., A. 3 ac.; (4) 1^l 7^s 10^d; (5) 13^s 11^d; (6) 3^l 2^s.

Mr George Story—(2) 6 yrs.; (3) 1 house, 1 outhouse, M. 7 ac., A. 2 ac., P.G. 2; (4) 1^l 13^s 4^d; (5) 8^s 4^d; (6) 3^l 0^s 8^d.

Idem—(2) 14 yrs.; (3) 1 outhouse, M. 3 ac.; (4) 13^s 4^d; (5) 3^s 4^d; (6) 18^s 8^d.

Idem—(2) 6 yrs.; (3) 1 house, M. 4 ac.; (4) 9^s 3^d; (5) 3^s 1^d; (6) 18^s 6^d.

James Buckle—(2) 6 yrs.; (3) 1 house, 2 outhouses, M. 18 ac., A. 7 ac., P.G. 2; (4) 3^l 4^s 8^d; (5) 16^s 2^d; (6) 5^l 3^s.

Leonard Butterfeild—(2) 6 yrs.; (3) 1 house, 1 outhouse, M. 8 ac., A. 2 ac.; (4) 1^l 5^s; (5) 8^s 4½^d; (6) 2^l 1^s 4^d.

Chrofer. Dodsworth—(2) —; (3) 1 house, 1 outhouse, M. 1 r.;
  (4) 8ˢ; (5) 4ˢ; (6) 5ˢ.

  Idem—(2) 10 yrs.; (3) 1 house, 1 outhouse, M. 9 ac., A. 6 ac.;
  (4) 13ˢ 8ᵈ; (5) 6ˢ 10ᵈ; (6) 2ˡ 17ˢ 4ᵈ.

John Preston—(2) 6 yrs.; (3) 1 house, 1 outhouse, M. 2 r.;
  (4) 1ˡ 17ˢ 4ᵈ; (5) 4ˢ 4ᵈ; (6) 6ˢ 8ᵈ.

  Idem—(2) 6 yrs.; (3) 3 houses, 2 outhouses, M. 18 ac., A. 10 ac.,
  P. 1 ac., P.G. 1; (4) 7ˡ 1ˢ 1½ᵈ; (5) 1ˡ 3ˢ 6¼ᵈ; (6) 5ˡ 18ˢ 8ᵈ.

Thomas Wray—(2) 6 yrs.; (3) 1 house, 1 outhouse, M. 6 ac.,
  A. 6 ac., P.G. 2; (4) 1ˡ 12ˢ 9ᵈ; (5) 10ˢ 11ᵈ; (6) 2ˡ 2ˢ.

Willm. Harison—(2) 6 yrs.; (3) 1 house, 1 outhouse, M. 3 ac.;
  (4) 17ˢ 4ᵈ; (5) 4ˢ 4ᵈ; (6) 15ˢ 4ᵈ.

Chrofer. Shepperdson—(2) 6 yrs.; (3) 1 house, 1 outhouse, M. 4 ac.;
  (4) 1ˡ; (5) 6ˢ 8ᵈ; (6) 1ˡ.

Thomas Hillary—(2) 6 yrs.; (3) 1 house, 1 outhouse, M. 1 r.;
  (4) 1ˢ; (5) 4ᵈ; (6) 2ˢ 6ᵈ.

Edmd. Wray—(2) 14 yrs.; (3) 1 house, 1 outhouse, M. 7 ac.,
  A. 2 ac.; (4) 1ˡ 11ˢ 6ᵈ; (5) 10ˢ 6ᵈ; (6) 1ˡ 17ˢ 4ᵈ.

Oswald Baynes—(2) 6 yrs.; (3) 1 house, 1 outhouse, M. 42 ac.,
  A. 4 ac., P. 1 ac.; (4) 4ˡ 17ˢ 3ᵈ; (5) 1ˡ 12ˢ 5ᵈ; (6) 9ˡ 6ˢ 8ᵈ.
  Idem—(2) 6 yrs.; (3) a brewing farme; (4) 2ˢ; (5) 1ˢ; (6) 5ˢ.

Antho: Atkinson—(2) 6 yrs.; (3) 1 house, 1 outhouse, M. 8 ac.;
  (4) 18ˢ; (5) 9ˢ; (6) 1ˡ 15ˢ 4ᵈ.

[p. 11

  Idem—(2) 6 yrs.; (3) 1 house, 1 outhouse, M. 10 ac., A. 2 ac.,
  P. 2 ac.; (4) 1ˡ 11ˢ 6ᵈ; (5) 9ˢ; (6) 1ˡ 15ˢ 4ᵈ.
  Idem—(2) 6 yrs.; (3) M. 5 ac.; (4) 15ˢ; (5) 5ˢ; (6) 1ˡ.
  Idem—(2) 6 yrs.; (3) M. 3 ac.; (4) 19ˢ; (5) 6ˢ 4ᵈ; (6) 15ˢ.

Thomas Scrafton—(2) 6 yrs.; (3) 1 house, 1 outhouse, M. 1 ac.;
  (4) 13ˢ 6ᵈ; (5) 4ˢ 6ᵈ; (6) 6ˢ 6ᵈ.

Thomas Tesmond—(2) 6 yrs.; (3) 1 house, 1 outhouse, M. 3 ac.,
  A. 1 ac., P. 1 ac.; (4) 14ˢ; (5) 7ˢ; (6) 1ˡ 2ˢ 4ᵈ.

Barth: Lowther—(2) 9 yrs.; (3) 1 house, 1 outhouse, M. 8 ac. 2 r.,
  A. 3 ac., P.G. 1; (4) 1ˡ 13ˢ 4ᵈ; (5) 8ˢ 4ᵈ; (6) 2ˡ 11ˢ 10ᵈ.

John Kidd—(2) 6 yrs.; (3) 1 house, 3 outhouses, M. 10 ac., A. 8 ac.;
  (4) 4ˡ 7ˢ 8ᵈ; (5) 1ˡ 1ˢ 11ᵈ; (6) 3ˡ 16ˢ 8ᵈ.

Geo. Metcalfe, gen.—(2) 33 yrs.; (3) 1 house, 4 outhouses, M. 34 ac.,
  P. 40 ac.; (4) 6ˡ; (5) 3ˡ; (6) 13ˡ 16ˢ.
  Idem—(2) 33 yrs.; (3) 1 house, M. 16 ac.; (4) 13ˢ 4ᵈ; (5) 6ˢ 8ᵈ;
  (6) 2ˡ 16ˢ.
  Idem—(2) 33 yrs.; (3) M. 5 ac.; (4) 1ˡ; (5) 10ˢ; (6) 1ˡ 5ˢ.

Chrofer. Metcalfe—(2) —; (3) 1 house, 1 outhouse; (4) 8ᵈ; (5) 4ᵈ;
  (6) 1ˢ.

Reynold Stanley—(2) 6 yrs.; (3) 1 house, 1 outhouse, M. 8 ac.,
  A. 4 ac.; (4) 1ˡ 2ˢ 7½ᵈ; (5) 7ˢ 6½ᵈ; (6) 2ˡ 7ˢ 4ᵈ.

G

Lawrence Terry—(2) 6 yrs.; (3) 1 house, M. 1 ac.; (4) 5ˢ; (5) 2ˢ 6ᵈ; (6) 6ˢ 8ᵈ.

Leonard Wray—(2) 6 yrs.; (3) M. 10 ac.; (4) 10ˢ 9ᵈ; (5) 5ˢ 4½ᵈ; (6) 2ˡ.

Total—46 tenants; 41 houses; 46 outhouses; 369 ac. 2 roods of Meadow; 132 acres of Arable; 45 ac. of Pasture; 21 Pasture Gates; £73 17ˢ 5ᵈ fines paid in 20 years; £23 6ˢ 3¾ᵈ yearly rent; £113 9ˢ 4ᵈ yearly value; Cleare Improvemᵗ 90ˡ 03ˢ 0¼ᵈ.

---

2. Swynninthwait.[1]

Leonard Spence—(2) 6 yrs.; (3) 1 house, 1 outhouse, M. 10 ac.; (4) 1ˡ 6ˢ 8ᵈ; (5) 6ˢ 8ᵈ; (6) 1ˡ 16ˢ 8ᵈ.

Philip Fidler—(2) 6 yrs.; (3) 1 house, 1 outhouse, M. 10 ac.; (4) 1ˡ 6ˢ 8ᵈ; (5) 6ˢ 8ᵈ; (6) 1ˡ 16ˢ 8ᵈ.

George Metcalfe—(2) 33 yrs.; (3) M. 8 ac.; (4) 1ˡ 6ˢ 8ᵈ; (5) 6ˢ 8ᵈ; (6) 1ˡ 12ˢ.

Willm. Wray—(2) 7 yrs.; (3) 1 house, 2 outhouses, M. 10 ac., A. 4 ac., P. 4 ac.; (4) 3ˡ 4ˢ 8ᵈ; (5) 16ˢ 2ᵈ; (3) 3ˡ 7ˢ.

James Wray—(2) 7 yrs.; (3) 1 house, 1 outhouse, M. 14 ac.; (4) 1ˡ 12ˢ 4ᵈ; (5) 16ˢ 2ᵈ; (6) 3ˡ 1ˢ.

Leonard Wray—(2) 7 yrs.; (3) 1 house, 2 outhouses, M. 12 ac., A. 6 ac., P. 2 ac.; (4) 1ˡ 12ˢ 4ᵈ; (5) 16ˢ 2ᵈ; (6) 3ˡ 17ˢ.

Willm. Barwick—(2) 6 yrs.; (3) 1 house, 1 outhouse, M. 14 ac., A. 6 ac., P.G. 1; (4) 1ˡ 8ˢ; (5) 14ˢ; (6) 4ˡ 4ˢ.

Lawrence Barwick—(2) 7 yrs.; (3) 1 house, 3 outhouses, M. 15 ac., A. 6 ac., P. 2 r.; (4) 1ˡ 8ˢ; (5) 14ˢ; (6) 4ˡ 4ˢ 8ᵈ.

John Hodgson—(2) 6 yrs.; (3) 1 house, 2 outhouses, M. 18 ac., A. 7 ac.; (4) 4ˡ; (5) 1ˡ; (6) 4ˡ 18ˢ.

Total: 9 tenants; 8 houses, 13 outhouses, 111 ac. of Meadow, 29 ac. of arable, 6 ac. 2 roods of Pasture, 1 Pasture Gate; £17 5ˢ 4ᵈ fines paid in 20 years; £5 16ˢ 6ᵈ yearly rent; £28 17ˢ yearly value.

Cleare Improvement £23 00ˢ 6ᵈ.

Demeasnes in both the Towneships. [p. 12

[2]The Towneships of Westwitton and Swynninthwait hold certeyne ground in Common called Penhill Parke[3] at yᵉ rent | 02ˡ 01ˢ 08ᵈ

It conteynes 250 acres of Pasture yearly worth | 06ˡ 05ˢ 08ᵈ

---

[1] Swinethwaite, or Swyingthwaite, hamlet in tnshp. and par. of West Witton.

[2] " The Cities " in the margin.

[3] First mentioned in 1465, enclosed in 1779 (*V.C.H., Yks., N.R.,* i, 287). Penhill is in the parishes of West Witton and Coverham.

There are certeyne payments yearly due to his M^tie
  by the Tennants of these two Towneshipes
  called fynes ℘ wards paid anciently in respect | 00^l 08^s 03½^d
  of some service they owe to the Castle of Rich-
  mond amounting to

There are likewise three freeholders in the Towne-
  ship of W. Witton who pay the yearly rent of | 00^l 04^s 10^d

The generall Abstract of West Witton being the Third Division of Midleham	Demeasnes	The number of Tennants—4
		Quantity of land—921 ac. ½
		Number of Beastgates—22—*nil vacat.*
		The yearly rent 20^l 08^s . 04^d
		The yearly value 158^l 11^s 08^d
		The Cleare Improve-
		ment 138^l 03^s 04^d
	Tenement Lands	The Number of Tennants—55
		Quantity of Land—693 ac.
		The Number of Beastgates—22
		Fynes and Wards 000^l 08^s 03½^d
		Fynes paid w^thin 20
		yeares 091^l 02^s 09^d
		The yearly Rent 029^l 02^s 09¾^d
		The yearly value 142^l 06^s 04^d
		The Cleare Improve-
		ment 113^l 03^s 06¼^d
	Freehold	The Number of Tennants—3
		The yearly free rent 00^l 04^s 10^d

[p. 13

4. Bishops dale Chace.[1]

This consists of Sixe Parts, viz.

1. Burton. 2. Walden. 3. Thorolby. 4. Bp^sdale. 5. Newbigging. 6. Aisgarthe.

1. Burton.[2]

Chrofer. Metcalfe—(2) —; (3) 1 house, 1 outhouse, M. 40 ac.,
  A. 16 ac., P. 20 ac., P.G. 17; (4) 4^l; (5) 2^l; (6) 12^s 8^d.
  Idem—(2) —; (3) 1 house, 1 outhouse, M. 17 ac., P.G. 10;
  (4) 4^l 2^s; (5) 11^s; (6) 4^l 4^s 4^d

[1] Leland mentions the red deer in the hills about Bishopsdale (*Itinerary*, Hearne's ed., v, 112).

[2] Or West Burton, in tnshp. of Burton with Walden, par. Aysgarth. Burton is the largest village in Bishopsdale, which extends 6 miles SW. into the hills from Aysgarth, which is at its lower end.

Jerome Wray—(2) —; (3) 1 house, 1 outhouse, M. 24 ac., A. 3 ac., P.G. 8; (4) 1^l 10^s; (5) 15^s; (6) 5^l 0^s 6^d.

John Mudd—(2) —; (3) 1 house, 1 outhouse, M. 24 ac., A. 6 ac., P.G. 6; (4) 3^l; (5) 15^s; (6) 7^l 0^s 8^d.

Jerome Simson—(2) —; (3) 1 house, 1 outhouse, M. 4 ac., A. 3 r., P. 2 r., P.G. 3; (4) 1^l 8^s; (5) 7^s; (6) 1^l 13^s.

Oswald Metcalfe—(2) —; (3) 1 house, 1 outhouse, M. 10 ac., P.G. 4; (4) 18^s; (5) 9^s; (6) 2^l 16^s 8^d.

Robt. Lodge—(2) —; (3) 1 house, 2 outhouses, M. 30 ac., A. 12 ac., P.G. 18; (4) 8^l 3^s 10^d; (5) 2^l 2^s 2$\frac{1}{2}$^{d}; (6) 10^l 15^s.

Thomas Sadler—(2) —; (3) 1 house, 2 outhouses, M. 13 ac., A. 5 ac., P.G. 4$\frac{3}{4}$; (4) 2^l 4^s 4^d; (5) 11^s 1^d; (6) 4^l 2^s 4^d.

Tho. Richardson—(2) —; (3) 1 house, 1 outhouse, M. 3 ac., A. 1 ac., P.G. 2; (4) 1^l 2^s; (5) 5^s 6^d; (6) 1^l 5^s.

Richard Murrey—(2) —; (3) 2 houses, 2 outhouses, M. 16 ac., A. 2 r., P.G. 8; (4) 2^l 8^s 9^d; (5) 16^s 3^d; (6) 4^l 15^s 11^d.

John Dixon—(2) —; (3) 1 house, 2 outhouses, M. 5 ac., A. 6 ac., P.G. 2; (4) 1^l 0^s 4^d; (5) 5^s 1^d; (6) 2^l 7^s 2^d.

John Tesmund—(2) —; (3) 1 house, 4 outhouses, M. 7 ac., P.G. 2; (4) 1^l; (5) 5^s; (6) 1^l 17^s 2^d.

Rich. Simson—(2) —; (3) 2 houses, 2 outhouses, M. 20 ac., A. 10 ac., P.G. 13; (4) 2^l 16^s 3^d; (5) 1^l 8^s 1$\frac{1}{2}$^{d}; (6) 7^l 15^s 8^d.

Jeffry Crookhay—(2) —; (3) 1 house, 2 outhouses, M. 16 ac., A. 1 ac. 1 r., P.G. 7; (4) 1^l 8^s 8^d; (5) 7^s 2^d; (6) 4^l 13^s 7^d.

John Jaque—(2) —; (3) 1 house, 2 outhouses, M. 8 ac., A. 7 ac., P.G. 6; (4) 1^l 6^s; (5) 13^s; (6) 3^l 16^s 4^d.

John Barwick—(2) —; (3) 1 house, 2 outhouses, M. 6 ac., A. 6 ac., P.G. 3; (4) 1^l 6^s; (5) 6^s 6^d; (6) 2^l 15^s 4^d.

John Sadler—(2) —; (3) 1 house, 1 outhouse, M. 5 ac., A. 5 ac., P.G. 2$\frac{1}{3}$; (4) 10^s 10^d; (5) 5^s 5^d; (6) 2^l 6^s 11^d.

Leonard Baynes—(2) —; (3) 1 house, 1 outhouse, M. 12 ac., A. 5 ac., P.G. 6$\frac{1}{4}$; (4) 1^l 4^s 6^d; (5) 12^s 3^d; (6) 4^l 6^s 4^d.

John Russell—(2) —; (3) 1 house, 3 outhouses, M. 14 ac., A. 10 ac., P.G. 9; (4) 3^l 9^s 4^d; (5) 17^s 4^d; (6) 5^l 17^s 6^d

Roger Baynes—(2) —; (3) 1 house, 1 outhouse, M. 2 ac., A. 2 ac., P.G. 1; (4) 11^s; (5) 2^s 9^d; (6) 1^l.

Chrofer. Richardson—(2) —; (3) 1 house, 1 outhouse, M. 4 ac., A. 6 ac., P.G. 3; (4) 14^s; (5) 7^s; (6) 2^l 1^s 4^d.

Tho. Richardson—(2) —; (3) 1 house, 2 outhouses, M. 2 ac., A. 8 ac., P.G. 3; (4) 14^s; (5) 7^s; (6) 2^l 7^s.

Robt. Calvert—(2) —; (3) 1 house, 3 outhouses, M. 12 ac., A. 2 ac., P.G. 10; (4) 5^l 11^s 8^d; (5) 1^l 2^s 4^d; (6) 4^l 12^s 4^d.

James Simson—(2) —; (3) 1 house, 4 outhouses, M. 12 ac., A. 1 ac., P.G. 6; (4) 1^l 16^s; (5) 12^s; (6) 3^l 16^s.

Henry Fletcher—(2) —; (3) 1 house, 3 outhouses, M. 8 ac., P.G. 2½; (4) 1^l 4^s; (5) 6^s; (6) 2^l 5^s 4^d.

Hen. Hodgson et al.—(2) —; (3) A Corne mill; (4) 3^l 13^s 4^d; (5) 1^l 6^s 8^d; (6) 8^l 10^s.

Tho. Crookehay—(2) —; (3) 1 house, 1 outhouse, M. 5 ac., A. 7 ac., P.G. 3½; (4) 14^s; (5) 7^s; (6) 2^l 6^s.

Total—27 tennants; 28 houses, 47 outhouses, 319 ac. of Meadow, 110 ac. 2 r. of Arrable, 20 ac. 2 r. of Pasture, 160¼ Pasture Gates; Fines paid in 20 years, 55^l 1^s 10^d; yearly rent 18^l 2^s 8^d; yearly value, 118^l 8^s 1^d. The Improvemt.—£100 5^s 5^d.

---

2. Walden.[1] [p. 14

John Robinson—(2) —; (3) 1 house, 1 outhouse, M. 7 ac., P.G. 5; (4) 1^l 8^s; (5) 7^s; (6) 2^l 7^s 2^d.

Idem—(2) —; (3) M. 4 ac., P.G. 3; (4) 1^l 4^s; (5) 6^s; (6) 1^l 6^s.

Idem—(2) —; (3) M. 3 ac., P.G. 2½; (4) 14^s; (5) 3^s 6^d; (6) 1^l 0^s 4^d.

Chrofer. Spence sen^r—(2) —; (3) 1 house, 5 outhouses, M. 30 ac., P.G. 32; (4) 4^l 6^s 8^d; (5) 2^l 3^s 4^d; (6) 11^l 11^s 8^d.

Idem—(2) —; (3) 1 house, 1 outhouse, M. 3 ac., P.G. 2; (4) 10^s 6^d; (5) 3^s 6^d; (6) 16^s 8^d.

Idem—(2) —; (3) 1 house, 1 outhouse, M. 12 ac., P.G. 6½; (4) 3^l 10^s; (5) 14^s; (6) 3^l 1^s 4^d.

Francis Scroop—(2) — (3) 1 house, 1 outhouse, M. 5 ac., P.G. 5; (4) 13^s 4^d; (5) 6^s 8^d; (6) 2^l.

John Swyndenbanke—(2) —; (3) 1 house, 3 outhouses, M. 10 ac., P.G. 11; (4) 3^l 4^s; (5) 6^s 8^d; (6) 4^l.

Stephen Spence—(2) —; (3) 1 house, 2 outhouses, M. 8 ac., P.G. 5½; (4) 16^s; (5) 8^s; (6) 2^l 13^s 8^d.

John Spence—(2) —; (3) 1 house, 3 outhouses, M. 10 ac., P.G. 4; (4) 1^l 4^s; (5) 12^s; (6) 2^l 16^s 8^d.

Chrofer. Spence, jun^r—(2) —; (3) 1 house, 4 outhouses, M. 12 ac., P.G. 7½; (4) 2^l 8^s; (5) 12^s; (6) 3^l 17^s 4^d.

Roger Spence—(2) —; (3) 1 house, 2 outhouses, M. 13 ac., P.G. 12; (4) 4^l 16^s; (5) 1^l 4^s; (6) 4^l 16^s.

Edward Danby—(2) — (3) 1 house, 3 outhouses, M. 18 ac., P.G. 10; (4) 3^l 6^s; (5) 16^s 6^d; (6) 5^l 10^s 4^d.

Richard Pullen—(2) —; (3) 1 house, 2 outhouses, M. 15 ac., P.G. 12; (4) 6^l; (5) 1^l; (6) 5^l 5^s.

George Harthford—(2) —; (3) 1 house, 2 outhouses, M. 12 ac., P.G. 10½; (4) 1^l 11^s; (5) 15^s 6^d; (6) 4^l 5^s 4^d.

John Jaque—(2) —; (3) M. 3 ac.; (4) 1^s 6^d; (5) 6^d; (6) 12^s.

[1] In tnshp. of Burton with Walden, par. Aysgarth.

Willm. Dixon—(2) —; (3) 1 house, 1 outhouse, M. 5 ac., P.G. 3; (4) 10^s; (5) 5^s; (6) 1^l 10^s.

Robert Dixon—(2) —; (3) M. 6 ac., P.G. 3; (4) 10^s; (5) 5^s; (6) 1^l 14^s.
    Idem—(2) —; (3) 1 house, 1 outhouse, M. 10 ac., P.G. 9$\frac{3}{4}$; (4) 1^l 3^s 6^d; (5) 11^s 9^d; (6) 3^l 15^s.

Richard Robinson—(2) —; (3) 1 house, 1 outhouse, M. 3 ac., P.G. 3$\frac{1}{2}$; (4) 1^l 4^s; (5) 6^s; (6) 1^l 6^s 2^d.

Adam Jaque—(2) —; (3) 1 house, 1 outhouse, M. 25 ac., P.G. 19; (4) 3^l 4^s; (5) 1^l 12^s; (6) 8^l 9^s 2^d.

    Total—21 Tenants; 17 houses, 34 outhouses, 214 acres of Meadow, 166$\frac{3}{4}$ Pasture Gates; £42 . 4 . 6 fines paid in 20 years; £13 . 08 . 3 yearly rent; £72 . 13 . 10 yearly value. The Improvement £59 05^s 07^d

---

3. Thorolby.[1]   [p. 15

Chrofer. Metcalfe—(2) —; (3) 1 house, 2 outhouses, M. 60 ac., P.G. 10; (4) 3^l; (5) 1^l 10^s; (6) 4^l 10^s.
    Idem—(2) —; (3) M. 30 ac., P.G. 14, (4) 4^l; (5) 2^l; (6) 7^l 2^s.
    Idem—(2) —; (3) M. 30 ac., P.G. 9; (4) 2^l 13^s 4^d; (5) 1^l 6^s 8^d; (6) 5^l 2^s.
    Idem—(2) —; (3) M. 8 ac.; (4) 2^l 6^s 8^d; (5) 1^l 3^s 4^d; (6) 1^l 12^s.

John Sadler—(2) —; (3) 1 house, M. 20 ac., P.G. 9; (4) 6^l 13^s 4^d; (5) 1^l 6^s 8^d; (6) 5^l 12^s.
    Idem—(2) —; (3) 1 house, 3 outhouses, M. 28 ac., A. 16 ac., P.G. 16; (4) 12^l 12^s 1^d; (5) 2^l 10^s 5^d; (6) 10^l 18^s.
    Idem—(2) —; (3) 2 houses, 3 outhouses, M. 22 ac., A. 13 ac., P.G. 10; (4) 6^l 9^s 6^d; (5) 1^l 9^s 10$\frac{1}{2}$^{d}; (6) 7^l 9^s 2^d.
    Idem—(2) —; (3) M. 20 ac., P.G. 5; (4) 2^l 18^s 4^d; (5) 14^s 7^d; (6) 4^l 16^s 8^d.
    Idem—(2) —; (3) 1 house, M. 3 ac., P.G. 1; (4) 7^s 6^d; (5) 2^s 6^d; (6) 17^s 4^d.
    Idem—(2) —; (3) 1 house, M. 2 ac., P.G. $\frac{1}{2}$; (4) 4^s; (5) 1^s 4^d; (6) 14^s 8^d.

Anth. Atkinson—(2) —; (3) 1 house, 1 outhouse, M. 4 ac., P.G. 1; (4) 13^s 8^d; (5) 3^s 5^d; (6) 1^l 1^s 10^d.

Bryan Calvert—(2) —; (3) 1 house, 1 outhouse, M. 11 ac., A. 1 ac., P.G. 3; (4) 19^s 9^d; (5) 9^s 10$\frac{1}{2}$^{d}; (6) 2^l 19^s 10^d.

Henry Gracethwayt—(2) —; (3) 1 house, 1 outhouse, M. 10 ac., A. 1 r., P.G. 3; (4) 19^s 9^d; (5) 9^s 10$\frac{1}{2}$^{d}; (6) 2^l 15^s 10^d.

John Dixon—(2) —; (3) M. 6 ac.; (4) 1^l 7^s 4^d; (5) 6^s 10^d; (6) 1^l 4^s.

Thomas Sadler—(2) —; (3) M. 6 ac.; (4) 1^l 7^s 4^d; (5) 6^s 10^d; (6) 1^l 4^s.

Richard Murrow—(2) —; (3) M. 6 ac.; (4) 1^l 7^s 4^d; (5) 6^s 10^d; (6) 1^l 4^s.

Jeffery Crookeaw—(2) —; (3) M. 4 ac.; (4) 9^s; (5) 3^s; (6) 16^s.

[1]Thoralby, par. of Aysgarth.

Geo: Dodsworth—(2) —; (3) 1 house, 2 outhouses, M. 34 ac.,
    P.G. 80; (4) 13^l 6^s 8^d; (5) 6^l 13^s 4^d; (6) 20^l 16^s.

Idem—(2) —; (3) 1 house, M. 4 ac., P.G. 1; (4) 7^s; (5) 3^s 6^d;
    (6) 1^l 2^s 8^d.

Idem—(2) —; (3) M. 25 ac., P.G. 8; (4) 2^l 8^s; (5) 1^l 4^s;
    (6) 6^l 6^s.

Idem—(2) —; (3) A Corne mill; (4) 8^l; (5) 4^l; (6) 10^l.

Edward Atkinson—(2) —; (3) 1 house, M. 14 ac., P.G. 7; (4)
    4^l 8^s 8^d; (5) 1^l 2^s 2^d; (6) 4^l 4^s 10^d.

Barth. Butterfeild—(2) —; (3) 1 house, 1 outhouse, M. 16 ac.,
    A 10 ac., P.G. 4$\frac{1}{2}$; (4) 2^l 18^s 4^d; (5) 14^s 7^d; (6) 5^l 13^s.

Adam Midleton, ar.—(2) —; (3) 1 house, 1 outhouse, M. 2 ac.,
    P.G. 1$\frac{1}{2}$; (4) 9^s 4^d; (5) 4^s 8^d; (6) 16^s 4^d.

Arthur Scathe—(2) —; (3) 1 house, 1 outhouse, M. 16 ac., A. 6 ac.,
    P.G. 9; (4) 5^l 3^s 6^d; (5) 1^l 5^s 10$\frac{1}{2}$^{d}; (6) 5^l 12^s 4^d.

Willm. Sadler—(2) —; (3) 1 house, 1 outhouse, M. 12 ac., A. 3 ac.,
    P.G. 4$\frac{1}{2}$; (4) 2^l 14^s 2^d; (5) 13^s 6$\frac{1}{2}$^{d}; (6) 3^l 13^s.

Bernard Spence—(2) —; (3) 1 house, 2 outhouses, M. 7 ac., A. 2 ac.,
    P.G. 3; (4) 1^l 10^s; (5) 10^s; (6) 2^l 16^s 4^d.

Idem—(2) —; (3) 1 outhouse, M. 5 ac., A. 1 r., P.G. 2$\frac{1}{2}$;
    (4) 1^l; (5) 6^s 8^d; (6) 1^l 11^s I^d.

Will. Wyreholme—(2) —; (3) 1 house, M. 4 ac., P.G. 1; (4) 13^s 8^d;
    (5) 3^s 5^d; (6) 1^l 1^s 10^d.

John Wray— (2) —; (3) 1 house, 3 outhouses, M. 20 ac., A. 7 ac.,
    P.G. 8; (4) 3^l 11^s 1$\frac{1}{2}$^{d}; (5) 1^l 3^s 8$\frac{1}{2}$^{d}; (6) 6^l 10^s 2^d.

Idem—(2) —; (3) 1 house, 2 outhouses, M. 7 ac., P.G. 3;
    (4) 1^l 5^s; (5) 3^s 4^d; (6) 2^l 0^s 6^d.

John Robinson—(2) —; (3) 1 house, 1 outhouse, M. 10 ac., P.G.
    6$\frac{1}{2}$; (4) 3^l; (5) 1^l; (6) 3^l 7^s 2^d.

Idem—(2) —; (3) $\frac{1}{2}$ house, M. 10 ac., P.G. 6$\frac{1}{2}$; (4) 3^l; (5) 1^l;
    (6) 3^l 8^s 4^d.

Francis Dodsworth—(2) —; (3) 1 house, 1 outhouse, M. (?) 2 r.,
    P.G. 1$\frac{1}{3}$; (4) 8^s 4^d; (5) 4^s 2^d; (6) 16^s 11^d.

Oliver Wray—(2) —; (3) 1 house, 1 outhouse, M. 16 ac., A. 8 ac.,
    P.G. 9; (4) 3^l 7^s 8$\frac{1}{2}$^{d}; (5) 1^l 7^s 1^d; (6) 6^l 1^s 4^d.

Idem—(2) —; (3) 1 house, M. 1 r., P.G. 1; (4) 6^s 6^d; (5) 2^s 2^d;
    (6) 6^s 8^d.

Willm. Dawson—(2) —; (3) 1 house, 2 outhouses, M. 12 ac.,
    A. 2 r., P.G. 4; (4) 2^l 6^s 8^d; (5) 11^s 8^d; (6) 3^l 6^s 2^d.

Edw. Robinson—(2) —; (3) 1 house, 3 outhouses, M. 11 ac.,
    A. 3 ac., P.G. 5; (4) 1^l 8^s; (5) 14^s; (6) 3^l 13^s.

Wm. Sadler, sen^r—(2) —; (3) 1 house, 3 outhouses, M. 12 ac.,
    A. 8 ac., P.G. 5; (4) 1^l 10^s; (5) 15^s; (6) 4^l 12^s 8^d.

Idem—(2) —; (3) 1 house, M. 4 ac., P.G. 2$\frac{1}{2}$; (4) 1^l 1^s 6^d;
    (5) 7^s 2^d; (6) 1^l 19^s 1^d

Myles Wyreholme—(2) —; (3) 1 house, 1 outhouse, M. 7 ac., P.G. 1⅓; (4) 16ˢ 8ᵈ; (5) 4ˢ 2ᵈ; (6) 1ˡ 15ˢ 5ᵈ.

James Byrode—·(2) —·; (3) 1 house, 2 outhouses, M. 14 ac., A. 4 ac., P.G. 5; (4) 3ˡ 0ˢ 8ᵈ; (5) 15ˢ 2ᵈ; (6) 4ˡ 8ˢ 8ᵈ.

Robt. Tomson—·(2) —·; (3) 1 house, 2 outhouses, M. 30 ac., A. 3 ac., P.G. 12; (4) 3ˡ 11ˢ 4ᵈ; (5) 1ˡ 15ˢ 8ᵈ; (6) 8ˡ 19ˢ.

Robert Lodge—·(2) —·; (3) M. 3 ac.; (4) 8ˢ; (5) 2ˢ; (6) 12ˢ.

John Barwicke—(2) —; (3) M. 3 ac.; (4) 8ˢ; (5) 2ˢ; (6) 12ˢ.

Roger Baynes—(2) —·; (3) M. 2 ac., A. 2 ac.; (4) 11ˢ; (5) 2ˡ 9ˢ; (6) 14ˢ.

Tho. Richardson—·(2) —; (3) M. 4 ac.; (4) 4ˢ; (5) 2ˢ; (6) 16ˢ.

Chrofer. Richardson—·(2) —·; (3) M. 4 ac.; (4) 4ˢ; (5) 2ˢ; (6) 16ˢ.

Chrofer. Topham—·(2) —·; (3) M. 4 ac., P.G. 2; (4) 15ˢ; (5) 5ˢ; (6) 1ˡ 2ˢ 8ᵈ

Edward Hogge—(2) —; (3) 1 house, 1 outhouse, M. 20 ac., P.G. 4½; (4) 3ˡ 13ˢ 4ᵈ; (5) 14ˢ 8ᵈ; (6) 5ˡ.
     Idem—(2) —; (3) M. 1 ac., P.G. 1; (4) 6ˢ 7½ᵈ; (5) 2ˢ 2½ᵈ; (6) 7ˢ 4ᵈ.
     Idem—(2) —·; (3) 1 house; (4) 1ˢ; (5) 6ᵈ; (6) 3ˢ 4ᵈ.

Francis Midleton—(2) —; (3) 1 house, 2 outhouses, M. 10 ac., A. 2 ac., P.G. 5; (4) 2ˡ 8ˢ 6ᵈ; (5) 16ˢ 2ᵈ; (6) 3ˡ 7ˢ.

Miles Bowes—(2) —; (3) 1 house, 1 outhouse, M. 12 ac., A. 6 ac., P.G. 3½; (4) 2ˡ 1ˢ 2ᵈ· (5) 10ˢ 3½ᵈ; (6) 4ˡ 1ˢ 4ᵈ.

Richard Hamond—(2) —; (3) M. 3 ac.; (4) 9ˢ; (5) 4ˢ 6ᵈ; (6) 12ˢ.

Tho. Crookeay—(2) —; (3) M. 10 ac., A. 2 ac. 2 r.; (4) 14ˢ 3ᵈ; (5) 5ˢ 9ᵈ; (6) 2ˡ 7ˢ 6ᵈ.

James Hamond—(2) —; (3) M. 3 ac.; (4) 9ˢ; (5) 4ˢ 6ᵈ; (6) 12ˢ.
                                         [p. 16

John Bowes—·(2) —·; (3) 1 house, 3 outhouses, M. 14 ac., A. 5 ac., P.G. 4½; (4) 2ˡ 18ˢ 4ᵈ; (5) 14ˢ 7ᵈ; (6) 4ˡ 19ˢ 4ᵈ.

Willm. Hogge—(2) —·; (3) 1 house, 2 outhouses, M. 14 ac., A. 5 ac., P.G. 4½; (4) 1ˡ 9ˢ 2ᵈ; (5) 14ˢ 7ᵈ; (6) 4ˡ 19ˢ 4ᵈ.

Michael Milner—·(2) —·; (3) 1 house, 1 outhouse, M. 3 ac., A. 3 ac., P.G. 2; (4) 12ˢ 5ᵈ; (5) 6ˢ 2½ᵈ; (6) 1ˡ 17ˢ 8ᵈ.

Sʳ Tho. Metcalfe—(2) —; (3) M. 50 ac., P.G. 14; (4) 4ˡ 1ˢ; (5) 2ˡ 0ˢ 6ᵈ; (6) 10ˡ 1ˢ 8ᵈ.
     Idem—(2) —·; (3) M. 18 ac.; (4) 1ˡ 2ˢ; (5) 11ˢ; (6) 3ˡ.

Jeffry Kirby—·(2) —; (3) 1 house, M. 6 ac., P.G. 5½; (4) 1ˡ 6ˢ 8ᵈ; (5) 13ˢ 4ᵈ; (6) 2ˡ 2ˢ 4ᵈ.
     Idem—·(2) —·; (3) M. 6 ac., P.G. 3; (4) 1ˡ; (5) 10ˢ; (6) 1ˡ 13ˢ.
     Idem—·(2) —; (3) M. 5 ac., P.G. 1½; (4) 8ˢ; (5) 4ˢ; (6) 1ˡ 4ˢ 6ᵈ,

Total— 65 Tenants; 44 houses, 51 outhouses, 759 ac. 3 r. of Meadow; 110 ac. 2 r. of Arrable; 324$\frac{1}{3}$ P.G.; £145 12^s 2$\frac{1}{2}$^{d} fines paid in 20 years; £51 10^s 7$\frac{1}{2}$^{d} yearly rent; £225 18^s 10^d yearly value.

The cleare Improvem^t is £174 8^s 3$\frac{1}{2}$^{d}.

---

4. Bishops dale.[1]

George Fawcet—(2) —; (3) 1 house, M. 80 ac.; (4) 26^l; (5) 8^l 13^s 4^d; (6) 13^l 6^s 8^d.

Idem—(2) —; (3) 1 house, 1 outhouse, M. 14 ac.; (4) 4^l 10^s· (5) 1^l 10^s; (6) 3^l 2^s 8^d.

Idem—(2) —; (3) M. 12 ac., (4) 1^l 10^s; (5) 10^s; (6) 2^l 8^s.

Idem—(2) —; (3) M. 4 ac., P.G. 6; (4) 1^l 2^s 6^d; (5) 7^s 6^d; (6) 1^l 16^s.

Idem—(2) —; (3) 3 P.G.; (4) 4^s; (5) 1^s 4^d; (6) 10^s.

Idem—(2) —; (3) 1 house, 1 outhouse, M. 10 ac., P.G. 4; (4) 4^l 10^s; (5) 1^l 10^s; (6) 2^l 19^s 8^d.

Idem—(2) —; (3) M. 6 ac., P.G. 2; (4) 8^s 4^d; (5) 4^s 2^d; (6) 1^l 10^s 8^d.

Idem—(2) —; (3) M. 20 ac., P.G. 22; (4) 3^l 13^s; (5) 1^l 11^s; (6) 7^l 13^s 4^d.

Gyles Fawcett—(2) 34 yrs.; (3) 1 house, 3 outhouses, M. 50 ac., P.G. 18$\frac{1}{2}$; (4) 9^l 3^s 4^d; (5) 2^l 5^s 10^d; (6) 13^l 8^s 10^d.

Idem—(2) 34 yrs; (3) 1 house, 1 outhouse, M. 50 ac., P.G. 18$\frac{1}{2}$; (4) 9^l 3^s 4^d; (5) 2^l 5^s 10^d; (6) 13^l 8^s 10^d.

Idem—(2) 34 yrs.; (3) M. 30 ac., P.G. 12; (4) 5^l 10^s; (5) 1^l 7^s 6^d; (6) 7^l 16^s

Henry Wray—(2) —; (3) 1 house, M. 12 ac., P.G. 10; (4) 4^l 2^s 6^d; (5) 16^s 6^d; (6) 3^l 12^s.

Laurence Metcalfe—(2) —; (3) 1 house, 1 outhouse, M. 11 ac., P.G. 5; (4) 2^l; (5) 10^s; (6) 2^l 17^s.

Henry Spence—(2) —; (3) 1 house, 1 outhouse, M. 18 ac., P.G. 16; (4) 3^l 6^s; (5) 1^l 13^s; (6) 6^l 6^s 8^d.

Idem—(2) —; (3) 1 house, M. 14 ac., P.G. 10; (4) 2^l 1^s 4^d; (5) 1^l 0^s 8^d; (6) 4^l 11^s.

Francis Dodsworth—(2) —; (3) 1 house, 1 outhouse, M. 20 ac., P.G. 20$\frac{1}{2}$; (4) 2^l 9^s; (5) 1^l 4^s 6^d; (6) 7^l 7^s 8^d.

John Horner—(2) —; (3) 1 house, 1 outhouse, P.G. 12; (4) 3^l 4^s; (5) 1^l 1^s 4^d; (6) 5^l 13^s.

Idem—(2) —; (3) M. 10 ac., P.G. 10; (4) 3^l; (5) 1^l; (6) 3^l 13^s 4^d.

Idem—(2) —; (3) 1 outhouse, M. 12 ac., P.G. 11; (4) 2^l 15^s; (5) 18^s 4^d; (6) 4^l 7^s 2^d.

Michael Dodsworth— (2) —; (3) 1 house, 4 outhouses, M. 55 ac., P.G. 63; (4) 8^l 18^s; (5) 4^l 9^s; (6) 18^l 0^s 10^d.

Idem—(2) —; (3) M. 16 ac., P.G. 6; (4) 2^l 11^s 9^d; (5) 17^s 3^d; (6) 3^l 4^s 2^d.

[1] Bishopdale, a tnshp. in par. of Aysgarth.

Bryan Dodsworth—(2) —; (3) 1 house, 1 outhouse, M. 30 ac. 2 r.,
P.G. 5; (4) 4^l 15^s; (5) 2^l 7^s 6^d; (6) 7^l 4^s 10^d.

Myles Faucett—(2) —; (3) 1 house, 1 outhouse, M. 15 ac., P.G. 4;
(4) 3^l; (5) 1^l 10^s; (6) 4^l 0^s 6^d.

Idem—(2) —; (3) 1 house, 1 outhouse, M. 17 ac., P.G. 9;
(4) 1^l 5^s; (5) 12^s 6^d; (6) 5^l 1^s 4^d.

Miles Spence—(2) —; (3) 1 house, 1 outhouse, M. 16 ac., P.G. 8;
(4) 1^l 12^s; (5) 16^s 8^d; (6) 4^s 16^s 2^d.

Idem—(2) —; (3) 1 house, 1 outhouse, M. 9 ac., P.G. 5;
(4) 1^l 8^s 6^d; (5) 9^s 6^d; (6) 2^l 16^s.

Thomas Spence—(2) —; (3) 1 house, M. 10 ac., P.G. 13;
(4) 2^l 11^s 9^d; (5) 17^s 3^d; (6) 4^l 7^s 4^d.

Jeffery Hamond—(2) —; (3) 1 house, M. 25 ac., P.G. 13;
(4) 2^l 13^s 4^d; (5) 1^l 6^s 8^d; (6) 7^l 9^s 4^d.

Idem—(2) —; (3) 1 house, 1 outhouse, M. 16 ac., P.G. 9;
(4) 2^l 12^s 6^d; (5) 17^s 6^d; (6) 4^l 19^s 3^d.

George Hamond—(2) —; (3) 1 house, M. 13 ac., P.G. 8$\frac{1}{3}$;
(4) 2^l 12^s 6^d; (5) 17^s 6^d; (6) 4^l 5^s.

Francis Harison—(2) —; (3) 1 house, 1 outhouse, M. 20 ac.;
(4) 3^l 5^s 2^d; (5) 1^l 12^s 7^d; (6) 4^l 7^s.

George Fryer—(2) —; (3) 1 house, 2 outhouses, M. 30 ac., P.G. 15;
(4) 3^l 11^s 2^d; (5) 1^l 15^s 7^d; (6) 8^l 16^s 8^d.

James Faucett—(2) —; (3) 1 house, 1 outhouse, M. 26 ac., P.G. 10;
(4) 2^l 15^s; (5) 1^l 7^s 6^d; (6) 7^l 0^s 8^d.

Idem—(2) —; (3) 1 house, M. 12 ac., P.G. 10; (4) 2^l 9^s 6^d;
(5) 16^s 6^d; (6) 10^l 18^s 8^d.

Total—34 Tenants; 26 houses, 25 outhouses, 700 ac. 2 r. of
Meadow, 359 Pasture gates; fines paid in 20 years,
£134 . 14 . 2; yearly rent, £49 . 4 . 4; yearly value,
£204 . 14 . 1.
Cleare Improvem^t £155 . 9^s 9^d.

5. Newbigging.[1]   [p. 17

John Gracethwait—(2) 6 yrs.; (3) 1 house, 1 outhouse, M. 10 ac.,
P.G. 3$\frac{1}{2}$; (4) 1^l 0^s 9^d; (5) 6^s 11^d; (6) 2^l 15^s.

John Jaques—(2) —; (3) M. 4 ac., A. 1 r., P.G. 2; (4) 7^s 4^d;
(5) 3^s 8^d; (6) 1^l 3^s.

Adam Jaques—(2) —; (3) 1 house, 1 outhouse, M. 13 ac., A. 1 ac.
1 r., P.G. 6$\frac{1}{2}$; (4) 1^l 2^s 5^d; (5) 11^s 2$\frac{1}{2}$^{d}; (6) 4^l 1^s 2^d.

Arthur Metcalfe—(2) —; (3) 1 house, 3 outhouses, M. 18 ac.,
A. 7 ac., P.G. 12$\frac{1}{3}$; (4) 4^l 2^s 8^d; (5) 1^l 0^s 8^d; (6) 6^l 16^s 8^d.

Richard Hammond—(2) —; (3) 1 house, 1 outhouse, M. 7 ac.,
A. 3 r., P.G. 5; (4) 1^l 0^s 1^d; (5) 10^s 2$\frac{1}{2}$^{d}; (6) 2^l 13^s 10^d.

Barth. Spence—(2) —; (3) 1 house, 1 outhouse, M. 6 ac., P.G. 4;
(4) 2^l 8^s 6^d; (5) 8^s 1^d; (6) 2^l 7^s 4^d.

[1] Newbiggin in Bishopdale, par. of Aysgarth.

Michael Sadler—(2) —; (3) 1 house, 1 outhouse, M. 12 ac., A. 4 ac., P.G. 8¼; (4) 1^l 4^s 10^d; (5) 12^s 5^d; (6) 4^l 10^s 10^d.

Myles Beane—(2) —; (3) 1 house, 1 outhouse, M. 24 ac., A. 7 ac., P.G. 14½; (4) 5^l 0^s 4^d; (5) 1^l 5^s 1^d; (6) 8^l 12^s.

Edward Wilkinson—(2) —; (3) 1 house, 1 outhouse, M. 13 ac., A. 4 ac., P.G. 11¾; (4) 1^l 19^s; (5) 19^s 6^d; (6) 5^l 13^s 2^d.

John Dixson, Junr—(2) —; (3) 1 house, 1 outhouse, M. 25 ac., A. 6 ac., P.G. 11; (4) 1^l 16^s 8^d; (5) 18^s 4^d; (6) 8^l 1^s 4^d.

Edward Taylor—(2) —; (3) 1 house, 2 outhouses, M. 8 ac., A. 7 ac., P.G. 12; (4) 4^l 2^s; (5) 1^l 0^s 6^d; (6) 6^l 19^s 8^d.

Chrofer. Hugginson— (2)—; (3) 1 house, 2 outhouses, M. 15 ac., A. 5 ac., P.G. 10; (4) 1^l 12^s 8^d; (5) 16^s 4^d; (6) 5^l 13^s 4^d.

Peter Taylor—(2) —; (3) 1 house, 2 outhouses, M. 15 ac., A. 9 ac., P.G. 8; (4) 1^l 7^s 4^d; (5) 13^s 8^d; (6) 5^l 18^s 8^d.

Roger Jackson—(2) —; (3) 1 house, 1 outhouse, M. 20 ac., A. 4 ac., P.G. 9; (4) 1^l 10^s 8^d; (5) 15^s 4^d; (6) 6^l 7^s 6^d.

Thomas Spence—(2) —; (3) 1 house, 1 outhouse, M. 19 ac., P.G. 11½; (4) 2^l 6^s; (5) 1^l 3^s; (6) 6^l 2^s 4^d.

Willm. Sadler—(2) —; (3) M. 5 ac., A. 1 ac. 2 r.; P.G. 2; (4) 12^s 7½^d; (5) 4^s 2½^d; (6) 1^l 12^s 10^d.

Roger Wilkinson—(2) —; (3) 1 house, 2 outhouses, M. 15 ac., A. 2 ac., P.G. 9; (4) 1^l 9^s 6^d; (5) 14^s 9^d; (6) 5^l 9^s 4^d.

James Hammond—(2) —; (3) 1 house, 1 outhouse, M. 21 ac., 2 r., A. 5 ac., P.G. 17½; (4) 4^l 6^s 10½^d; (5) 1^l 8^s 11½^d; (6) 8^l 6^s 8^d.

James Spence—(2) —; (3) 1 house, 1 outhouse, M. 16 ac., A. 4 ac., P.G. 14; (4) 2^l 8^s; (5) 1^l 4^s; (6) 6^l 12^s 8^d.

Miles Dixson—(2) —; (3) 1 house, 1 outhouse, M. 20 ac., A. 7 ac., P.G. 9; (4) 2^l 2^s; (5) 14^s; (6) 6^l 15^s.

Roger Dixson—(2) —; (3) 1 house, 1 outhouse, M. 7 ac., A. 5 ac., P.G. 6½; (4) 1^l 11^s 6^d; (5) 10^s 6^d; (6) 3^l 11^s 4^d.

John Taylor—(2) —; (3) 1 house, M. 6 ac., A. 1 ac., P.G. 4; (4) 1^l 4^s; (5) 8^s; (6) 2^l 4^s 4^d.

Gyles Fryer—(2) —; (3) 1 house, 1 outhouse, M. 7 ac., P.G. 4; (4) 1^l 5^s 3^d; (5) 8^s 5^d; (6) 2^l 4^s 8^d.

Idem—(2) —; (3) 1 house, 1 outhouse, M. 12 ac., A. 2 ac., P.G. 6½; (4) 2^l 4^s; (5) 11^s; (6) 4^l 0^s 4^d.

Leonard Wilkinson—(2) —; (3) 1 house, 1 outhouse, M. 10 ac., A. 4 ac., P. G. 9½; (4) 1^l 10^s 6^d; (5) 15^s 3^d; (6) 4^l 10^s 4^d.

John Dixson, senr.—(2) —; (3) 1 house, 2 outhouses, M. 15 ac., A. 5 ac., P.G. 11; (4) 1^l 16^s 8^d; (5) 18^s 4^d; (6) 6^l 1^s 8^d.

John Scarre—(2) —; (3) 1 house, 2 outhouses, M. 17 ac., A. 8 ac., P,G. 12; (4) 1^l 16^s 8^d; (5) 18^s 4½^d; (6) 6^l 19^s 8^d.

Total—27 Tenants; 25 houses, 32 outhouses; 370 ac. 2 roods of Meadow; 98 ac. 3 roods of Arrable; 234½ pasture gates; fines paid in 20 years, £53 . 9 . 2; yearly rent, £20 . 0 . 8½; yearly value, £113 . 5 . 4.

Cleare Improvem^t—£93 . 4 . 7½.

---

6. Aysgarth.[1]

Chrofer. Simson—(2) —; (3) 1 house, 2 outhouses, M. 30 ac., A. 10 ac., P.G. 5¼; (4) 4^l 2^s 6^d; (5) 1^l 1^s; (6) 9^l 6^s 4^d.

John Faucett—(2) —; (3) 1 house, 2 outhouses, M. 30 ac., P.G. 3¾; (4) 1^l 10^s; (5) 15^s; (6) 6^l 19^s 2^d.

John Tunstell—(2) —; (3) 1 house, 2 outhouses, M. 14 ac., P.G. 4¼; (4) 1^l 16^s; (5) 9^s; (6) 3^l 13^s 6^d.

Roger Spence—(2) —; (3) 1 house, 1 outhouse, M. 8 ac., A. 1 ac., P.G. 2; (4) 1^l 4^s; (5) 8^s; (6) 2^l 11^s.

Leonard Spence—(2) —; (3) 1 house, M. 4 ac., P.G. 1½; (4) 12^s; (5) 6^s; (6) 1^l 4^s 4^d.

Thomas Milner—(2) —; (3) 1 house; (4) 1^s 4^d; (5) 8^d; (6) 3^s 4^d.

Anthony Atkinson—(2) —; (3) 1 house, 1 outhouse, M. 8 ac., P.G. 2; (4) 1^l 12^s; (5) 8^s; (6) 2^l 2^s 8^d.

Idem—(2) —; (3) 1 house, M. 10 ac., P.G. 1¼; (4) 15^s; (5) 5^s; (6) 2^l 6^s 10^d.

Willm. Terry—(2) —; (3) 1 house, 1 outhouse, M. 6 ac., A. 1 ac. 2 r., P.G. 1¼; (4) 10^s; (5) 5^s; (6) 1^l 15^s 2^d.

Willm. Scarre—(2) —; (3) 1 house, M. 7 ac., P.G. 1¼; (4) 10^s; (5) 5^s; (6) 1^l 14^s 8^d.

Tristram Beverley—(2) —; (3) 1 house, M. 12 ac., A. 5 ac., P.G. 3¼; (4) 2^l 16^s; (5) 14^s; (6) 3^l 17^s 10^d.

Robert Dixson—(2) —: (3) a Corne mill; (4) 3^l 16^s; (5) 3^s 4^d; (6) 1^l 10^s.

Total—12 Tenants; 11 houses, 8 outhouses, 129 acres of Meadow, 19 ac. 2 roods of arrable; 26 Pasture Gates; fines paid in 20 years, £19 . 4 . 10; yearly rent £5; yearly value £37 . 4 . 10.

Cleare Improvem^t—£32 . 4 . 10.

The generall Abstract of Bishopsdale Chace being the fourth division of Midleham	The Number of tennants	186		
	Quantity of ground	2852 ac. 2 r.		
	Beastgates pasture	1271	*l.*	*s.*	*d.*
	Fynes paid in 20 years past	450	06	08
	The yearly rent	157	06	07
	The yearly value	772	05	00
	The cleare yearly Improvem^t	614	18	05

[1] A parish town. The ancient parish included the whole valley of the Ure from a point just above Castle Bolton to the heights of Ure head and covers about 80,000 acres.

[p. 18

5. Wensladale forest.[1]

This consists of 22 parts, viz.

1. Bainbrigg Towne	9. Birkrigg	17. Burrisgaris
2. Woodall	10. Mosedale	18. Burghill
3. Counterside	11. Snaisholme	19. Cravenholme
4. Buske	12. Butterside	20. Holmehouse
5. Marsett	13. Bainbrigg Ings	21. Bleasings
6. Gaile	14. Worton Barony	22. Cubeckings
7. Hawes	15. Cubecke	
8. Aperside	16. Kitlaide	

1. Bainbrigg Towne.[2]

Sir Tho. Metcalfe—(2) —; (3) a Corne Mill; (4) 7^l 13^s 4^d; (5) 3^l 16^s 8^d; (6) 16^l.

Chrofer. Metcalfe—(2) —; (3) 1 house, 2 outhouses, M. and A. 6 ac., P.G. 10; (4) 1^l 9^s $8\frac{1}{2}^d$; (5) 9^s $10\frac{1}{2}^d$; (6) 2^l 10^s.

Chrofer. Metcalfe—(2) —; (3) 1 house, 1 outhouse, M. & A. 8 ac., P.G. $9\frac{1}{2}$; (4) 1^l 18^s 8^d; (5) 9^s 8^d; (6) 2^l 14^s 6^d.

Robert Nicolson—(2) —; (3) 1 house, M. & A. 4 ac., P.G. 6; (4) 12^s 5^d; (5) 6^s $2\frac{1}{2}^d$; (6) 1^l 10^s 4^d

Antho. Stirkehead—(2) —; (3) 1 house, 2 outhouses, M. & A. 12 ac., P.G. 15; (4) 1^l 10^s 11^d; (5) 15^s $5\frac{1}{2}^d$; (6) 3^l 18^s 6^d.

Richard Metcalfe—(2) —; (3) 1 house, 1 outhouse, M. & A. 20 ac., P.G. 20; (4) 1^l 19^s 6^d; (5) 19^s 9^d; (6) 5^l 15^s.

John Metcalfe, junr.—(2) —; (3) 1 house, 1 outhouse, M. & A. 6 ac., P.G. 6; (4) 1^l 4^s; (5) 6^s; (6) 1^l 17^s.

Alex. Metcalfe—(2) —; (3) 1 house, 1 outhouse, M. & A. 10 ac., P.G. 12; (4) 2^l 18^s 8^d; (5) 14^s 8^d; (6) 3^l 5^s.

Idem—(2) —; (3) 1 house, M. & A. 8 ac., P.G. 8; (4) 2^l; (5) 10^s; (6) 2^l 7^s 2^d.

Idem—(2) —; (3) 1 house, 1 outhouse, M. & A. 10 ac., P.G. 4; (4) 1^l 8^s; (5) 5^s 2^d; (6) 2^l 2^s.

Roger Scott—(2) —; (3) 1 house, 1 outhouse, M. & A. 6 ac., P.G. $4\frac{1}{2}$; (4) 1^l 16^s; (5) 6^s; (6) 1^l 18^s 6^d.

Willm. Stockdale—(2) —; (3) 1 house, 3 outhouses, M. & A. 6 ac., P.G. 4; (4) 15^s 9^d; (5) 5^s 3^d; (6) 1^l 16^s 6^d.

John Cooper—(2) —; (3) 1 house, 1 outhouse, M. & A. 6 ac., P.G. $8\frac{1}{2}$; (4) 17^s 7^d; (5) 8^s $9\frac{1}{2}^d$; (6) 2^l 15^s 4^d.

Edmd. Nicholson—(2) —; (3) 1 house, 1 outhouse, M. & A. 10 ac., P.G. 10; (4) 2^l 13^s 4^d; (5) 10^s 8^d; (6) 3^l 14^s.

James Mason—(2) —; (3) 1 house, 1 outhouse, M. & A. 8 ac., P.G. 4; (4) 1^l; (5) 5^s; (6) 2^l 2^s 6^d.

[1] This forest was of great extent and occupied much of the valley of the Ure above Bainbridge. The boundaries in the early thirteenth century are set out in *V.C.H., Yks., N.R.*, i, 200–201.

[2] Bainbridge Town in par. of Aysgarth. It was the headquarters of the forest government.

John Aigland—(2) —; (3) 1 house, $\frac{1}{2}$ outhouse, M. & A. 12 ac., P.G. 15$\frac{1}{2}$; (4) 1^l 10^s 11^d; (5) 15^s 5$\frac{1}{2}$^{d}; (6) 5^l 2^s.

Francis Metcalfe—(2) —; (3) 1 house, 2 outhouses, M. & A. 12 ac., P.G. 16; (4) 6^l 4^s 9^d; (5) 1^l 9$\frac{1}{2}$^{d}; (6) 5^l 5^s.

Percivall Ingram—(2) —; (3) 1 house, 1 outhouse, M. & A. 3 ac., P.G. 2$\frac{1}{2}$; (4) 6^s 8^d; (5) 3^s 4^d; (6) 1^l 1^s 6^d.

 Idem—(2) —; (3) 1 house, M. & A. 3 ac., P.G. 3; (4) 7^s 4^d; (5) 3^s 8^d; (6) 1^l 3^s 6^d.

John Metcalfe, sen.—(2) —; (3) 1 house, 2 outhouses, M. & A. 10 ac., P.G. 9$\frac{1}{2}$; (4) 1^l 18^s 8^d; (5) 9^s 8^d; (6) 3^l 12^s.

Alex^r Ingram—(2) —; (3) 1 house, 2 outhouses, M. & A. 10 ac., P.G. 14; (4) 1^l 7^s 10^d; (5) 13^s 11^d; (6) 4^l 10^s.

 Idem—(2) —; (3) 1 outhouse, M. & A. 6 ac., P.G. 5; (4) 1^l 6^s 3^d; (5) 5^s 3^d; (6) 1^l 18^s.

Willm. Nicholson—(2) —; (3) 1 house, M. & A. 5 ac., P.G. 5; (4) 1^l 4^s 10^d; (5) 6^s 2$\frac{1}{2}$^{d}; (6) 1^l 17^s 6^d.

Chrofer. Thistlethwait—(2) —; (3) 1 house, M. & A. 4 ac., P.G. 5; (4) 18^s; (5) 6^s; (6) 1^l 15^s 4^d.

James Metcalfe—(2) —; (3) 1 house, 2 outhouses, M. & A. 9 ac., P.G. 10; (4) 1^l 19^s 6^d; (5) 9^s 10$\frac{1}{2}$^{d}; (6) 3^l 10^s 4^d.

 Idem—(2) —; (3) M. & A. 1 ac. 2 r.; (4) 1^s 10^d; (5) 11^d; (6) 4^s 6^d.

Margaret Blaides—(2) —; (3) 1 house, 1 outhouse, M. & A. 6 ac., P.G. 6; (4) 13^s 4^d; (5) 6^s 8^d; (6) 2^l 7^s.

John Tuke—(2) —; (3) 1 house, 3 outhouses, M. & A. 8 ac., P.G. 14; (4) 3^l 14^s 2^d; (5) 14^s 10^d; (6) 4^l 4^s.

 Total—28 Tenants; 25 houses, 30$\frac{1}{2}$ outhouses, 209 acres 2 roods of Meadow and Arrable; 228 Pasture Gates; fynes paid in 20 years, 51^l 11^s 10$\frac{1}{2}$^{d}; yearly rent 16^l 5^s 9^d; yearly value 90^l 17^s 2^d.

 The Clere Improvem^t £74 . 11^s 5^d.

---

2. Woodall.[1]

Edmund Metcalfe—(2) —; (3) 1 house, 1 outhouse, M. & A. 12 ac., P.G. 3; (4) 2^l 18^s 8^d; (5) 14^s 8^d; (6) 2^l 11^s 4^d.

 Idem—(2) —; (3) 1 house, 2 outhouses, M. & A. 30 ac., P.G. 7; (4) 3^l 17^s 3^d; (5) 1^l 5^s 9^d; (6) 6^l 3^s.

Geo. Metcalfe, jun^r.—(2) —; (3) 1 house, M. & A. 24 ac., P.G. 5; (4) 3^l 17^s 3^d; (5) 1^l 5^s 9^d; (6) 4^l 12^s 6^d.

Martin Faucet—(2) 6 yrs.; (3) 1 house, 3 outhouses, M. & A. 51 ac., P.G. 6; (4) 10^l 4^s; (5) 2^l 11^s; (6) 8^l 19^s 8^d.

Peter Hawkins—(2) —; (3) M. & A. 8 ac.; (4) 13^s 4^d; (5) 6^s 8^d; (6) 1^l 1^s 6^d.

[1] Woodhall in tnshp. of Askrigg.

James Gricethwait—(2) —; (3) 1 house, 3 outhouses, M. & A.
16 ac., P.G. 4; (4) 6^l 1^s 3^d; (5) 1^l 4^s 3^d; (6) 3^l 9^s 2^d.

Alex^r Metcalfe—(2) 9 yrs; (3) 1 house, 1 outhouse, M. & A. 16 ac.,
P.G. 4; (4) 2^l 8^s 6^d; (5) 1^l 4^s 3^d; (6) 3^l 9^s 2^d.

George Metcalfe—(2) —; (3) 1 house, M. & A. 37 ac., P.G. 7;
(4) 4^l 17^s; (5) 2^l 8^s 6^d; (6) 7^l 1^s.

Idem—(2) —; (3) 1 house, 3 outhouses, M. & A. 27 ac.,
P.G. 5½; (4) 3^l 13^s 8^d; (5) 1^l 16^s 10^d; (6) 6^l 3^s.

Sr Tho. Metcalfe—(2) — (3) M. & A. 30 ac., P.G. 8; (4) 5^l 3^s;
(5) 2^l 11^s 6^d; (6) 8^l 12^s.

All the tennants there—(2) —; (3) M. & A. 1 ac.; (4) 8^d; (5) 4^d;
(6) 3^s.

Total: 11 Tenants; 8 houses, 13 outhouses, 252 acres of
meadow and arrable; 49½ Pasture Gates; fines paid in
20 years, £43 13^s 7^d; yearly rent, £15 9^s 6^d; yearly
value £52 10^s 4^d.

The Cleere Improvem^t £37 0^s 10^d.

Demeasnes.

[1]Sr Tho. Metcalfe holdeth Woodall parke for 10
yrs to come at the rent of   02^l 00^s 00^d

[2]The quantity is 60 beast gates worth yearly   15^l 00^s 00^d

The Improvem^t 13^l 00^s 00^d

After the expiracon of the lease Sr Hen. Linley
hath it in fee ferme, at ye rent of   04^l 00^s 00^d

---

3. Counterside.[3]   [p. 19

Augustine Metcalfe—(2) 6 yrs; (3) 1 house, 1 outhouse, M. 30 ac.,
P.G. 13; (4) 2^l 17^s 8^d; (5) 14^s 5^d; (6) 3^s 14^s.

Idem—(2) 6 yrs; (3) 1 house, 1 outhouse, M. 13 ac., P.G. 11;
(4) 2^l 16^s 8^d; (5) 14^s 2^d; (6) 2^l 19^s 8^d.

Idem—(2) 6 yrs; (3) 1 house, M. 8 ac., P.G. 3; (4) 1^l; (5) 6^s 8^d;
(6) 1^l 19^s.

Idem—(2) 6 yrs; (3) M. 10 ac., P.G. 4½; (4) 1^l 1^s; (5) 10^s;
(6) 2^l 8^s.

Edmund Harison—(2) 6 yrs; (3) 1 house, 1 outhouse, M. 30 ac.,
P.G. 9; (4) 1^l 18^s 4^d; (5) 19^s 2^d; (6) 6^l 3^s 8^d.

James Metcalfe—(2) —; (3) 1 house, 1 outhouse, M. 10 ac.,
P.G. 15; (4) 3^l; (5) 15^s; (6) 3^l 19^s.

Thomas Harison—(2) —; (3) 1 house, 2 outhouses, M. 25 ac.,
P.G. 9; (4) 2^l; (5) 1^l; (6) 5^l 16^s.

Richard Metcalfe—(2) —; (3) 1 house, 1 outhouse, M. 12 ac.,
P.G. 11½; (4) 1^l 8^s 10½^d; (5) 14^s 5¼^d; (6) 4^l 6^s.

---

[1] "Not ye Cities, as is said" in the margin.

[2] "Worth 20^{ll}" in the margin.

[3] Countersett, a hamlet in the tnshp. of Bainbridge.

Mathew Metcalfe—(2) —; (3) 1 house, 1 outhouse, M. 10 ac.,
P.G. 15½; (4) 1ˡ 8ˢ 4ᵈ; (5) 14ˢ 2ᵈ; (6) 4ˡ 15ˢ 4ᵈ.
Idem—(2) —; (3) 1 outhouse, M. 20 ac., P.G. 21¼; (4) 3ˡ 15ˢ;
(5) 1ˡ 5ˢ; (6) 7ˡ 5ˢ.
John Ingram—(2) —; (3) 1 house, M. 25 ac., P.G. 6; (4) 2ˡ 3ˢ 3ᵈ;
(5) 14ˢ 5½ᵈ; (6) 5ˡ 10ˢ 8ᵈ.
Alexʳ Metcalfe, jun.—(2) —; (3) 1 house, 2 outhouses, M. 40 ac.,
P.G. 30; (4) 5ˡ 3ˢ 4ᵈ; (5) 2ˡ 11ˢ 8ᵈ; (6) 13ˡ 3ˢ 4ᵈ.
George Metcalfe—(2) —; (3) 1 house,.M. 12 ac., P.G. 5; (4) 1ˡ 3ˢ 4ᵈ;
(5) 11ˢ 8ᵈ; (6) 2ˡ 19ˢ 4ᵈ.
Barth. Harison—(2) —; (3) 1 house, M. 22 ac., P.G. 6; (4) 2ˡ 10ˢ;
(5) 12ˢ 6ᵈ; (6) 4ˡ 15ˢ.
Augustine Metcalfe—(2) —; (3) 1 house, 2 outhouses, M. 50 ac.,
P.G. 33; (4) 7ˡ 13ˢ 4ᵈ; (6) 3ˡ 16ˢ 8ᵈ; (6) 14ˡ 12ˢ.

Total—15 Tenants; 13 houses, 15 outhouses; 297 acres of
meadow; 192¾ Pasture Gates; fynes paid in 20 years
£39 19ˢ 1½ᵈ; yearly rent, £15 19ˢ 11¾ᵈ; (6) £84 . 6 . 0.
Cleere Improvemᵗ—£68 . 6ˢ 0¼ᵈ.

---

4. Buske.[1]

James Lobley—(2) —; (3) 1 house, 4 outhouses, M. 40 ac., P.G. 37;
(4) 4ˡ 18ˢ 4ᵈ; (5) 2ˡ 9ˢ 2ᵈ; (6) 12ˡ 13ˢ 4ᵈ.
Idem—(2) —; (3) M. 1 ac.; (4) 1ˢ; (5) 6ᵈ; (6) 4ˢ.
Idem—(2) —; (3) M. 2 ac.; (4) 2ˢ; (5) 1ˢ; (6) 4ˢ.
Tho. Metcalfe, sen.—(2) —; (3) 1 house, 2 outhouses, M. 30 ac.,
P.G. 20; (4) 2ˡ 16ˢ 8ᵈ; (5) 1ˡ 8ˢ 4ᵈ; (6) 9ˡ 1ˢ 6ᵈ.
Augustine Carlile—(2) —; (3) 1 house, 1 outhouse, M. 8 ac.,
P.G. 5; (4) 1ˡ 8ˢ 4ᵈ; (5) 7ˢ 1ᵈ; (6) 2ˡ 7ˢ 4ᵈ.
Willm. Scarre—(2) —; (3) 1 house, 1 outhouse, M. 14 ac., P.G. 10;
(4) 2ˡ 16ˢ 8ᵈ; (5) 14ˢ 2ᵈ; (6) 4ˡ 7ˢ.
Tho. Metcalfe, jun.—(2) 5 yrs; (3) 1 house, 2 outhouses, M. 10 ac.,
P.G. 6½; (4) 1ˡ 15ˢ 5ᵈ; (5) 8ˢ 10¼ᵈ; (6) 2ˡ 19ˢ 4ᵈ.
Bryan Wilson—(2) —; (3) 1 house, 2 outhouses, M. 13 ac., P.G.
10; (4) 1ˡ 9ˢ 2ᵈ; (5) 19ˢ 7ᵈ; (6) 4ˡ 4ˢ.
Willm. Hunter—(2) —; (3) 1 house, 1 outhouse, M. 10 ac., P.G.
7½; (4) 2ˡ 2ˢ 10ᵈ; (5) 10ˢ 8¼ᵈ; (6) 3ˡ 5ˢ.
Francis Tomson—(2) —; (3) 1 house, M. 8 ac., P.G. 5; (4) 1ˡ 8ˢ 4ᵈ;
(5) 17ˢ 1ᵈ; (6) 2ˡ 7ˢ 4ᵈ.
John Metcalfe— (2) 5 yrs; (3) 1 house, 1 outhouse, M. 8 ac.,
P.G. 5; (4) 1ˡ 1ˢ 3ᵈ; (5) 7ˢ 1ᵈ (6) 2ˡ 7ˢ 4ᵈ.
Ralphe Lobley—(2) —; (3) 1 house, 1 outhouse, M. 11 ac., P.G.
8½; (4) 2ˡ; (5) 10ˢ; (6) 3ˡ 17ˢ.
Idem—(2) —; (3) 1 house, 1 outhouse, M. 9 ac., P.G. 8½;
(4) 1ˡ 10ˢ; (5) 10ˢ; (6) 3ˡ 7ˢ

[1] Stalling or Stallion Busk, a hamlet in tnshp. of Bainbridge.

Willm. Jackson—(2) —; (3) 1 house, M. 6 ac., P.G. 3; (4) 12ˢ 6ᵈ;
    (5) 4ˢ 2ᵈ; (6) 1ˡ 12ˢ 6ᵈ.

Jeffery Walker— (2) —; (3) 1 house, M. 14 ac., P.G. 16; (4)
    3ˡ 3ˢ 9ᵈ; (5) 1ˡ 1ˢ 3ᵈ; (6) 5ˡ 11ˢ.

Mr. Symon Haddocke—(2) —; (3) 1 house, M. 8 ac., P.G. 10;
    (4) 2ˡ; (5) 13ˢ 4ᵈ; (6) 3ˡ 9ˢ.

    Idem—(2) —; (3) 1 house, M. 9 ac., P.G. 7½; (4) 1ˡ 9ˢ 0¾ᵈ;
    (5) 9ˢ 8¼ᵈ; (6) 2ˡ 17ˢ.

Willm. Slinger— (2) —; (3) 1 house, 1 outhouse, M. 7 ac., P.G. 5;
    (4) 14ˢ 2ᵈ; (5) 7ˢ 1ᵈ; (6) 2ˡ 3ˢ.

Edmd. Metcalfe— (2) —; (3) 1 house, M. 3 ac., P.G. 2½; (4) 12ˢ 6ᵈ;
    (5) 4ˢ 2ᵈ; (6) 1ˡ 1ˢ 6ᵈ.

Total: 19 Tenants; 17 houses, 17 outhouses; 211 acres of
    meadow; 167 Pasture Gates; fynes paid in 20 years,
    £32 1ˢ 11¾ᵈ; yearly rent £11 8ˢ 3ᵈ; yearly value,
    £67 14ˢ 2ᵈ.
        Cleere Improvemᵗ £56 5ˢ 11ᵈ.

---

5. Marcette.[1]   [p. 20

Francis Lambert—(2) —; (3) 1 house, 1 outhouse, M. 12 ac.,
    P.G. 14; (4) 1ˡ 6ˢ 8ᵈ; (5) 13ˢ 4ᵈ; (6) 4ˡ 3ˢ.

    Idem—(2) —; (3) M. 5 ac., P.G. 4; (4) 13ˢ 4ᵈ; (5) 6ˢ 8ᵈ;
    (6) 1ˡ 11ˢ.

    Idem—(2) —; (3) M. 5 ac., P.G. 4; (4) 1ˡ; (5) 6ˢ 8ᵈ; (6) 1ˡ 11ˢ.

Alexʳ Thwait—(2) —; (3) 1 house, M. 9 ac., P.G. 4; (4) 2ˡ 6ˢ 8ᵈ;
    (5) 6ˢ 8ᵈ; (6) 2ˡ 3ˢ.

John Metcalfe—(2) —; (3) 1 house, 2 outhouses, M. 16 ac., P.G.
    14; (4) 1ˡ 6ˢ 8ᵈ; (5) 13ˢ 4ᵈ; (6) 4ˡ 18ˢ.

    Idem—(2) —; (3) 1 house, M. 6 ac., P.G. 4; (4) 1ˡ; (5) 6ˢ 8ᵈ;
    (6) 1ˡ 13ˢ 10ᵈ.

    Idem—(2) —; (3) M. 4 ac., P.G. 1; (4) 3ˢ 4ᵈ; (5) 1ˢ 8ᵈ; (6)
    15ˢ 4ᵈ.

James Tomson, jun.—(2) 5 yrs.; (3) 1 house, 2 outhouses, M.
    16 ac., P.G. 14; (4) 2ˡ; (5) 13ˢ 4ᵈ; (6) 5ˡ 8ˢ.

John Tomson—(2) —; (3) 1 house, 1 outhouse, M. 11 ac., P.G. 13;
    (4) 1ˡ 0ˢ 8ᵈ; (5) 10ˢ 4ᵈ; (6) 4ˡ 8ˢ 4ᵈ.

Thomas Tomson—(2) —; (3) 1 house, 1 outhouse, M. 17 ac.,
    P.G. 14½; (4) 3ˡ 6ˢ 8ᵈ; (5) 16ˢ 8ᵈ; (6) 5ˡ 4ˢ 4ᵈ.

Sʳ Tho. Metcalfe—(2) —; (3) 1 house, M. 30 ac., P.G. 50;
    (4) 6ˡ 13ˢ 4ᵈ; (5) 3ˡ 6ˢ 8ᵈ; (6) 13ˡ 3ˢ 4ᵈ.

    Idem in Radale[2]—(2) —; (3) 1 house, 1 outhouse, M. 110 ac.,
    P.G. 140; (4) 21ˡ 6ˢ 8ᵈ; (5) 10ˡ 13ˢ 4ᵈ; (6) 34ˡ 5ˢ.

---

[1] Marsett, a hamlet in tnshp. of Bainbridge, 4 m. from Hawes.
[2] Raydale, a dale in the tnshp. of Bainbridge.

H

Anthony Atkinson—(2) —; (3) M. 13 ac., P.G. 14; (4) 1^l 6^s 8^d;
    (5) 13^s 4^d; (6) 4^l 15^s.
Chrofer. Cunnell—(2) —; (3) 1 house, M. 10 ac., P.G. 9; (4) 1^l;
    (5) 10^s; (6) 3^l 0^s 4^d.
Chrofer. Metcalfe—(2) —; (3) 1 house, M. 12 ac., P.G. 3; (4) 13^s 4^d;
    (5) 6^s 8^d; (6) 2^l 6^s.
George Lambert—(2) —; (3) 1 house, 2 outhouses, M. 13 ac.,
    P.G. 14; (4) 2^l 13^s 4^d; (5) 13^s 4^d; (6) 4^l 9^s.
   Idem—(2) —; (3) M. 5 ac., P.G. 4; (4) 13^s 4^d; (5) 6^s 8^d;
    (6) 1^l 8^s 4^d.
Thomas Metcalfe—(2) —; (3) 1 house, M. 12 ac., P.G. 8; (4) 1^l 6^s 8^d;
    (5) 13^s 4^d; (6) 3^l 7^s 8^d.
   Idem—(2) —; (3) 1 house, 1 outhouse, M. 5 ac., P.G. 4;
    (4) 13^s 4^d; (5) 6^s 8^d; (6) 1^l 13^s 4^d.
James Tomson, sen^r—(2) —; (3) 1 house, 1 outhouse, M. 18 ac.,
    P.G. 14; (4) 1^l; (5) 10^s; (6) 5^l 13^s 4^d.
John Lambert—(2) —; (3) 1 house, 2 outhouses, M. 25 ac.,
    P.G. 22; (4) 1^l 13^s 4^d; (5) 13^s 4^d; (6) 7^l 13^s 4^d.
Thomas Tomson—(2) —; (3) 1 house, 1 outhouse, M. 20 ac.,
    P.G. 18; (4) 2^l; (5) 10^s; (6) 6^l 3^s 4^d.
James Tomson—(2) —; (3) M. 5 ac., P.G. 2$\frac{1}{2}$; (4) 6^s 8^d; (5) 1^s 8^d;
    (6) 1^l 3^s 4^d.
Thomas Weste—(2) —; (3) 1 house, 1 outhouse; (4) 1^s; (5) 6^d;
    (6) 3^s.
   Total—24 Tenants; 18 houses, 16 outhouses; 379 ac. of
    Meadow; 389 Pasture Gates; fynes paid in 20 yeares,
    £55 11^s 8^d; yearly rent £24 0^s 10^d; yearly value,
    £121 0^s 2^d
      The Clere Improvement—£96 19^s 4^d.

---

6. Gayle.[1]   [p. 21

Owen Dinsdale—(2) —; (3) 1 house, 2 outhouses, M. 16 ac.,
    P.G. 18; (4) 1^l 18^s 9$\frac{1}{2}$^{d}; (5) 15^s 3^d; (6) 4^l 8^s.
Roger Sturdy—(2) —; (3) 1 house, M. 8 ac., P.G. 21$\frac{1}{2}$; (4) 1^l 17^s 6^d;
    (5) 12^s 6^d; (6) 3^l 11^s.
Michael Metcalfe—(2) —; (3) 1 house, 1 outhouse, M. 10 ac.,
    P.G. 10; (4) 15^s 4^d; (5) 7^s 8^d; (6) 2^l 7^s 4^d.
Reignold Metcalfe—(2) —; (3) 1 house, 4 outhouses, M. 13 ac.,
    P.G. 14$\frac{1}{2}$; (4) 1^l 4^s 10^d; (5) 12^s 5^d; (6) 3^l 6^s 6^d.
James Dinsdale—(2) —; (3) 1 house, 1 outhouse, M. 22 ac.,
    P.G. 15$\frac{1}{2}$; (4) 2^l 6^s 6^d; (5) 15^s 6^d; (6) 4^l 11^s.
Edmund Metcalfe—(2) 10 yrs.; (3) 1 house, 1 outhouse, M. 20 ac.,
    P.G. 38; (4) 3^l 3^s 9^d; (5) 1^l 1^s 3^d; (6) 6^l 1^s.

[1] Hamlet in township of Hawes.

Sr Thomas Metcalfe—(2) —; (3) M. 4 ac., P.G. 4; (4) 12^s; (5) 6^s; (6) 1^l 4^s.

Nynian Metcalfe—(2) —; (3) 1 house, M. 16 ac., P.G. 9; (4) 2^l 6^s 3^d; (5) 9^s 3^d; (6) 3^l 10^s.

Idem—(2) —; (3) 1 house, 1 outhouse, M. 40 ac., P.G. 6; (4) 2^l; (5) 13^s 4^d; (6) 4^l 17^s.

Chrofer. Tenant—(2) —; (3) 1 house, 3 outhouses, M. 23 ac., P.G. 16; (4) 2^l 9^s; (5) 14^s 6^d; (6) 4^l 16^s.

Tho: Dinsdale, jun.—(2) —; (3) 1 house, 4 outhouses, M. 25 ac., P.G. 18; (4) 2^l 14^s 10^d; (5) 17^s 8^d; (6) 5^l 9^s.

Bryan Wynne—(2) —; (3) 1 house, 3 outhouses, M. 14 ac., P.G. 16; (4) 2^l 9^s 8^d; (5) 12^s 5^d; (6) 3^l 12^s.

Gilbert Atkinson—(2) —; (3) M. 5 ac., P.G. 3$\frac{1}{2}$; (4) 7^s; (5) 3^s 6^d; (6) 19^s 6^d.

Richard Carre—(2) —; (3) 1 house, 1 outhouse, M. 5 ac., P.G. 8; (4) 1^l 1^s; (5) 7^s; (6) 1^l 11^s 10^d.

Richard Wynne—(2) —; (3) 1 house, 1 outhouse, M. 24 ac., P.G. 30; (4) 3^l 16^s 3^d; (5) 1^l 5^s 6^d; (6) 6^l 6^s 8^d.

Francis Wynne—(2) —; (3) 1 house, 1 outhouse, M. 10 ac., P.G. 11$\frac{1}{2}$; (4) 1^l 15^s 3^d; (5) 11^s 9^d; (6) 2^l 17^s.

John Wynne—(2) —; (3) 1 house, M. 7 ac., P.G. 9; (4) 1^l 7^s; (5) 9^s; (6) 2^l 2^s 4^d.

Roger Dawson—(2) —; (3) 1 house, M. 6 ac., P.G. 15$\frac{1}{2}$; (4) 1^l 1^s; (5) 7^s; (6) 2^l 9^s 4^d.

Jasper Busheles—(2) —; (3) 1 house, 1 outhouse, M. 16 ac., P.G. 27; (4) 4^l 16^s; (5) 1^l 4^s; (6) 5^l 2^s.

Robert Busheles—(2) —; (3) 1 house, M. 18 ac., P.G. 21$\frac{1}{2}$; (4) 3^l 18^s; (5) 19^s 6^d; (6) 4^l 12^s.

Michael Metcalfe—(2) —; (3) 1 house, M. 5 ac., P.G. 8; (4) 15^s; (5) 5^s; (6) 1^l 11^s.

Idem—(2) —; (3) M. 2 ac., P.G. 2; (4) 4^s; (5) 2^s; (6) 9^s.

George Rowthe—(2) —; (3) 1 house, 1 outhouse, M. 24 ac., P.G. 20; (4) 1^l 8^s; (5) 14^s; (6) 4^l 14^s.

Reignall Dinsdale—(2) —; (3) 1 house, M. 9 ac., P.G. 6; (4) 13^s 4^d; (5) 6^s 8^d; (6) 1^l 17^s.

Peter Metcalfe—(2) —; (3) 1 house, 1 outhouse, M. 10 ac., P.G. 9; (4) 15^s 4^d; (5) 7^s 8^d; (6) 2^l 6^s 4^d.

Augustine Wynne—(2) —; (3) 1 house, 2 outhouses, M. 10 ac., P.G. 14$\frac{1}{2}$; (4) 1^l 8^s 4^d; (5) 14^s 2^d; (6) 2^l 18^s 6^d.

George Dinsdale—(2) —; (3) M. 12 ac., P.G. 9$\frac{1}{2}$; (4) 1^l 17^s 6^d; (5) 12^s 6^d; (6) 2^l 14^s.

Nicolas Metcalfe—(2) —; (3) 1 house, 2 outhouses, M. 12 ac., P.G. 13; (4) 1^l 14^s 2^d; (5) 8^s 6$\frac{1}{2}$^{d}; (6) 2^l 19^s 4^d.

Richard Dinsdale—(2) —; (3) 1 house, 1 outhouse, M. 8 ac., P.G. 8; (4) 12^s 8^d; (5) 6^s 4^d; (6) 1^l 19^s 4^d.

Peter Wynne—(2) —; (3) 1 house, 1 outhouse, M. 8 ac., P.G. 10; (4) 14^s; (5) 7^s; (6) 2^l 3^s 4^d.

Chrofer. Glover—(2) —; (3) 1 house, 2 outhouses, M. 12 ac., P.G. 16; (4) 1^l 12^s 6^d; (5) 10^s 6^d; (6) 3^l 5^s 4^d.

Chrofer. Metcalfe—(2) —; (3) 1 house, 1 outhouse, M. 10 ac., P.G. 12$\frac{1}{2}$; (4) 19^s 3^d; (5) 9^s 7$\frac{1}{2}$^{d}; (6) 2^l 13^s 4^d.

George Metcalfe—(2) —; (3) 1 house, 1 outhouse, M. 10 ac., P.G. 12$\frac{1}{4}$; (4) 18^s 7^d; (5) 9^s 3$\frac{1}{2}$^{d}; (6) 2^l 12^s 10^d.

George Dinsdale—(2) —; (3) 1 house, 4 outhouses, M. 25 ac., P.G. 33; (4) 2^l 14^s 6^d; (5) 18^s 2^d; (6) 6^l 3^s 6^d.

Rowland Syll—(2) —; (3) 1 house, 1 outhouse, M. 30 ac., P.G. 56; (4) 9^l 14^s 2^d; (5) 1^l 18^s 10^d; (6) 9^l 12^s.

George Dinsdale—(2) —; (3) 1 house, 1 outhouse, M. 8 ac., P.G. 6; (4) 1^l 6^s 8^d; (5) 6^s 8^d; (6) 1^l 15^s 4^d.

Willm. Dinsdale—(2) —; (3) 1 house, M. 10 ac., P.G. 12$\frac{1}{2}$; (4) 1^l 1^s; (5) 10^s 6^d; (6) 2^l 16^s.

James Wynne—(2) —; (3) 1 house, 1 outhouse, M. 8 ac., P.G. 5; (4) 10^s; (5) 5^s; (6) 1^l 12^s 6^d.

George Metcalfe, jun^r—(2) —; (3) 1 house, 1 outhouse, M. 10 ac., P.G. 15; (4) 1^l 17^s; (5) 9^s 3^d; (6) 2^l 19^s 4^d.

Isaac Dinsdale—(2) —; (3) 1 house, 1 outhouse, M. 5 ac., P.G. 7$\frac{1}{2}$; (4) 1^l 5^s 4^d; (5) 6^s 4^d; (6) 1^l 10^s.

James Metcalfe—(2) —; (3) 1 house, 1 outhouse, M. 8 ac., P.G. 10$\frac{1}{2}$; (4) 2^l; (5) 10^s; (6) 2^l 4^s 4^d.

Jeffery Sturdy—(2) —; (3) 1 house, 2 outhouses, M. 13 ac., P.G. 13$\frac{1}{2}$; (4) 1^l 3^s; (5) 11^s 6^d; (6) 3^l 4^s 6^d.

Henry Becke—(2) —; (3) 1 house, 1 outhouse, M. 8 ac., P.G. 8$\frac{3}{4}$; (4) 17^s; (5) 8^s 6^d; (6) 2^l.

Roger Bradly—(2) —; (3) 1 house, 1 outhouse, M. 29 ac., P.G. 18$\frac{1}{2}$; (4) 2^l 1^s; (5) 13^s 8^d; (6) 5^l 0^s 4^d.

 Total—44 Tenants; 40 houses, 50 outhouses; 583 acres of Meadow; 639$\frac{1}{2}$ Pasture Gates; fynes paid in 20 years £90 2^s 3$\frac{1}{2}$^{d}; annual rent £25 16^s 8$\frac{1}{2}$^{d}; annual value £144 14^s 8^d.

 The Clere Improvement—£118 17^s 11$\frac{1}{2}$^{d}.

---

7. Hawes.[1]   [p. 22

Richard Rowthe—(2) —; (3) $\frac{1}{2}$ house, M. 6 ac., P.G. 6$\frac{1}{2}$; (4) 11^s 3^d; (5) 5^s 7$\frac{1}{2}$^{d}; (6) 1^l 10^s 6^d.

 Idem—(2) —; (3) 1 house; (5) 4^s; (6) 3^s 4^d.

Richard Dinsdale—(2) —; (3) $\frac{1}{2}$ house, M. 8 ac., P.G. 8; (4) 1^l 1^s 1$\frac{1}{2}$^{d}; (5) 7^s 0$\frac{1}{2}$^{d}; (6) 1^l 18^s 6^d.

[1] A market town in par. of Aysgarth, 5 m. from Askrigg.

Nynian Stockdale—(2) —; (3) M. 12 ac., P.G. 6; (4) 1^l 18^s;
  (5) 12^s 8^d; (6) 2^l 2^s.

William Binkes—(2) —; (3) 1 house, 1 outhouse, M. 8 ac., P.G. 7;
  (4) 1^l 1^s 1½^d; (5) 7^s 0½^d; (6) 1^l 17^s 4^d.

Michael Rowth, sen^r—(2) —; (3) 1 house, M. 8 ac., P.G. 5;
  (4) 16^s 10½^d; (5) 5^s 7½^d; (6) 1^l 13^s 4^d.

Tho. Rowth, sen^r—(2) —; (3) 1 house, 2 outhouses, M. 18 ac.,
  P.G. 14; (4) 1^l 11^s 3^d; (5) 15^s 7½^d; (6) 3^l 18^s.

Michael Rowth, jun^r—(2) —; (3) 1 house, 2 outhouses, M. 13 ac.,
  P.G. 12; (4) 1^l 6^s 11^d; (5) 13^s 5½^d; (6) 3^l 0^s 6^d.

Thomas Rowth, jun^r—(2) —; (3) ½ house, M. 5 ac., P.G. 6½;
  (4) 11^s 3^d; (5) 5^s 7½^d; (6) 1^l 8^s.

Thomas Metcalfe—(2) —; (3) 1 house, 2 outhouses, M. 20 ac.,
  P.G. 14; (4) 1^l 5^s 3^d; (5) 12^s 10^d; (6) 4^l 2^s.

Oswald Rowth—(2) —; (3) 1 outhouse, M. 12 ac., P.G. 10;
  (4) 1^l 13^s 3^d; (5) 11^s 1^d; (6) 2^l 14^s.

John Rowth—(2) —; (3) 1 house, 1 outhouse, M. 20 ac., P.G. 17⅓;
  (4) 2^l 10^s 8^d; (5) 12^s 8^d; (6) 4^l 4^s 2^d.

Chrofer. Rowth, jun^r—(2) —; (3) 1 house, 2 outhouses, M. 20 ac.,
  P.G. 10; (4) 2^l 13^s; (5) 13^s 3^d; (6) 3^l 15^s.

Chrofer. Rowth, sen^r—(2) —; (3) 1 house, 2 outhouses, M. 22 ac.,
  P.G. 14; (4) 1^l 5^s 1^d; (5) 12^s 6½^d; (6) 4^l 7^s.

Thomas Banks—(2) —; (3) 1 house, 2 outhouses, M. 10 ac.,
  P.G. 7; (4) 1^l 4^s; (5) 6^s 2^d; (6) 2^l 1^s 6^d.

John Metcalfe, jun^r—(2) —; (3) 1 house, 2 outhouses, M. 22 ac.,
  P.G. 17½; (4) 3^l 16^s 4^d; (5) 19^s 1^d; (6) 4^l 15^s.

John Metcalfe, sen^r—(2) —; (3) M. 8 ac., P.G. 1; (4) 13^s 4^d;
  (5) 6^s 8^d; (6) 1^l 2^s.

Matheu Jobson—(2) —; (3) 1 house, 1 outhouse, M. 23 ac., P.G.
  28; (4) 3^l 11^s 9^d; (5) 1^l 3^s 11^d; (6) 6^l 12^s 2^d.

Francis Pert—(2) —; (3) 1 house, M. 11 ac., P.G. 3½; (4) 16^s 10½^d;
  (5) 5^s 7½^d; (6) 1^l 17^s.

Anthony Metcalfe—(2) —; (3) 1 house, 5 outhouses, M. 16 ac.,
  P.G. 7; (4) 2^l 4^s 4^d; (5) 11^s 1^d; (6) 2^l 19^s.

Total—20 Tenants; 15½ houses, 22 outhouses, 262 acres of
  Meadow, 199⅓ Pasture Gates; fynes paid in 20 years,
  £13 12^s 1^d; yearly rent, £10 7^s 11½^d; yearly value,
  £56 0^s 4^d.
    The Cleere Improvem^t—£45 12^s 4½^d.

---

8. Apersyde.[1]

Gawen Roger—(2) —; (3) 1 house, 1 outhouse, M. 10 ac., P.G. 8
  (4) 2^l 0^s 8^d; (5) 10^s 2^d; (6) 2^l 5^s.

[1] Appersett, hamlet in tnshp. of Bainbridge, 2 m. from Hawes.

Mathew Roger—(2) —; (3) 1 house, M. 5 ac., P.G. 3; (4) 18^s; (5) 6^s; (6) 1^l 1^s.

Thomas Sedgwick—(2) —; (3) 1 house, 3 outhouses, M. 30 ac., P.G. 21; (4) 6^l 17^s 11^d; (5) 1^l 7^s 7^d; (6) 6^l 3^s 8^d.

Tho. Whaley, jun^r—(2) —; (3) 1 house, 2 outhouses, M. 24 ac., P.G. 28; (4) 6^l 4^s 10^d; (5) 1^l 11^s 2$\frac{1}{2}$^{d}; (6) 6^l 2^s 8^d.

Henry Metcalfe—(2) —; (3) 1 house, 2 outhouses, M. 24 ac., P.G. 15; (4) 3^l 8^s; (5) 17^s; (6) 4^l 13^s 4^d.

John Thorneton—(2) —; (3) 1 house, 2 outhouses, M. 25 ac., P.G. 14; (4) 4^l 5^s; (5) 17^s; (6) 4^l 13^s 10^d.

Thomas Whaley—(2) —; (3) 1 house, 3 outhouses, M. 30 ac., P.G. 25; (4) 3^l 2^s 5^d; (5) 1^l 11^s 2$\frac{1}{2}$^{d}; (6) 6^l 11^s 8^d.

Gawen Metcalfe—(2) —; (3) 1 house, 3 outhouses, M. 25 ac., P.G. 22; (4) 2^l 15^s; (5) 1^l 7^s 6^d; (6) 5^l 11^s 6^d.

Edmd. Metcalfe—(2) —; (3) 1 house, 3 outhouses, M. 40 ac., P.G. 31$\frac{1}{2}$; (4) 3^l 7^s; (5) 1^l 13^s 6^d; (6) 8^l 8^s.

John Harison—(2) —; (3) 1 house, 3 outhouses, M. 12 ac., P.G. 10; (4) 1^l 10^s 6^d; (5) 10^s 2^d; (6) 2^l 15^s.

Total—10 tenants; 10 houses, 22 outhouses; 225 ac. of Meadow; 177$\frac{1}{2}$ Pasture Gates; fynes paid in 20 years, £34 9^s 4^d; yearly rent, £10 11^s 4^d; yearly value £48 5^s 8^d.

The Cleere Improvem^t—£37 14^s 4^d.

---

9. Birckrigge.[1]

John Metcalfe—(2) —; (3) 1 house, M. 26 ac., P.G. 22; (4) 1^l 11^s 3^d; (5) 15^s 7$\frac{1}{2}$^{d}; (6) 5^l 14^s.

Richard Sedgwick—(2) —; (3) 1 house, M. 22 ac., P.G. 15$\frac{1}{2}$; (4) 2^l 16^s 3^d; (5) 9^s 4$\frac{1}{2}$^{d}; (6) 3^l 10^s.

Total—2 Tenants; 2 houses, 48 ac. of Meadow, 37$\frac{1}{2}$ Pasture Gates; fynes paid in 20 years £4 7^s 6^d; yearly rent, 1^l 5^s; yearly value 9^l 4^s.

The cleere Improvem^t—£7 19^s 0^d.

---

10. Mosdale.[2]　　　　　[p. 23

James Aspinall—(2) —; (3) 1 house, 2 outhouses, M. 50 ac., P.G. 30; (4) 8^l; (5) 1^l 6^s 8^d; (6) 8^l 15^s.

Richard Metcalfe—(2) —; (3) 1 house, 3 outhouses, M. 26 ac., P.G. 13$\frac{1}{2}$; (4) 1^l 19^s; (5) 13^s; (6) 4^l 17^s.

Alex^r Metcalfe—(2) —; (3) 1 house, 1 outhouse, M. 17 ac., P.G. 13$\frac{1}{2}$; (4) 1^l 17^s 6^d; (5) 12^s 6^d; (6) 3^l 13^s 6^d.

[1] Birk Rigg in tnshp. of High Abbotside, 2$\frac{1}{2}$ m. from Hawes.
[2] Mossdale in tnshp. of Hawes.

Chrofer. Whaley—(2) —; (3) 1 house, 4 outhouses, M. 24 ac.,
P.G. 22; (4) 4^l 11^s 4^d; (5) 1^l 2^s 10^d; (6) 5^l 9^s.

Total—4 Tenants; 4 houses, 10 outhouses, 117 ac. of meadow,
79 Pasture gates; fynes paid in 20 years, £16 7^s 10^d;
yearly rent, £3 15^s 0^d; yearly value £22 14^s 6^d.

The cleere Improvem^t—£18 19^s 6^d.

---

11. Snailsholme.[1]

James Dinsdale—(2) —; (3) 1 house, 5 outhouses, M. 24 ac.,
P.G. 20; (4) 2^l 5^s; (5) 15^s; (6) 4^l 15^s.

Francis Allen, sen^r—(2) —; (3) 1 house, 8 outhouses, M. 28 ac.,
P.G. 26; (4) 2^l 6^s 6^d; (5) 19^s 6^d; (6) 6^l 8^s 8^d.

Francis Allen, jun^r—(2) —; (3) 1 house, 4 outhouses, M. 20 ac.,
P.G. 12½; (4) 2^l 11^s 4^d; (5) 12^s 10^d; (6) 4^l.

Leonard Allen—(2) —; (3) 1 house, 1 outhouse, M. 16 ac., P.G. 8;
(4) 19^s 2^d; (5) 7^s 1^d; (6) 3^l.

Thomas Sym—(2) —; (3) 1 house, 1 outhouse, M. 8 ac., P.G. 3;
(4) 10^s; (5) 5^s; (6) 1^l 8^s 6^d.

James Bellassis, gen.—(2) —; (3) 1 house, 5 outhouses, M. 40 ac.,
P.G. 22; (4) 2^l 18^s 1½^d; (5) 19^s 4½^d; (6) 6^l 19^s 8^d.

Edmund Allen—(2) —; (3) M. 8 ac., P.G. 5; (4) 8^s; (5) 4^s;
(6) 1^l 7^s 6^d.

Philip Allen—(2) —; (3) 1 house, 3 outhouses, M. 14 ac., P.G. 16;
(4) 2^l 11^s 4^d; (5) 12^s 10^d; (6) 3^l 4^s.

Robert Wadeson—(2) —; (3) 1 house, 3 outhouses, M. 110 ac.,
P.G. 84; (4) 9^l 13^s 1½^d; (5) 3^l 4^s 4½^d; (6) 20^l 1^s.

Total—9 tenants; 8 houses, 30 outhouses, 268 acres of
Meadow, 196½ Pasture gates; fynes paid in 20 years,
£23 17^s 7^d; yearly rent £8; yearly value, £51 4^s 4^d.

Improvement—£43 4^s 4^d.

---

12. Butterside.[2]

[3]Jeffry Scarre—(2) —; (3) 1 house, 1 outhouse, M. 14 ac., P.G. 5;
(4) 1^l 14^s 3½^d; (5) 17^s 1¾^d; (6) 2^l 10^s.

Nynian Stockdale—(2) —; (3) 1 house, 3 outhouses, M. 20 ac.,
P.G. 5; (4) 3^l 5^s 3^d; (5) 16^s 5^d; (6) 3^l 5^s.

Jenkyn Stockdale—(2) —; (3) 1 house, 2 outhouses, M. 14 ac.,
P.G. 4; (4) 1^l 7^s 10^d; (5) 13^s 11^d; (6) 2^l 8^s 6^d.

Nynian Stockdale, sen^r—(2) —; (3) 1 house, 3 outhouses, M. 16 ac.,
P.G. 5; (4) 1^l 12^s 10^d; (5) 16^s 5^d; (6) 2^l 15^s.

---

[1] Snaizeholme, hamlet in tnshp. of Hawes.
[2] Burtersett, hamlet in tnshp. of Hawes.
[3] " Butterside " in the margin opposite this entry.

Mathew Scarre—(2) —; (3) 1 house, 2 outhouses, M. 16 ac., P.G. 8; (4) 3^l 8^s 7^d; (5) 17^s $1\frac{3}{4}^d$; (6) 3^l 2^s 8^d.

James Scarre—(2) —; (3) 1 house, 2 outhouses, M. 4 ac., P.G. 1; (4) 9^s 6^d; (5) 4^s 9^d; (6) 14^s 9^d.

John Buckle—(2) —; (3) 1 house, 1 outhouse, M. 16 ac., P.G. 3; (4) 1^l 8^s 9^d; (5) 14^s $4\frac{1}{2}^d$; (6) 2^l 13^s.

Jenkyn Scarre—(2) —; (3) 1 house, 2 outhouses, M. 30 ac., P.G. $5\frac{1}{2}$; (4) 3^l 4^s 10^d; (5) 16^s $2\frac{1}{2}^d$; (6) 4^l 10^s.

John Scarre—(2) —; (3) 1 house, 1 outhouse, M. 20 ac., P.G. $4\frac{1}{2}$; (4) 3^l 1^s 2^d; (5) 15^s $3\frac{1}{2}^d$; (6) 3^l 1^s.

Thomas Colton—(2) —; (3) 1 house, 2 outhouses, M. 20 ac., P.G. 5; (4) 1^l 12^s 6^d; (5) 16^s 3^d; (6) 3^l 5^s.

Roger Taylor—(2) —; (3) 1 house, 1 outhouse, M. 16 ac., P.G. 4; (4) 2^l 13^s 10^d; (5) 13^s $5\frac{1}{2}^d$; (6) 2^l 12^s.

Thomas Taylor—(2) —; (3) 1 house, 2 outhouses, M. 16 ac., P.G. 4; (4) 2^l 13^s 10^d; (5) 13^s $5\frac{1}{2}^d$; (6) 2^l 12^s.

Jeffry Coulton—(2) —; (3) 1 house, 2 outhouses, M. 14 ac., P.G. 6; (4) 3^l 3^s 10^d; (5) 15^s $11\frac{1}{2}^d$; (6) 2^l 12^s.

Richard Coulton—(2) —; (3) 1 house, 1 outhouse, M. 16 ac., P.G. 5; (4) 3^l 3^s 10^d; (5) 15^s $11\frac{1}{2}^d$; (6) 2^l 15^s.

Alex. Stockdale—(2) —; (3) 1 house, 2 outhouses, M. 20 ac., P.G. 4; (4) 2^l 11^s; (5) 12^s 9^d; (6) 3^l 2^s 6^d.

Nynian Stockdale—(2) —; (3) 1 house, 2 outhouses, M. 12 ac., P.G. 2; (4) 16^s 9^d; (5) 8^s $4\frac{1}{2}^d$; (6) 1^l 17^s 4^d.

Willm. Allen—(2) —; (3) 1 house, M. 8 ac., P.G. 2; (4) 1^l 8^s 3^d; (5) 6^s $4\frac{1}{2}^d$; (6) 1^l 7^s 4^d.

Tho. Robinson—(2) —; (3) 1 house, 4 outhouses, M. 8 ac., P.G. $5\frac{1}{2}$; (4) 2^l 8^s 9^d; (5) 16^s 3^d; (6) 3^l 1^s.

Henry Robinson—(2) —; (3) M. 12 ac., P.G. 3; (4) 1^l 10^s; (5) 10^s; (6) 1^l 16^s.

George Faucett—(2) —; (3) 1 house, 2 outhouses, M. 20 ac., P.G. 5; (4) 2^l 18^s 6^d; (5) 16^s 3^d; (6) 3^l 6^s 8^d.

James Coulton—(2) —; (3) 1 house, M. 20 ac., P.G. 5; (4) 3^l 5^s; (5) 16^s 3^d; (6) 3^l 5^s.

Chrofer. Frankland—(2) —; (3) 1 house, 2 outhouses, M. 12 ac., P.G. 3; (4) 1^l; (5) 10^s; (6) 1^l 18^s 6^d.

---

13. Bainbrigg Inge.

[1]Francis Metcalfe—(2) —; (3) M. 3 ac., P.G. 1; (4) 4^s 6^d; (5) 1^s $1\frac{1}{4}^d$; (6) 10^s 6^d.

Alex[r] Metcalfe—(2) —; (3) M. 6 ac., P.G. $2\frac{1}{4}$; (4) 15^s 8^d; (5) 3^s 11^d; (6) 19^s 6^d.

[1] " Bainbrig Ings " in the margin opposite this entry.

James Metcalfe—(2) —; (3) M. 1 ac. 2 r., P.G. 1; (4) 1ˢ 10ᵈ; (5) 11ᵈ; (6) 6ˢ 9ᵈ.

Richard Metcalfe—(2) —; (3) M. 3 ac., P.G. 1; (4) 4ˢ; (5) 2ˢ; (6) 11ˢ 6ᵈ.

John Metcalfe, junʳ—(2) —; (3) M. 1 ac. 2 r., P.G. 1; (4) 2ˢ 2ᵈ; (5) 1ˢ 1ᵈ; (6) 6ˢ 9ᵈ.

Chrofer. Metcalfe—(2) —; (3) M. 1 ac., P.G. ½; (4) 1ˢ 11ᵈ; (5) 11½ᵈ; (6) 5ˢ 6ᵈ.

Total for Butterside and Bainbrigg Inge.

28 Tenants; 21 houses, 37 outhouses, 370 acres of meadow, 101¼ pasture gates; fynes paid in 20 years £50 19ˢ 7½ᵈ; yearly rent £15 13ˢ 0ᵈ; yearly value £61 10ˢ 9ᵈ.

The cleere Improvemᵗ £45 17ˢ 9ᵈ.

[p. 24

14. Worton Baronry.[1]   15. Cubeck.[2]   16. Kitlaid.[3]   17. Burrisgaris.

Anthony Besson, gen.—(2) —; (3) 1 house, 5 outhouses, M. 80 ac., P.G. 158; (4) 16ˡ; (5) 8ˡ; (6) 27ˡ 16ˢ.

Owen Coulton—(2) 8 yrs.; (3) 1 house, 3 outhouses, M. 16 ac., P.G. 12; (4) 1ˡ 10ˢ; (5) 15ˢ; (6) 3ˡ 8ˢ 6ᵈ.

Antho. Nicolson—(2) —; (3) 1 house, 2 outhouses, M. 24 ac., P.G. 18½; (4) 5ˡ 12ˢ 6ᵈ; (5) 1ˡ 8ˢ 1½ᵈ; (6) 5ˡ 3ˢ 8ᵈ.

Willm. Metcalfe—(2) —; (3) 1 house, 2 outhouses, M. 16 ac., P.G. 5; (4) 2ˡ 5ˢ; (5) 15ˢ; (6) 2ˡ 15ˢ.

Edmd. Nicolson—(2) —; (3) 1 house, 2 outhouses, M. 12 ac., P.G. 7; (4) 2ˡ 6ˢ 10ᵈ; (5) 11ˢ 8½ᵈ; (6) 2ˡ 9ˢ.

Thomas Scarre—(2) —; (3) 1 house, M. 15 ac., P.G. 8½; (4) 1ˡ 9ˢ 7ᵈ; (5) 14ˢ 9½ᵈ; (6) 3ˡ 1ˢ.

John Aigland—(2) —; (3) 1 house, 2 outhouses, M. 14 ac., P.G. 8½; (4) 3ˡ 15ˢ; (5) 15ˢ; (6) 2ˡ 17ˢ.

Margaret Blaides—(2) —; (3) M. 3 ac., P.G. 2; (4) 6ˢ 8ᵈ; (5) 3ˢ 4ᵈ; (6) 11ˢ 6ᵈ.

James Connell—(2) —; (3) 1 house, 1 outhouse, M. 10 ac., P.G. 10 (4) 2ˡ 5ˢ; (5) 15ˢ; (6) 2ˡ 10ˢ.

Idem—(2) —; (3) 1 house, 2 outhouses, M. 10 ac., P.G. 6; (4) 1ˡ 10ˢ; (5) 10ˢ; (6) 2ˡ 1ˢ.

Edmund Tomson—(2) —; (3) 1 house, 1 outhouse, M. 14 ac., P.G. 7; (4) 2ˡ 13ˢ 4ᵈ; (5) 13ˢ 4ᵈ; (6) 2ˡ 11ˢ.

[1] Hamlet in tnshp. of Bainbridge, 5 m. from Hawes, often, with probably the surrounding district, referred to from an early date as the barony of Worton, but the reason is unknown (*V.C.H., Yks., N.R.*, i, 210).

[2] Near Worton.

[3] Kitlade in Askrigg. A dispute in 1616 about the lease of a farm in Kitlade in Askrigg is mentioned in *Metcalfe Records* (p. 127).

Thomas Coulton—(2) —; (3) 1 house, M. 5 ac., P.G. 3; (4) 14ˢ 6ᵈ; (5) 4ˢ 10ᵈ; (6) 16ˢ.

Chrofer. Metcalfe—(2) —; (3) 1 house, 1 outhouse, M. 14 ac., P.G. 7½; (4) 1ˡ 19ˢ 4½ᵈ; (5) 13ˢ 1½ᵈ; (6) 2ˡ 14ˢ.

   Idem—(2) —; (3) 1 outhouse, M. 9 ac., P.G. 5¾; (4) 1ˡ 8ˢ 9ᵈ; (5) 9ˢ 7ᵈ; (6) 1ˡ 17ˢ 10ᵈ.

Robt. Wadeson—(2) —; (3) 1 house, 1 outhouse, M. 13 ac., P.G. 6; (4) 1ˡ 15ˢ 1½ᵈ; (5) 12ˢ 8½ᵈ; (6) 2ˡ 9ˢ 3ᵈ.

James Skarre—(2) —; (3) 1 house, 2 outhouses, M. 9 ac., P.G. 6; (4) 1ˡ; (5) 10ˢ; (6) 1ˡ 18ˢ 4ᵈ.

John Skarre—(2) —; (3) 1 house, 3 outhouses, M. 25 ac., P.G. 9; (4) 1ˡ 16ˢ 8ᵈ; (5) 18ˢ 4ᵈ; (6) 4ˡ 2ˢ.

John Stockdale—(2) —; (3) 1 house, 1 outhouse, M. 1 ac. 2 r., P.G. 1¾; (4) 10ˢ; (5) 3ˢ 4ᵈ; (6) 10ˢ 6ᵈ.

Tho. Midleton—(2) —; (3) 1 house, M. 34 ac., P.G. 35; (4) 10ˡ 3ˢ 4ᵈ; (5) 2ˡ 10ˢ 10ᵈ; (6) 7ˡ 4ˢ 2ᵈ.

James Metcalfe—(2) —; (3) 1 house, 1 outhouse, M. 24 ac., P.G. 20; (4) 2ˡ 10ˢ 10ᵈ; (5) 1ˡ 5ˢ 5ᵈ; (6) 4ˡ 15ˢ.

James Tomson—(2) —; (3) 1 house, 1 outhouse, M. 30 ac., P.G. 20; (4) 6ˡ 1ˢ 8ᵈ; (5) 1ˡ 5ˢ 5ᵈ; (6) 5ˡ 10ˢ.

Symon Rudd—(2) —; (3) 1 house, M. 30 ac., P.G. 41½; (4) 10ˡ; (5) 2ˡ 10ˢ; (6) 10ˡ 19ˢ 4ᵈ.

   Idem—(2) —; (3) M. 5 ac., P.G. 5; (4) 2ˡ; (5) 6ˢ 8ᵈ; (6) 1ˡ 7ˢ 6ᵈ.

John Metcalfe—(2) —; (3) 1 house, M. 26 ac., P.G. 17; (4) 2ˡ 7ˢ; (5) 1ˡ 3ˢ 6ᵈ; (6) 5ˡ 9ˢ.

Elizab: Metcalfe—(2) —; (3) 1 house, M. 16 ac., P.G. 10; (4) 4ˡ; (5) 1ˡ; (6) 3ˡ 15ˢ.

Alexʳ Ingram—(2) —; (3) 1 outhouse, M. 10 ac., P.G. 8; (4) 1ˡ 6ˢ 8ᵈ; (5) 13ˢ 4ᵈ; (6) 2ˡ 6ˢ.

Edmd. Metcalfe—(2) —; (3) M. 5 ac., P.G. 4; (4) 1ˡ; (5) 6ˢ 8ᵈ; (6) 1ˡ 0ˢ 6ᵈ.

Ingram Nicolson—(2) —; (3) 1 house, M. 24 ac., P.G. 16; (4) 4ˡ 13ˢ 4ᵈ; (5) 1ˡ 3ˢ 4ᵈ; (6) 4ˡ 15ˢ 4ᵈ.

Edmd. Skarre—(2) —; (3) 1 house, 2 outhouses, M. 13 ac., P.G. 8½; (4) 3ˡ 13ˢ 11½ᵈ; (5) 14ˢ 9½ᵈ; (6) 2ˡ 14ˢ.

   Idem—(2) —; (3) 1 house, M. 12 ac., P.G. 7½; (4) 2ˡ 12ˢ 6ᵈ; (5) 13ˢ 1½ᵈ; (6) 2ˡ 11ˢ.

   Total: 30 Tenants; 25 houses, 34 outhouses, 520 acres 2 roods of meadow, 474 pasture gates; fynes paid in 20 years, £99 9ˢ 7½ᵈ; yearly rent, £32 5ˢ 3½ᵈ; yearly value, £121 18ˢ 5ᵈ.

     The cleere Improvemᵗ £89 13ˢ 1½ᵈ.

[p. 25

18. Burghill.¹   19. Cravenholme.²   20. Holmehouse.³
21. Bleasings.   22. Cubeckings.

⁴John Metcalfe—(2) —; (3) 1 house, 4 outhouses, M. 20 ac.
P.G. 12; (4) 4¹; (5) 1¹; (6) 4¹ 12ˢ 8ᵈ.

Edmd. Metcalfe—(2) —; (3) 1 house, 2 outhouses, M. 18 ac.,
P.G. 12; (4) 4¹; (5) 1¹; (6) 3¹ 15ˢ.

⁵Thomas Metcalfe—(2) —; (3) 1 house, 5 outhouses, M. 30 ac.,
P.G. 26; (4) 4¹ 6ˢ 8ᵈ; (5) 2¹ 3ˢ 4ᵈ; (6) 6¹ 17ˢ.

⁶Alexʳ Metcalfe—(2) —; (3) 1 house, 2 outhouses, M. 53 ac.,
P.G. 38; (4) 12¹ 13ˢ 4ᵈ; (5) 3¹ 3ˢ 4ᵈ; (6) 10¹ 16ˢ 8ᵈ.

John Metcalfe—(2) —; (3) 1 house, 1 outhouse, M. 36 ac., P.G.
22; (4) 2¹ 17ˢ; (5) 1¹ 8ˢ 6ᵈ; (6) 6¹ 9ˢ 8ᵈ.

Idem—(2) —; (3) 1 house, 1 outhouse, M. 12 ac., P.G. 12½;
(4) 1¹ 17ˢ 6ᵈ; (5) 12ˢ 6ᵈ; (6) 3¹.

Chrofer. Dawson—(2) —; (3) 1 house, 1 outhouse, M. 12 ac.,
P.G. 12½; (4) 1¹ 5ˢ; (5) 12ˢ 6ᵈ; (6) 3¹.

John Metcalfe—(2) —; (3) 1 house, 1 outhouse, M. 17 ac., P.G. 11;
(4) 1¹ 8ˢ 4ᵈ; (5) 14ˢ 2ᵈ; (6) 3¹.

Tho. Metcalfe—(2) —; (3) 1 house, 2 outhouses, M. 34 ac., P.G. 22;
(4) 2¹ 17ˢ; (5) 1¹ 8ˢ 6ᵈ; (6) 8¹ 1ˢ.

Jeffry Metcalfe—(2) —; (3) M. 2 ac., P.G. 17; (4) 10ˢ; (5) 5ˢ;
(6) 1ˢ 6ᵈ.

Augustine Metcalfe—(2) —; (3) 1 house, 1 outhouse, M. 20 ac.,
P.G. 13; (4) 1¹ 6ˢ 8ᵈ; (5) 13ˢ 4ᵈ; (6) 4¹ 1ˢ.

John Metcalfe, senʳ—(2) —; (3) 1 house, M. 22 ac., P.G. 12½;
(4) 1¹ 7ˢ 6ᵈ; (5) 13ˢ 9ᵈ; (6) 4¹ 4ˢ.

Chrofer. Metcalfe—(2) —; (3) 1 house, 1 outhouse, M. 20 ac.,
P.G. 11; (4) 1¹ 8ˢ 4ᵈ; (5) 14ˢ 2ᵈ; (6) 4¹ 8ˢ.

John Metcalfe, junʳ—(2) —; (3) 1 house, 1 outhouse, M. 20 ac.,
P.G. 13½; (4) 1¹ 8ˢ 4ᵈ; (5) 14ˢ 2ᵈ; (6) 5¹ 2ˢ 8ᵈ.

Willm. Ingram—(2) —; (3) 1 house, 1 outhouse, M. 20 ac., P.G. 13;
(4) 3¹ 8ˢ 9ᵈ; (5) 13ˢ 9ᵈ; (6) 4¹ 15ˢ 8ᵈ.

Anthony Smith—(2) —; (3) 1 house, 1 outhouse, M. 12 ac.,
P.G. 3; (4) 12ˢ; (5) 4ˢ; (6) 2¹ 2ˢ 4ᵈ.

Alexʳ Metcalfe—(2) —; (3) M. 10 ac., P.G. 6½; (4) 2¹ 13ˢ 4ᵈ;
(5) 13ˢ 4ᵈ; (6) 2¹ 3ˢ.

¹ Brough hill, nr. Bainbridge.
² In tnshp. of Bainbridge.
³ In tnshp. of Bainbridge. Langdale (*Top. Dict. of Yorkshire*, 1822) appears
to consider that Cravenholme and Holmehouse as one and the same place.
Probably they were close together.
⁴ " Burghill " in the margin.
⁵ " Cravenholme " in the margin as if this entry referred to that place.
⁶ " Holmehouse " in the margin as if the entry referred to that place.

Percival Ingram—(2) —; (3) 1 outhouse, M. 6 ac., P.G. 6$\frac{1}{2}$; (4) 1^l 0^s 4^d; (5) 10^s 2^d; (6) 1^l 14^s 6^d.

Idem—(2) —; (3) M. 5 ac., P.G. 3; (4) 11^s 4^d; (5) 5^s 8^d; (6) 1^l 1^s 6^d.

Roger Scott—(2) —; (3) M. 2 ac. 2 r., P.G. 1$\frac{1}{2}$; (4) 6^s; (5) 3^s; (6) 10^s 9^d.

Willm. Stockdale—(2) —; (3) M. 5 ac., P.G. 3; (4) 11^s 9^d; (5) 5^s 10$\frac{1}{2}$^{d}; (6) 1^l 1^s 6^d.

Alexr. Ingram—(2) —; (3) M. 4 ac., P.G. 2$\frac{1}{2}$; (4) 15^s; (5) 5^s; (6) 17^s 6^d.

Tho. Stirkhead—(2) —; (3) M. 6 ac., P.G. 5; (4) 2^l; (5) 10^s; (6) 1^l 10^s.

Agnes Metcalfe—(2) —; (3) M. 6 ac., P.G. 4; (4) 16^s; (5) 8^s; (6) 1^l 7^s.

James Metcalfe—(2) —; (3) M. 4 ac., P.G. 1; (4) 10^s; (5) 2^s 6^d; (6) 13^s.

John Metcalfe—(2) —; (3) 1 outhouse, M. 8 ac., P.G. 11$\frac{1}{2}$; (4) 3^l 16^s; (5) 19^s; (6) 3^l 4^s 6^d.

James Mason—(2) —; (3) M. 4 ac., P.G. 2; (4) 15^s 2^d; (5) 3^s 9$\frac{1}{2}$^{d}; (6) 16^s.

Edmd. Metcalfe—(2) —; (3) 1 outhouse, M. 10 ac., P.G. 2$\frac{1}{2}$; (4) 1^l 15^s 8$\frac{3}{4}$^{d}; (5) 5^s 1$\frac{1}{4}$^{d}; (6) 1^l 12^s 6^d.

Idem—(2) —; (3) M. 4 ac., P.G. 2; (4) 11^s 4$\frac{1}{2}$^{d}; (5) 3^s 9$\frac{1}{2}$^{d}; (6) 16^s.

Idem—(2) —; (3) M. 4 ac., P.G. 2; (4) 5^s 7$\frac{1}{2}$^{d}; (5) 1^s 10$\frac{1}{2}$^{d}; (6) 16^s.

Roger Nicolson—(2) —; (3) M. 6 ac., P.G. 2$\frac{1}{2}$; (4) 1^l 6^s 8^d; (5) 6^s 8^d; (6) 1^l 2^s 6^d.

Willm. Metcalfe—(2) —; (3) M. 3 ac., P.G. 1$\frac{3}{4}$; (4) 7^s 7^d; (5) 3^s 9$\frac{1}{2}$^{d}; (6) 12^s 9^d.

Richard Metcalfe—(2) —; (3) M. 3 ac., P.G. 2$\frac{1}{2}$; (4) 10^s; (5) 5^s; (6) 15^s.

John Jaques—(2) —; (3) M. 2 ac., P.G. 1$\frac{1}{4}$; (4) 7^s 6^d; (5) 2^s 6^d; (6) 8^s 9^d.

John Metcalfe—(2) —; (3) M. 10 ac., P.G. 3$\frac{1}{2}$; (4) 1^l 8^s; (5) 7^s; (6) 1^l 15^s 6^d.

Total—35 Tenants; 15 houses, 27 outhouses, 460 acres 2 roods of meadow, 315$\frac{1}{2}$ pasture gates; fynes paid in 20 years £85 13^s 9$\frac{3}{4}$^{d}; yearly rent, £22 3^s 0$\frac{3}{4}$^{d}; yearly value, £99 12^s 11^d.

The Cleere Improvem^t—£77 9^s 10$\frac{1}{4}$^{d}.

Demeasnes.   [p. 26

The Tennantes of Wensladale on ye Northside of Yore: |

These tenants hold by a lease from Q. Elizabethe	£	s.	d.
dated the 16th of March the xxxvth of her raigne	10	00	00

for 40 yeares the Agistment of that part of the
forest of Wensladale wch. lyeth on the North
side of Yore, upon the rent of

It is yearly worth	40	00	00

The Lord Duke[1]:
> chalengeth the same by vertue of his graunt made
> by King James of the Mannor of Wensladale. The
> land passed in that graunt was sometyme lett in
> Leasse for a yearly rent to the Abbey of Jervax
> as parcell of the honor of Richmond, and (for
> ought appeareth to us to the contrary) ever was,
> ℘ now is part of the same honor.

John Metcalfe, gen.:

holdeth the Agistment of the said forest on
the Southside of Yore wthout leasse at the
rent of · · · · · · · · · · · · · · · 03^l 06^s 08^d

It is yearly worth · · · · · 10 . 00 . 00

John Dynsdale:

holdeth a Toll called Gatelaw Toll[2] at the
rent of · · · · · · · · · · · · · · 02^l 00^s 00^d

It is yearly worth · · · · · 03^l 00^s 00^d

The Tenants of Bainbrig, Counterside, Burterside
and Gayle:

hold a sheep rake[3] upon Canine called
Caninegate and pay yearly for the same · · 00^l 06^s 08^d

It is yearly worth · · · · · 01^l 00^s 00^d

The generall
Abstract of
Wensladale
forest being
ye fifth
division of
Midleham.

Demeasnes.

The whole rent of these demeasnes is	15^l	13^s	4^d
The yearly value	54^l	00^s	00^d
The Improvemt is	38^l	06^s	8^d

Tenement
Lands.

The Number of Tennants	269		
Quantity of Ground	3977 ac.		
Pasture gates	3053¼		
Fynes paid in 20 yeares	£587	06^s	06^d
The yearly rent	£202	10^s	04^d
The yearly value	£983	07^s	09^d
The Cleere yearly Improvement	£780	17^s	05^d

---

[1] Ludovick Stuart, Duke of Lennox, who had a grant of the manor of Wensleydale from James I in 1603.

[2] Gatelaw—toll, or right of way, toll paid for this (*N.E.D.*; see Gate, 10).

[3] A course, or path, especially of cattle in pasturing, hence pasture ground, right of pasture (*N.E.D.*).

6—1 The Mannor of Cracall[1] wth. 2 Rand,[2] 3 Kettlewell, 4 Could Conystone 5 and Scale Parke.

1. Cracall.

John Day—(2) 37 years; (3) 1 house, 1 outhouse, M. & A. 12 ac., P.G. 5½; (4) 1ˡ 12ˢ 8ᵈ; (5) 16ˢ 4ᵈ; (6) 3ˡ 13ˢ 8ᵈ.

George Cooke—(2) 37 years; (3) 1 house, 2 outhouses, M. & A. 18 ac., P.G. 9; (4) 2ˡ 9ˢ 6ᵈ; (5) 1ˡ 4ˢ 9ᵈ; (6) 5ˡ 11ˢ.

Willm. Jackson—(2) 37 years; (3) 1 house, 1 outhouse, M. & A. 1 ac., P.G. 3; (4) 12ˢ; (5) 4ˢ; (6) 19ˢ.

Luke Jackson—(2) —; (3) 1 house, 1 outhouse, M. & A. 3 ac., P.G. 2; (4) 6ˢ 6ᵈ; (5) 3ˢ 3ᵈ; (6) 16ˢ 9ᵈ.

George Mason—(2) —; (3) 1 house, 1 outhouse, M. & A. 2 r., P.G. 2; (4) 7ˢ; (5) 3ˢ 6ᵈ; (6) 13ˢ 10ᵈ.

Willm. Jackson—(2) —; (3) 1 house, 1 outhouse, M. & A. 5 ac. 3 r., P.G. 4½; (4) 1ˡ; (5) 10ˢ; (6) 2ˡ 3ˢ 9ᵈ.

George Storer—(2) —; (3) 1 house, 1 outhouse, M. & A., 1 ac. 1 r., P.G. 2; (4) 12ˢ; (5) 4ˢ; (6) 16ˢ 4ᵈ.

Willm. Jackson—(2) —; (3) M. & A. 20 ac., P.G. 8; (4) 2ˡ 6ˢ 6ᵈ; (5) 1ˡ 3ˢ 3ᵈ; (6) 5ˡ 5ˢ 4ᵈ.

George Storer—(2) —; (3) 1 house, 1 outhouse, M. & A. 20 ac., P.G. 12; (4) 3ˡ 12ˢ; (5) 1ˡ 16ˢ; (6) 6ˡ 11ˢ 4ᵈ.

Willm. Storer—(2) —; (3) 1 house, 1 outhouse, M. & A. 21 ac., P.G. 10; (4) 4ˡ 16ˢ; (5) 1ˡ 4ˢ; (6) 6ˡ 5ˢ.

George Storer—(2) —; (3) 1 house, M. & A. 5 ac., P.G. 2; (4) 1ˡ; (5) 10ˢ; (6) 1ˡ 17ˢ.

Willm. Ward—(2) —; (3) 1 house, 1 outhouse, M. & A. 13 ac., P.G. 8; (4) 2ˡ 6ˢ 3ᵈ; (5) 1ˡ 3ˢ 1½ᵈ; (6) 4ˡ 14ˢ 8ᵈ.

Richard Ward—(2) —; (3) 1 house, 1 outhouse, M. & A. 2 r., P.G. 1½; (4) 5ˢ; (5) 2ˢ 6ᵈ; (6) 10ˢ 2ᵈ.

Richard Mason—(2) —; (3) 1 house, 1 outhouse, M. & A., 24 ac., P.G. 11½; (4) 3ˡ 5ˢ; (5) 1ˡ 12ˢ 6ᵈ; (6) 7ˡ 2ˢ 8ᵈ.

Willm. Jackson, jun.—(2) —; (3) 1 house, M. & A. 30 ac., P.G. 11½; (4) 2ˡ 12ˢ 8ᵈ; (5) 1ˡ 6ˢ 4ᵈ; (6) 6ˡ 19ˢ 4ᵈ.

　　Idem—(2) —; (3) 1 house, 1 outhouse, M. & A. 15 ac., P.G. 5½; (4) 4ˡ; (5) 2ˡ; (6) 4ˡ 5ˢ 9ᵈ.

Marmaduke Kettlwell—(2) —; (3) M. & A. 1 ac.; (4) 2ˢ; (5) 1ˢ; (6) 5ˢ.

Dorothy Jackson—(2) —; (3) 1 house, 1 outhouse, M. & A. 34 ac., P.G. 16; (4) 10ˡ 3ˢ 6ᵈ; (5) 2ˡ 10ˢ 10½ᵈ; (6) 10ˡ 4ˢ.

Willm. Clapham—(2) —; (3) 1 house, 1 outhouse, M. & A. 34 ac., P.G. 12½; (4) 3ˡ 18ˢ 4ᵈ; (5) 1ˡ 19ˢ 2ᵈ; (6) 9ˡ 10ˢ.

---

[1] Great Crakehall, par. Bedale.

[2] Rand grange, tnshp. of Crakehall, par. Bedale.

George Storer—(2) —; (3) 1 house, 1 outhouse, M. & A. $\frac{1}{2}$ ac., P.G. $2\frac{1}{2}$; (4) 15ˢ; (5) 5ˢ; (6) 18ˢ 4ᵈ.

George Hill—(2) —: (3) 1 house, 1 outhouse, M. & A. 2 r., P.G. 2; (4) 10ˢ; (5) 2ˢ 6ᵈ; (6) 12ˢ 2ᵈ.

Willm. Clarke—(2) —; (3) 1 house, 1 outhouse, M. & A. 25 ac., P.G. $11\frac{1}{2}$; (4) 7ˡ 5ˢ; (5) 1ˡ 16ˢ 3ᵈ; (6) 7ˡ 4ˢ 4ᵈ.

George Whitehorne—(2) —; (3) 1 house, M. & A. 7 ac., P.G. $4\frac{1}{2}$; (4) 2ˡ 3ˢ; (5) 10ˢ 9ᵈ; (6) 2ˡ 8ˢ.

Thomas Whitton—(2) —; (3) 1 house, 1 outhouse, M. & A. 7 ac., P.G. 6; (4) 1ˡ 8ˢ 4ᵈ; (5) 14ˢ 2ᵈ; (6) 3ˡ 14ˢ.

Richard Ellis—(2) —; (3) 1 house, M. & A. 1 r., P.G. 2; (4) 6ˢ 8ᵈ; (5) 3ˢ 4ᵈ; (6) 12ˢ.

Thomas Harison—(2) —; (3) 1 house, 1 outhouse, M. & A. 27 ac., P.G. $17\frac{1}{2}$; (4) 6ˡ 8ˢ 8ᵈ; (5) 1ˡ 12ˢ 2ᵈ; (6) 8ˡ 16ˢ 4ᵈ.

John Richardson—(2) —; (3) 1 house, M. & A. 2 ac., P.G. 2; (4) 10ˢ; (5) 5ˢ; (6) 1ˡ 1ˢ 4ᵈ.

Willm. Rowle—(2) —; (3) 1 house, 1 outhouse, M. & A. 1 ac., P.G. 2; (4) 6ˢ 8ᵈ; (5) 3ˢ 4ᵈ; (6) 13ˢ 4ᵈ

John Dodsworth—(2) 27 years; (3) a Corne mill; (4) 7ˡ 6ˢ 8ᵈ; (5) 3ˡ 13ˢ 4ᵈ; (6) 16ˡ.

Miles Metcalfe—(2) —; (3) 1 house, 2 outhouses, M. & A. 42 ac., P.G. 12; (4) 8ˡ 5ˢ 4ᵈ; (5) 4ˡ 2ˢ 8ᵈ; (6) 12ˡ 8ˢ.

Symon Metcalfe—(2) 33 years; (3) a bakehouse, M. & A. 20 ac. 2 r., P.G. 10; (4) 2ˡ 18ˢ 4ᵈ; (5) 1ˡ 9ˢ 2ᵈ; (6) 8ˡ 1ˢ 6ᵈ.

Total—31 Tenants; 27 houses, 23 outhouses, 392 acres and 1 rood of meadow and arable, $198\frac{1}{2}$ pasture gates; fynes paid in 20 years, £83 10ˢ 7ᵈ; yearly rent, £33 12ˢ 3ᵈ; yearly value £140 13ˢ 11ᵈ.

The Cleere Improvemᵗ—£107 1ˢ 8ᵈ.

There are 2 freeholders in Cracall wch. pay rent—[blank].

2. Rand.

The Lord Scroope[1] holdeth the Rand and payeth

yearly rent for it		£6	13ˢ 4ᵈ
Medow belonging to it	70 acres		
Arrable land	12 acres		
Pasture beast gates	97		
All these worth yearly		£32	19ˢ 4ᵈ
Fynes paid in 20 yeares		£13	06ˢ 8ᵈ
The Improvement		£26	06ˢ 0ᵈ

[1] Thomas, 10th Lord Scrope of Bolton, died 1609; mar. Philadelphia, dau. of Hen. Carey, 1st Lord Hunsdon (Clay, J. W., *Extinct and Dormant Peerages*, p. 201).

3. Kettlewell.[1] [p. 28

John Stapper—(2) 6 years; (3) 1 house, 3 outhouses, M. & A. 11 ac., P.G. 15; (4) 4^l 4^s; (5) 14^s; (6) 3^l 7^s.

Gregory Scot—(2) 6 years; (3) 1 house, 5 outhouses, M. & A. 19 ac., P.G. 16; (4) 2^l 1^s; (5) 14^s; (6) 4^l 8^s.

Idem—(2) 6 years; (3) 1 house, 1 outhouse, P.G. 1; (4) 3^s; (5) 1^s; (6) 4^s.

Idem—(2) 6 years; (3) 1 house; (4) 2^s 6^d; (5) 6^d; (6) 2^s.

Ralph Clarke—(2) —; (3) 1 house, 1 outhouse, M. & A. 9 ac., P.G. 4; (4) 10^s 6^d; (5) 3^s 6^d; (6) 1^l 14^s 6^d.

Humfry Faucet—(2) —; (3) 1 house, 4 outhouses, M. & A. 28 ac., P.G. 11; (4) 1^l; (5) 10^s; (6) 4^l 6^s 4^d.

Idem—(2) —; (3) 1 house, 2 outhouses, M. & A. 29 ac., P.G. $11\frac{1}{2}$; (4) 1^l; (5) 10^s; (6) 4^l 5^s 4^d.

Idem—(2) —; (3) 1 house, 1 outhouse, M. & A. 1 ac., P.G. 2; (4) 3^s; (5) 1^s 6^d; (6) 10^s.

Leonard Ibotson—(2) —; (3) 1 house, 1 outhouse, M. & A. 5 ac. 1 r., P.G. 5; (4) 12^s; (5) 3^s; (6) 1^l 2^s 4^d.

Laurence Topham—(2) —; (3) 1 house, 2 outhouses, M. & A. 20 ac., P.G. 9; (4) 1^l 4^s; (5) 8^s; (6) 2^l 18^s.

Robert Smithson—(2) —; (3) 1 house, 3 outhouses, M. & A. 38 ac., P.G. $22\frac{1}{2}$; (4) 2^l 2^s; (5) 1^l 1^s; (6) 7^l 16^s.

Idem—(2) —; (3) 1 outhouse; (4) 1^s; (5) 6^d; (6) 2^s 6^d.

Peter Snell—(2) —; (3) 1 house, 4 outhouses, M. & A. 16 ac., P.G. 16; (4) 1^l 6^s 10^d; (5) 13^s 5^d; (6) 3^l 17^s 9^d.

Steph. Ibotson, sen.—(2) —; (3) 1 house, 4 outhouses, M. & A. 14 ac. 2 r., P.G. $15\frac{1}{2}$; (4) 1^l 10^s; (5) 15^s; (6) 3^l 13^s 4^d.

Chrofer. Ibotson—(2) —; (3) 1 house, 3 outhouses, M. & A. 7 ac. 2 r., P.G. $5\frac{1}{2}$; (4) 1^l; (5) 5^s; (6) 1^l 13^s 4^d.

Roger Bowland—(2) —; (3) 1 house, 4 outhouses, M. & A. 12 ac. 2 r., P.G. $7\frac{1}{2}$; (4) 2^l 9^s; (5) 7^s; (6) 2^l 11^s 7^d.

Chrofer. Settell—(2) —; (3) 1 house, 2 outhouses, M. & A. 21 ac. 1 r., P.G. 15; (4) 2^l 16^s; (5) 14^s; (6) 4^l 13^s.

Rich. Riply *als.* Clark—(2) —; (3) M. & A. 3 ac. 2 r., P.G. 2; (4) 8^s 8^d; (5) 2^s 2^d; (6) 13^s 6^d.

Rich. Costentyde—(2) —; (3) M. & A. 7 ac., P.G. $3\frac{1}{2}$; (4) 10^s; (5) 3^s 4^d; (6) 1^l 5^s.

John Bowland—(2) —; (3) 1 house, 4 outhouses, M. & A. 23 ac. 2 r., P.G. 14; (4) 1^l 6^s; (5) 13^s; (6) 4^l 17^s 6^d.

James Coates—(2) —; (3) M. & A. 19 ac., P.G. $7\frac{1}{2}$; (4) 2^l 2^s; (5) 7^s; (6) 3^l 7^s.

Idem—(2) —; (3) 1 house, 2 outhouses, M. & A. 2 ac., P.G. 5; (4) 16^s 6^d; (5) 2^s 9^d; (6) 18^s.

---

[1] A market and parish town in the W.R., 14 m. from Hawes, 15 m. from Middleham.

Idem—(2) —; (3) 1 house, 2 outhouses, M. & A. 2 ac. 1 r., P.G. 5; (4) 16ˢ 6ᵈ; (5) 2ˢ 9ᵈ; (6) 18ˢ 4ᵈ.

Edmd. Smithson—(2) —; (3) 1 outhouse, M. & A. 8 ac., P.G. 4; (4) 10ˢ 10½ᵈ; (5) 3ˢ 7½ᵈ; (6) 1ˡ 14ˢ.

James Tenant—(2) —; (3) 1 house, M. & A. 53 ac., P.G. 22½; (4) 2ˡ 1ˢ 4ᵈ; (5) 1ˡ 0ˢ 8ᵈ; (6) 7ˡ 16ˢ.

Idem—A Corne mill; (4) 3ˡ 13ˢ 4ᵈ; (5) 1ˡ 16ˢ 8ᵈ; (6) 6ˡ 13ˢ 4ᵈ.

John Jackson—(2) —; (3) 1 house, 3 outhouses, M. & A. 1 ac., P.G. 5; (4) 8ˢ; (5) 2ˢ; (6) 15ˢ.

Robt. Staney—(2) —; (3) 1 house, 1 outhouse; (4) 1ˢ; (5) 6ᵈ; (6) 2ˢ 6ᵈ.

Stephen Ibotson—(2) —; (3) 1 house, 5 outhouses, M. & A. 18 ac., P.G. 5; (4) 1ˡ 8ˢ; (5) 7ˢ; (6) 2ˡ 15ˢ 6ᵈ.

Steven Johnson—(2) 6 years; (3) 1 house, 3 outhouses, M. & A. 14 ac., P.G. 7; (4) 14ˢ; (5) 7ˢ; (6) 2ˡ 10ˢ 6ᵈ.

Thomas Ripley—(2) 6 years; (3) 1 house, 2 outhouses, M. & A. 25 ac., P.G. 15; (4) 1ˡ 8ˢ; (5) 14ˢ; (6) 4ˡ 14ˢ.

Robt. Williamson—(2) 6 years; (3) 1 house, 3 outhouses, M. & A. 16 ac., P.G. 16; (4) 2ˡ 10ˢ; (5) 12ˢ 6ᵈ; (6) 3ˡ 14ˢ.

John Horseman—(2) 6 years; (3) 1 house, M. & A. 1 ac., P.G. 2; (4) 4ˢ; (5) 1ˢ 4ᵈ; (6) 8ˢ 6ᵈ.

Tho. Topham—(2) 6 years; (3) 1 house, 2 outhouses, M. & A. 8 ac., P.G. 7; (4) 13ˢ 4ᵈ; (5) 6ˢ 8ᵈ; (6) 1ˡ 16ˢ 4ᵈ.

Willm. Ripley—(2) —; (3) 1 house, 1 outhouse, M. & A. 6 ac., P.G. 7; (4) 1ˡ 9ˢ; (5) 7ˢ 3ᵈ; (6) 1ˡ 11ˢ 4ᵈ.

Robt. Constantine—(2) —; (3) 1 house, 5 outhouses, M. & A. 22 ac., P.G. 13; (4) 1ˡ 4ˢ; (5) 12ˢ; (6) 4ˡ 2ˢ.

Idem—(3) A Brewing farme; (4) 2ˢ; (5) 1ˢ; (6) 10ˢ.

Bernard Calvert—(2) —; (3) M. & A. 4 ac.; (4) 18ˢ; (5) 6ˢ; (6) 12ˢ.

Robt. Procter—(2) —; (3) 1 house, 1 outhouse, M. & A. 14 ac., P.G. 7; (4) 14ˢ; (5) 7ˢ; (6) 3ˡ 0ˢ 4ᵈ.

Humfry Tennant—(2) 17 years; (3) M. & A. 4 ac.; (4) 4ˢ 8ᵈ; (5) 2ˢ 4ᵈ; (6) 10ˢ.

Edward Ward—(2) —; (3) 1 house, M. & A. 1 ac., P.G. 5; (4) 9ˢ; (5) 3ˢ; (6) 15ˢ 6ᵈ.

Humfry Snell—(2) —; (3) 1 house, 4 outhouses, M. & A. 12 ac., P.G. 7; (4) 14ˢ; (5) 7ˢ; (6) 2ˡ 6ˢ.

Idem—(2) —; (3) ½ house, ½ outhouse, M. & A. 6 ac., P.G. 4; (4) 12ˢ; (5) 4ˢ; (6) 1ˡ 6ˢ 4ᵈ.

Wm. Fulshawe—(2) —; (3) 1 house; (4) 1ˢ; (5) 4ᵈ; (6) 2ˢ.

Edmd. Caytham—(2) —; (3) ½ house, ½ outhouse, M. & A. 3 ac., P.G. 4½; (4) 16ˢ; (5) 4ˢ; (6) 18ˢ 6ᵈ.

Thomas Hulley—(2) —; (3) 1 house, 2 outhouses, M. & A. 22 ac., P.G. 11; (4) 1ˡ 1ˢ; (5) 10ˢ. 6ᵈ; (6) 3ˡ 16ˢ 6ᵈ.

I

Alice Hogge—(2) —; (3) 1 house, 2 outhouses, M. & A. 17 ac., P.G. 11; (4) 2^l 10^s; (5) 10^s; (6) 3^l 3^s 6^d.

Chrofer. Snell—(2) --; (3) 1 house, 1 outhouse, M. & A. 1 ac., P.G. 5; (4) 5^s 6^d; (5) 2^s 9^d; (6) 14^s.

    Idem—(2) —; (3) 1 outhouse, M. & A. 6 ac., P.G. 3; (4) 7^s; (5) 3^s 6^d; (6) 1^l 2^s 6^d.

Chrofer. Ripley—(2) —; (3) 1 house; (4) 2^s; (5) 1^s; (6) 5^s.

Nicolas Hewett—·(2) —; (3) 1 house, 2 outhouses, M. & A. 17 ac., P.G. 13; (4) 1^l 14^s 6^d; (5) 11^s 6^d; (6) 3^l 11^s 6^d.

    Idem—(2) 6 years; (3) M. & A., 4 ac.; (4) 18^s; (5) 6^s; (6) 12^s 6^d.

Abraham Snell—(2) 6 years; (3) 1 house, 2 outhouses, M. & A. 7 ac., P.G. 3½; (4) 18^s 1½^d; (5) 3^s 7½^d; (6) 1^l 6^s.

    Total—53 tenants; 41 houses, 81 outhouses, 579 acres 1 rood of Meadow and Arrable, 370 pasture gates; fynes paid in 20 years, £56 16^s 2^d; yearly rent, £19 6^s 2^d; yearly value, £122 9^s 7^d.

    The Cleere Improvem^t £103 3^s 5^d.

There 10 freeholders heire wch. pay yearly 2^s 10^d ℮ a payre of gloves. ——————

4. Could Conistone.[1]   [p. 29

Willm. Holmes—(2) 31 years; (3) 1 house, 1 outhouse, M. & A. 40 ac. 1 r., P.G. 20; (4) 4^l 10^s 8^d; (5) 1^l 2^s 8^d; (6) 6^l 8^s 6^d.

Richard Greene—(2) 31 years; (3) 1 house, 1 outhouse, M. & A. 40 ac., P.G. 30; (4) 6^l 4^s 8^d; (5) 1^l 11^s 2^d; (6) 7^l 6^s 8^d.

Thomas Hardy—·(2) 31 years; (3) 1 house, 1 outhouse, M. & A. 12 ac., P.G. 8; (4) 16^s; (5) 8^s; (6) 2^l 3^s 4^d.

John Hardy—·(2) 31 years; (3) 1 house, 2 outhouses, M. & A. 12 ac., P.G. 8; (4) 16^s; (5) 8^s; (6) 2^l 4^s.

Stephen Hogge—(2) 31 years; (3) M. & A. 1 ac.; (4) 1^s; (5) 6^d; (6) 2^s 6^d.

    Total—5 Tenants; 4 houses, 5 outhouses, 105 acres 1 rood of Meadow & Arrable land, 66 pasture gates; fynes paid in 20 years, £12 8^s 4^d; yearly rent, £3 1^s 4^d; yearly value, £18 5^s 0^d.

    The Cleere Improvement—£15 3^s 8^d.

——————

5. Scale Parke.[2]—Demeasnes.

[3]Mr. Emanuel Scroope[4] holdeth the same ℮ cer- teyne gates in Carnie at the rent of   £17 06^s 08^d

---

[1] In par. of Gargrave (W.R.).

[2] In par. of Kettlewell. So called from the long and steep ascent within it from Craven into Coverdale (Whitaker, T. D., *History of Craven Deanery*, 3rd ed., by A. W. Morant, p. 563).

[3] " 520^{li} offered for this to ye Committee, but it is too late " in the margin.

[4] Son of Thomas, 10th Lord Scrope, by Philadelphia, dau. of Henry, Lord Hunsdon. He became 11th Lord Scroope and died 1630 (Clay, J. W., *Dugdale's Visitation*, 1665-6, ii, 9).

Demeasnes. The Parke conteynes in quantity

600 acres

Pasture gates 16

It is yearly worth   £61 12ˢ 00ᵈ

The Improvemᵗ   £44 05ˢ 04ᵈ

The generall Abstract of Cracall etc. being the sixth division of Midleham.	Tenemᵗ lands	The number of Tennants 90		
		Quantity of ground	1158 ac. 3 r.	
		Number of Beast gates	731½	
			£	s. d.
		Fynes paid in 20 yeares	166	01 09
		The yearly rent	062	13 01
		The yearly value	301	01 03
		The cleere Improvemᵗ	251	14 09

7. Tenements in Carperby,[1] Laborne[2] and Scotton.[3]

[4]Peter Hawkins—(2) 26 years; (3) 1 house, 2 outhouses, M. & A. 36 ac., P.G. 13; (4) 4ˡ 10ˢ; (5) 1ˡ 10ˢ; (6) 8ˡ 14ˢ.

Reignald Russell—(2) 30 years; (3) 1 house, 4 outhouses, M. & A. 20 ac., P.G. 8½; (4) 2ˡ 6ˢ; (5) 1ˡ 3ˢ; (6) 4ˡ 13ˢ 4ᵈ.

[5]Percivall Jefferson—(2) 30 years; (3) 1 house, 2 outhouses, M. & A. 26 ac., P.G. 7; (4) 4ˡ; (5) 1ˡ; (6) 5ˡ 11ˢ 4ᵈ.

John Brockall—(2) 30 years; (3) 2 houses, 3 outhouses, M. & A. 60 ac., P.G. 17; (4) 6ˡ 1ˢ 11ᵈ; (5) 3ˡ; (6) 13ˡ 14ˢ 8ᵈ.

John Rooke—(2) —; (3) 1 house, 4 outhouses, P.G. 8; (4) 10ˡ 5ˢ 4ᵈ; (5) 2ˡ 11ˢ 4ᵈ; (6) 10ˡ.

John Tenant—(2) —; (3) 4 houses, 8 outhouses, M. & A. 47 ac., P.G. 12; (4) 7ˡ 2ˢ; (5) 2ˡ 7ˢ 4ᵈ; (6) 12ˡ 19ˢ 8ᵈ.

Total—6 Tenants; 10 houses, 20 outhouses, 189 acres of Meadow & arrable land, 65½ pasture gates; fynes paid in 20 years £34 5ˢ 3ᵈ; yearly rent, £11 12ˢ 7½ᵈ; yearly value £55 13ˢ 0ᵈ.

The Cleere Improvemᵗ is £44 00ˢ 04½ᵈ.

The Summary of the whole Mannor of Midleham	Demeasnes	The yearly rent	£99 16ˢ 00ᵈ
		The yearly value	£674 18ˢ 04ᵈ
		The Cleere yearly Improvemᵗ	£575 02ˢ 04ᵈ
		The quantity of land—2840 ac. 2 r.	
		The whole number of Tennants	753

[1] In par. of Aysgarth.   [2] A market town in the par. of Wensley.

[3] In par. of Catterick.

[4] "Carperby" in the margin.   [5] "Laborne" in the margin.

Tenement Lands	Meadow, arrable, & pasture	11,256 acres
	Beast gates in pasture	5884

Fynes paid wthin
  20 yeares   £1757 13ˢ 10ᵈ
The yearly rent is   £597 09ˢ 06¾ᵈ
The yearly value   £2836 16ˢ 05ᵈ
The Cleere yearly
  Improvemᵗ is   £2239 06ˢ 10¼ᵈ

Freehold   The number of Tennants—68
The yearly rent   £00 07ˢ 08ᵈ
              and a payre of gloves

[p. 30

2. RICHMOND.

This Mannor is divided into 3 principall partes
viz.

1. **Bowes,**[1] and this
   is subdivided into

   1 **Bowes Towne**
   2 **Slightholme**
   3 **Boulrond**
   4 **Stonikeld**
   5 **Spittle**

2. **Arkengarth** and
   this into

   1 **Arkengarthdale**
   2 **New forest**
   3 **Hope**
   4 **Crackpott**

3. **Certaine tenements**
   in

   1 **Helae**
   2 **Reath**
   3 **Harkerside**

1. The Towneship of Bowes. [p. 31

Wᵐ Cotes fil. Roberti—(2) 8 years; (3) 1 house, 3 outhouses,
    M. 29 ac. 2 r., P.G. 8; (4) 3ˡ 13ˢ; (5) 12ˢ 2ᵈ; (6) 5ˡ 5ˢ 6ᵈ.
Anthony Bainbrigg—(2) 9 years; (3) 1 house, 4 outhouses,
    M. 40 ac., P.G. 9; (4) 2ˡ 1ˢ 8ᵈ; (5) 13ˢ 2ᵈ; (6) 8ˡ 19ˢ 4ᵈ.
  Idem—(2) 9 years; (3) M. 5 ac.; (4) 2ˢ; (5) 6ᵈ; (6) 5ˢ.
  Idem—(2) —; (3) M. 7 ac.; (4) 2ˢ 8ᵈ; (5) 8ᵈ; (6) 7ˢ.
Thomas Dent—(2) 8 years; (3) 1 house, 4 outhouses, M. 21 ac.
    3 r., P.G. 4; (4) 1ˡ 4ˢ 8ᵈ; (5) 6ˢ 2ᵈ; (6) 4ˡ 0ˢ 1ᵈ.

[1] A parish town 4 m. from Barnard Castle.

Thomas Leadman—(2) 11 years; (3) 1 house, 4 outhouses, M. 34 ac.
1 r., P.G. 7; (4) 2^l 7^s 4^d; (5) 11^s 11^d; (6) 5^l 15^s 9^d.

Reignald Leadman—(2) 8 years; (3) 1 house, 2 outhouses, M. 20 ac.
2 r., P.G. 4; (4) 1^l 6^s; (5) 6^s 6^d; (6) 3^l 9^s 6^d.

Symon Hanby—(2) —; (3) 1 house, 5 outhouses, M. 39 ac., P.G. 8;
(4) 1^l 11^s; (5) 12^s 4^d; (6) 7^l 8^s.
Idem—(2) —; (3) M. 2 r.; (4) 2^d; (5) 1^d; (6) 1^s.

Anthony Hanby—(2) —; (3) 1 house, 1 outhouse; (4) 8^d; (5) 4^d;
(6) 1^s 3^d.

Chrofer. Dent—(2) 8 years; (3) 1 house, 1 outhouse, M. 17 ac.,
P.G. 4; (4) 1^l 0^s $4\frac{1}{2}^d$; (5) 6^s $9\frac{1}{2}^d$; (6) 3^l 17^s.

Anthony Greene—(2) —; (3) 1 house; (4) 2^s 6^d; (5) 10^d; (6) 2^s 6^d.

John Turner—(2) —; (3) 1 house; (4) 2^s; (5) 8^d; (6) 2^s 6^d.

Willm. Baker—(2) —; (3) 1 house; (4) 1^s; (5) 6^d; (6) 2^s 6^d.

Willm. Baker—(2) —; (3) 1 house; (4) 1^s; (5) 6^d; (6) 2^s 6^d.

Willm. Buckle—(2) —; (3) 1 house; (4) 4^d; (5) 2^d; (6) 2^s 6^d.

John Leadman fil. Anth.—(2) —; (3) 1 house, 2 outhouses,
M. 31 ac. 2 r., P.G. 7; (4) 1^l 4^s 8^d; (5) 6^s 2^d; (6) 5^l 17^s 2^d.

John Bainbrigg—(2) —; (3) 1 house, 3 outhouses, M. 17 ac. 1 r.;
(4) 6^s; (5) 1^s 6^d; (6) 2^l 17^s 6^d.

Willm. Leadman—(2) —; (3) 1 house, 5 outhouses, M. 38 ac. 1 r.,
P.G. 8; (4) —; (5) 10^s; (6) 6^l 17^s 9^d.

Willm. Peacocke—(2) 8 years; (3) 1 house, 2 outhouses, M. 23 ac.
2 r., P.G. 4; (4) 12^s 4^d; (5) 6^s 2^d; (6) 3^l 19^s 6^d.
Idem—(2) —; (3) M. 2 ac.; (4) 8^d; (5) 4^d; (6) 2^s.

Thomas Leadman—(2) —; (3) 1 house, 4 outhouses, M. 31 ac.,
P.G. 8; (4) 16^s; (5) 11^s 10^d; (6) 5^l 11^s.

Thomas Thomson—(2) —; (3) 1 house, 3 outhouses, M. 24 ac. 1 r.,
P.G. 4; (4) 14^s 6^d; (5) 7^s 3^d; (6) 3^l 9^s $7\frac{1}{2}^d$.

Tho. Leadman fil. Jo'is—(2) —; (3) 1 house, 3 outhouses, M. 19 ac.
1 r., P.G. 3; (4) 12^s 4^d; (5) 6^s 2^d; (6) 3^l 1^s 9^d.

Thomas Slater—(2) 8 years; (3) 1 house, 2 outhouses, M. 40 ac.
1 r., P.G. 8; (4) 1^l 15^s 8^d; (5) 8^s 8^d; (6) 5^l 18^s $7\frac{1}{2}^d$.

John Blades—(2) —; (3) 1 house, 1 outhouse, M. 14 ac. 1 r.;
(4) 8^s; (5) 2^s 8^d; (6) 1^l 15^s $7\frac{1}{4}^d$.

Willm. Tomson—(2) —; (3) M. 6 ac. 2 r.; (4) 3^s 6^d; (5) 1^s 2^d;
(6) 19^s 6^d

Thomas Slater—(2) 8 years; (3) 1 house, M. 8 ac., P.G. $2\frac{1}{2}$;
(4) 13^s 8^d; (5) 3^s 5^d; (6) 1^l 7^s 4^d.

George Aldersey—(2) —; (3) 1 house, 5 outhouses, M. 22 ac. 3 r.,
P.G. 5; (4) 1^l 5^s 8^d; (5) 6^s 5^d; (6) 3^l 10^s $10\frac{1}{2}^d$.

Philip Brumskill—(2) —; (3) 1 house, 2 outhouses, M. 38 ac. 2 r.,
P.G. 8; (4) 4^l 18^s 8^d; (5) 12^s 4^d; (6) 5^l 14^s 3^d.

John Leadman fil. Bart.—(2) —; (3) 1 house, 6 outhouses, M. 15 ac.,
P.G. 4; (4) 12ˢ 4ᵈ; (5) 6ˢ 2ᵈ; (6) 2ˡ 9ˢ 10ᵈ.
Idem—(2) —; (3) M. 3 ac.; (4) 8ᵈ; (5) 4ᵈ; (6) 3ˢ.

John Hanby—(2) —; (3) 1 house, 1 outhouse, M. 15 ac., P.G. 4;
(4) 18ˢ; (5) 6ˢ; (6) 2ˡ 9ˢ 10ᵈ.
Idem—(2) —; (3) M. 1 r.; (4) 4ᵈ; (5) 2ᵈ; (6) 1ˢ.

Charles Kipling—(2) —; (3) M. 10 ac., P.G. 1; (4) 9ˢ 3ᵈ; (5) 3ˢ 1ᵈ;
(6) 1ˡ 10ˢ.

Henry Pinkney—(2) —; (3) 1 house, 2 outhouses, M. 3 ac., P.G. 1;
(4) 4ˢ 4ᵈ; (5) 2ˢ 2ᵈ; (6) 11ˢ 4ᵈ.

Anthony Alderson— (2) —; (3) 1 house, 4 outhouses, M. 32 ac.,
P.G. 8; (4) 1ˡ 17ˢ; (5) 12ˢ 4ᵈ; (6) 5ˡ 1ˢ 4ᵈ.

Willm. Alderson—(2) 8 years; (3) 1 house, 3 outhouses, M. 30 ac.,
P.G. 7½; (4) 2ˡ 4ˢ 4ᵈ; (5) 12ˢ 7ᵈ; (6) 4ˡ 16ˢ 4ᵈ.
Idem—(2) 8 years; (3) M. 3 ac.; (4) 2ˢ; (5) 6ᵈ; (6) 3ˢ.

John Leadman—(2) 8 years; (3) 1 house, 5 outhouses, M. 28 ac.,
P.G. 7; (4) 1ˡ 2ˢ 6ᵈ; (5) 11ˢ 3ᵈ; (6) 4ˡ 6ˢ 2ᵈ.
Idem—(2) 8 years; (3) M. 4 ac.; (4) 1ˢ 2ᵈ; (5) 7ᵈ; (6) 4ˢ.

Xpofer. Ward—(2) 8 years; (3) 1 house, 2 outhouses, M. 18 ac.,
P.G. 4; (4) 1ˡ 4ˢ; (5) 6ˢ; (6) (? 2)ˡ 16ˢ 6ᵈ.

Willm. Slater—(2) 8 years; (3) 1 house, 5 outhouses, M. 26 ac.,
P.G. 4; (4) 13ˢ 4ᵈ; (5) 6ˢ 8ᵈ; (6) 3ˡ 16ˢ 6ᵈ.

Tho. Dodsworth—(2) —; (3) 1 house, 5 outhouses, M. 80 ac.,
P.G. 17; (4) 3ˡ 6ˢ 8ᵈ; (5) 1ˡ 6ˢ 8ᵈ; (6) 11ˡ 19ˢ 10ᵈ.

John Leadman—(2) 8 years; (3) 1 house, 3 outhouses, M. 20 ac.,
P.G. 4; (4) 1ˡ 4ˢ 8ᵈ; (5) 6ˢ 2ᵈ; (6) 3ˡ 5ˢ 8ᵈ.

Willm. Park—(2) —; (3) 1 house; (4) 1ˢ 6ᵈ; (5) 6ᵈ; (6) 3ˢ 4ᵈ.
Idem—(2) —; (3) 1 outhouse, M. 4 ac.; (4) 8ᵈ; (5) 4ᵈ; (6) 6ˢ.

Leonard Tomson—(2) 8 years; (3) M. 7 ac.; (4) 5ˢ 8ᵈ; (5) 2ˢ 10ᵈ;
(6) 17ˢ 6ᵈ.

Anthony Buckle—(2) —; (3) 1 house; (4) 1ˢ 4ᵈ; (5) 4ᵈ; (6) 3ˢ 4ᵈ.

Xpofer Denham—(2) —; (3) 1 house; (4) 1ˢ; (5) 4ᵈ; (6) 3ˢ 4ᵈ

Willm. Kipling—(2) —; (3) 1 house, 2 outhouses, M. 14 ac.;
(4) 6ˢ 2ᵈ; (5) 3ˢ 1ᵈ; (6) 2ˡ.

Willm. Cotes—(2) —; (3) M. 2 ac.; (4) 4ᵈ; (5) 2ᵈ; (6) 3ˢ.

Richard Rayldon—(2) —; (3) 1 house, 4 outhouses, M. 18 ac.,
P.G. 3; (4) 11ˢ; (5) 1ˢ 10ᵈ; (6) 2ˡ 0ˢ 11ᵈ.

John Copland—(2) —; (3) 1 house, 3 outhouses, M. 34 ac., P.G. 2;
(4) 1ˡ 4ˢ 8ᵈ; (5) 12ˢ 4ᵈ; (6) 4ˡ 17ˢ.

Wᵐ Cotes fil. Geor.—(2) —; (3) 1 house, 2 outhouses, M. 25 ac.,
P.G. 14; (4) 2ˡ 4ˢ 9ᵈ; (5) 14ˢ 11ᵈ; (6) 4ˡ 14ˢ 8ᵈ.
Idem—(2) —; (3) M. 3 ac.; (4) 2ˢ 2ᵈ; (5) 10ᵈ; (6) 7ˢ 6ᵈ.

Geo. Cotes fil. Will.—(2) —; (3) 1 house, M. 12 ac., P.G. 5;
(4) 12ˢ 4ᵈ; (5) 6ˢ 2ᵈ; (6) 2ˡ 6ˢ 6ᵈ.
Idem—(2) —; (3) 2 outhouses, M. 4 ac.; (4) 1ˢ; (5) 6ᵈ; (6) 6ˢ.

Anthony Hanby—(2) —; (3) 1 house; (4) 8ᵈ; (5) 4ᵈ; (6) 3ˢ 4ᵈ.

Wm. Bainbrigge—(2) 14 years; (3) 1 house, 3 outhouses, M. 50 ac., P.G. 10½; (4) —; (5) 16ˢ 2ᵈ; (6) 7ˡ 14ˢ 10ᵈ.

Robert Ward—(2) 8 years; (3) 1 house, M. 18 ac., P.G. 4; (4) 12ˢ 4ᵈ; (5) 6ˢ 2ᵈ; (6) 2ˡ 17ˢ 4ᵈ.

Idem—(2) 8 years; (3) 1 outhouse, M. 4 ac.; (4) 8ᵈ; (5) 4ᵈ; (6) 8ˢ.

Total—62 Tenants; 46 houses, 109 outhouses, 1024 acres of meadow, 201½ pasture gates; fynes paid in 20 years, £47 17ˢ 2½ᵈ; yearly rent £16 6ˢ 4½ᵈ; yearly value £166 3ˢ 11ᵈ

The Cleere Improvement—£149 17ˢ 6½ᵈ.

---

2. Slightholme.¹   3. Boulrond.²   [p. 32

³Nicholas Alderson—(2) 28 years; (3) 1 house, 6 outhouses, M. 34 ac.; (4) 3ˡ 8ˢ 8ᵈ; (5) 17ˢ 2ᵈ; (6) 4ˡ 11ˢ 8ᵈ.

Reginald Alderson—(2) 8 years; (3) M. 12 ac.; (4) 4ˢ; (5) 2ˢ; (6) 1ˡ 4ˢ.

Roger Alderson—(2) 28 years; (3) 1 house, 6 outhouses, M. 44 ac.; (4) 2ˡ 11ˢ 6ᵈ; (5) 17ˢ 2ᵈ; (6) 5ˡ 15ˢ.

Idem—(2) 8 years; (3) 2 outhouses, M. 10 ac.; (4) 6ˢ 8ᵈ; (5) 1ˢ 8ᵈ; (6) 10ˢ.

Richard Alderson—(2) —; (3) 1 house, M. 20 ac.; (4) 4ˢ 8ᵈ; (5) 2ˢ 4ᵈ; (6) 1ˡ.

Idem—(2) —; (3) 1 house, M. 5 ac.; (4) 8ᵈ; (5) 4ᵈ; (6) 5ˢ.

Richard Leadman—(2) 8 years; (3) 1 house, 3 outhouses, M. 16 ac.; (4) 4ˢ 2ᵈ; (5) 2ˢ 1ᵈ; (6) 16ˢ.

John Musgrave—(2) —; (3) M. 22 ac.; (4) 6ˢ; (5) 2ˢ; (6) 11ˢ.

Anthony Alderson—(2) —; (3) 2 houses, 3 outhouses, M. 64 ac.; (4) 3ˡ 8ˢ 8ᵈ; (5) 1ˡ 14ˢ 4ᵈ; (6) 7ˡ 12ˢ 4ᵈ.

⁴Lionel Michell—(2) 8 years; (3) 1 house, 2 outhouses, M. 42 ac., P.G. 14; (4) 2ˡ 17ˢ 4ᵈ; (5) 14ˢ 4ᵈ; (6) 6ˡ 1ˢ.

Richard Wilson—(2) 8 years; (3) 1 house, 4 outhouses, M. 34 ac., P.G. 14; (4) 2ˡ 9ˢ 4ᵈ; (5) 12ˢ 4ᵈ; (6) 5ˡ 3ˢ.

Thomas Michell—(2) 8 years; (3) 1 house, 3 outhouses, M. 40 ac., P.G. 14; (4) 1ˡ 9ˢ 2ᵈ; (5) 14ˢ 7ᵈ; (6) 5ˡ 19ˢ 8ᵈ.

Michael Clarkson—(2) 8 years; (3) 1 house, 2 outhouses, M. 36 ac., P.G. 14; (4) 1ˡ 17ˢ; (5) 12ˢ 4ᵈ; (6) 5ˡ 9ˢ 8ᵈ.

Thomas Clarkson—(2) 8 years; (3) 1 house, 2 outhouses, M. 30 ac., P.G. 11; (4) 2ˡ 6ˢ 3ᵈ; (5) 9ˢ 3ᵈ; (6) 4ˡ 10ˢ 6ᵈ.

¹ Sleightholme in tnshp. of Bowes.

² Boldron, par. Bowes: it has since been transferred to Startforth parish.

³ "Slightholme" in the margin.

⁴ "Boulrond" in the margin, as if the entries relating to "Sleightholme" ended with the previous one and those for "Boulrond" began at this point.

James Richardson—(2) 8 years; (3) 1 house, 2 outhouses, M. 30 ac., P.G. 11; (4) 1¹ 17ˢ; (5) 9ˢ 3ᵈ; (6) 4¹ 10ˢ 6ᵈ.

John Wharleton—(2) 8 years; (3) 1 house, 3 outhouses, M. 21 ac., P.G. 7; (4) 12ˢ 4ᵈ; (5) 6ˢ 2ᵈ; (6) 3¹ 3ˢ 6ᵈ.

John Atkin—(2) 8 years; (3) 1 house, P.G. ⅔ of 7; (4) 6ˢ; (5) 2ˢ; (6) 8ˢ 2ᵈ.

Chrofer. Boswell—(2) 8 years; (3) 1 outhouse, P.G. ⅔ of 7; (4) 4ˢ; (5) 2ˢ; (6) 8ˢ 2ᵈ.

Total—18 Tenants; 15 houses, 39 outhouses, 460 acres of meadow, 92 and ⅓ of 7 pasture gates; fynes paid in 20 years, £24 13ˢ 5ᵈ; yearly rent, £8 1ˢ 4ᵈ; yearly value, £57 19ˢ 2ᵈ.

Improvement—£49 17ˢ 10ᵈ.

---

4. Stonikeld.[1]   5. The Spittle.[2]

Robert Peacocke—(2) 8 years; (3) 1 house, 1 outhouse, M. 20 ac., P.G. 4; (4) 1¹ 4ˢ 8ᵈ; (5) 6ˢ 2ᵈ; (6) 2¹ 9ˢ.

Idem—(2) —; (3) M. 16 ac.; (4) 1ˢ 4ᵈ; (5) 8ˢ; (6) 13ˢ 2ᵈ.

John Jackson—(2) 8 years; (3) 1 house, 3 outhouses, M. 14 ac.; (4) 3ˢ; (5) 1ˢ; (6) 11ˢ 10ᵈ.

Leonard Binkes—(2) 8 years; (3) 2 houses, M. 14 ac.; (4) 3ˢ 8ᵈ; (5) 11ᵈ; (6) 11ˢ 4ᵈ.

Idem—(2) —; (3) M. 2 ac.; (4) 2ᵈ; (5) 1ᵈ; (6) 1ˢ 4ᵈ.

Robert Binks—(2) 8 years; (3) 1 house, 2 outhouses, M. 14 ac.; (4) 2ˢ; (5) 1ˢ; (6) 11ˢ 10ᵈ.

Idem—(2) —; (3) M. 2 ac.; (4) 4ᵈ; (5) 2ᵈ; (6) 1ˢ 4ᵈ.

John Bailife—(2) 8 years; (3) 1 house, M. 12 ac.; (4) 2ˢ; (5) 6ᵈ; (6) 10ˢ.

Willm. Rayne—(2) —; (3) 1 house, 1 outhouse, M. 12 ac.; (4) 4ˢ; (5) 1ˢ; (6) 10ˢ 6ᵈ.

Chrofer. Cotes—(2) 8 years; (3) M. 6 ac.; (4) 2ˢ; (5) 1ˢ; (6) 9ˢ.

Idem—(2) 8 years; (3) 1 outhouse, M. 6 ac.; (4) 1ˢ 8ᵈ; (5) 10ᵈ; (6) 11ˢ.

Idem—(2) —; (3) M. 2 ac.; (4) 6ᵈ; (5) 3ᵈ; (6) 2ˢ.

Richard Catterick—(2) 8 years; (3) 1 house, 1 outhouse, M. 6 ac.; (4) 8ᵈ; (5) 4ᵈ; (6) 4ˢ.

Idem—(2) —; (3) M. 3 ac.; (4) 4ᵈ; (5) 2ᵈ; (6) 2ˢ.

Anthony Binks—(2) 8 years; (3) 1 house, 2 outhouses, M. 14 ac.; (4) 3ˢ 4ᵈ; (5) 1ˢ 8ᵈ; (6) 11ˢ 10ᵈ.

Idem—(2) —; (3) M. 3 ac.; (4) 6ᵈ; (5) 3ᵈ; (6) 2ˢ.

John or Jenkin Kipling—(2) 8 years; (3) 1 house, 2 outhouses, M. 12 ac.; (4) 2ˢ; (5) 8ᵈ; (6) 15ˢ 6ᵈ.

Ralph Binkes—(2) 8 years; (3) 1 house, 2 outhouses, M. 12 ac.; (4) 4ˢ; (5) 1ˢ; (6) 10ˢ 6ᵈ.

[1] In tnshp. of Bowes.   [2] Spital house. tnshp. of Bowes.

Nicolas Sawyer—(2) —; (3) 1 house, M. 7 ac.; (4) 1ˢ 6ᵈ; (5) 6ᵈ;
(6) 5ˢ 8ᵈ.

Idem—(2) 8 years; (3) M. 8 ac.; (4) 1ˢ; (5) 4ᵈ; (6) 5ˢ.

Chrofer. Buckle—(2) —; (3) M. 100 ac.; (4) 1ˡ 11ˢ 8ᵈ; (5) 15ˢ 10ᵈ;
(6) 8ˢ 10ᵈ.

Total—21 tenants; 12 houses, 15 outhouses, 285 acres of
meadow; 4 pasture gates; fynes paid in 20 years,
£4 10ˢ 4ᵈ; yearly rent, £2 1ˢ 8ᵈ; yearly value, £18 8ˢ 10ᵈ.
Improvemᵗ—£16 7ˢ 2ᵈ.

Deameasnes.

Philip Brumskill[1]—holdeth the Toll ℮ Tallage of Bowes, the mill
℮ common furnace oven or bakehouse, a close of land ℮
pasture under the castle cont. 6 acres by lres. patent from
Q. Eliz. 30 Aug. 36 regni for 21 years from the date at the
rent of—   £20 00ˢ 00ᵈ
It is worth yearly   £30 00ˢ 00ᵈ

Freeholds. There are 27 freeholders wthin this first part of Richmond wch. doe theyre service ℮ pay a yearly rent of—
£04 15ˢ 08½ᵈ.

---

2. ARKENGARTH.

1. Arkengarth dale.[2]   [p. 33

John Collin—(2) 6 years; (3) 1 house, 3 outhouses, M. 24 ac.,
P.G. 16; (4) 1ˡ 7ˢ 4ᵈ; (5) 13ˢ 8ᵈ; (6) 3ˡ 17ˢ.

Chrofer. Cotes—(2) —; (3) 1 house, 2 outhouses, M. 24 ac., P.G. 16;
(4) 3ˡ 2ˢ 8ᵈ; (5) 15ˢ 8ᵈ; (6) 4ˡ 5ˢ 4ᵈ.

James Cotes—(2) —; (3) 1 house, 3 outhouses, M. 30 ac., P.G. 12;
(4) 1ˡ 17ˢ 6ᵈ; (5) 18ˢ 9ᵈ; (6) 4ˡ 3ˢ.

James Collin—(2) —; (3) 1 house, 2 outhouses, M. 24 ac., P.G. 16;
(4) 1ˡ 12ˢ 10ᵈ; (5) 16ˢ 5ᵈ; (6) 3ˡ 18ˢ 8ᵈ.

William Hall—(2) —; (3) 1 house, 1 outhouse, M. 12 ac., P.G. 5;
(4) 19ˢ; (5) 6ˢ 4ᵈ; (6) 1ˡ 14ˢ 10ᵈ.

Chrofer. Hutchinson—(2) —; (3) 1 house, 3 outhouses, M. 20 ac.,
P.G. 8; (4) 2ˡ 18ˢ 4ᵈ; (5) 14ˢ 7ᵈ; (6) 2ˡ 17ˢ.

Bryan Scott—(2) —; (3) 1 house, 3 outhouses, M. 16 ac., P.G. 10;
(4) 1ˡ 8ˢ 8ᵈ; (5) 7ˢ 2ᵈ; (6) 2ˡ 13ˢ 8ᵈ.

Idem—(2) —; (3) 1 outhouse, M. 5 ac.; (4) 6ˢ 8ᵈ; (5) 1ˢ 8ᵈ;
(6) 11ˢ 2ᵈ.

---

[1] Of Barnard Castle. The eldest son of Reynold B. of Barnard Castle.
He mar. Christian, dau. of Roger Alderson, and died in 1634. He purchased
the manor and advowson of Bowes from John Dalston in 1593 (Clay, J. W.,
Dugdale's Visitation of Yorkshire, i, 108).

[2] The valley of the river Arkle, and a parish, 3 m. from Reeth.

Idem—(2) —; (3) 1 house, 4 outhouses, M. 26 ac., P.G. 6; (4) 2^l; (5) 6^s 8^d; (6) 3^l 6^s.

Wm. Robinson, Alderman—(2) —; (3) 1 house, 4 outhouses, M. 40 ac., P.G. 10; (4) 2^l 10^s 4^d; (5) 1^l 5^s 2^d; (6) 5^l 1^s 8^d.

Idem—(2) —; (3) M. 600 ac.; (4) 6^l 13^s 4^d; (5) 1^l 6^s 8^d; (6) 15^l

Idem—(2) —; (3) 1 house, 3 outhouses, M. 36 ac., P.G. 10; (4) 7^l 5^s 10^d; (5) 1^l; (6) 4^l 12^s.

John Peacocke—(2) —; (3) 1 house, 1 outhouse, M. 26 ac., P.G. 8; (4) 3^l 3^s 4^d; (5) 15^s 10^d; (6) 3^l 10^s 8^d.

James Hutchinson—(2) —; (3) 1 house, 12 outhouses, M. 16 ac., P.G. 3; (4) 1^l 5^s; (5) 6^s 3^d; (6) 1^l 19^s.

Elizabeth Scott—(2) —; (3) 1 house, 1 outhouse, M. 10 ac., P.G. $1\frac{1}{2}$; (4) 13^s 4^d; (5) 3^s 4^d; (6) 1^l 3^s 3^d.

William Heard—(2) —; (3) 1 house, 4 outhouses, M. 20 ac., P.G. 9; (4) 3^l; (5) 15^s; (6) 2^l 15^s 6^d.

Robert Tomson—(2) —; (3) 1 house, 3 outhouses, M. 12 ac., P.G. $2\frac{1}{2}$; (4) 1^l; (5) 6^s 8^d; (6) 1^l 11^s 1^d.

Idem—(2) —; (3) M. 3 ac. 1 r.; (4) 5^s; (5) 1^s 8^d; (6) 6^s 4^d.

Idem ℮ Jennet Scott—(2) —; (3) 1 house, 2 outhouses, M. 16 ac., P.G. $3\frac{1}{2}$; (4) 1^l 6^s 8^d; (5) 6^s 8^d; (6) 1^l 19^s 9^d.

George Carter—(2) —; (3) 1 house, 2 outhouses, M. 30 ac., P.G. 16; (4) 2^l 1^s 8^d; (5) 1^l 0^s 10^d; (6) 4^l 14^s.

George Cotes—(2) —; (3) 1 house, 3 outhouses, M. 28 ac., P.G. 8; (4) 3^l 6^s 8^d; (5) 16^s 8^d; (6) 3^l 13^s.

John Cotes—(2) —; (3) 1 house, 2 outhouses, M. 36 ac., P.G. 12; (4) 3^l; (5) 1^l; (6) 4^l 15^s.

George Scott—(2) —; (3) 1 house, 1 outhouse, M. 16 ac., P.G. 1; (4) 1^l 6^s 8^d; (5) 6^s 8^d; (6) 2^l 0^s 2^d.

James Scott, jun^r—(2) —; (3) 1 house, 3 outhouses, M. 34 ac., P.G. 10; (4) 2^l 13^s 2^d; (5) 13^s 4^d; (6) 4^l 9^s 8^d.

James Hutchenson, sen^r—(2) —; (3) 1 house, 2 outhouses, M. 14 ac., P.G. 2; (4) 1^l 4^s 3^d; (5) 8^s 1^d; (6) 1^l 14^s 4^d.

Idem—(2) —; (3) 1 house, 2 outhouses, M. 18 ac., P.G. 2; (4) 18^s 9^d; (5) 6^s 3^d; (6) 2^l 2^s 4^d.

Robert Hutchenson—(2) —; (3) 1 house, 2 outhouses, M. 24 ac., P.G. 24; (4) 2^l 13^s 4^d; (5) 13^s 4^d; (6) 4^l 9^s.

John Savile—(2) —; (3) 1 house, 1 outhouse, M. 16 ac., P.G. 10; (4) 2^l 13^s 4^d; (5) 13^s 4^d; (6) 2^l 12^s.

Cutbert Hall—(2) —; (3) 1 house, 2 outhouses, M. 14 ac., P.G. 4; (4) 18^s 9^d; (5) 6^s 3^d; (6) 1^l 16^s 6^d.

James Peacock, jun^r—(2) —; (3) 1 house, 3 outhouses, M. 3 ac., P.G. 8; (4) 1^l 11^s 4^d; (5) 15^s 8^d; (6) 3^l 17^s.

James Carter—(2) —; (3) 1 house, 2 outhouses, M. 26 ac., P.G. 44; (4) 1^l 10^s 6^d; (5) 1^l 5^s 3^d; (6) 6^l 1^s.

James Scott, senr—(2) —; (3) 1 house, 4 outhouses, M. 20 ac., P.G. 3; (4) 14s; (5) 7s; (6) 2l 17s 6d.

Raphe Peacocke—(2) —; (3) 1 house, 3 outhouses, M. 10 ac., P.G. 20; (4) 16s 8d; (5) 8s 4d; (6) 1l 12s 6d.

Willm. Garthe—(2) —; (3) 1 house, 2 outhouses, M. 20 ac., P.G. 16; (4) 1l 6s 11d; (5) 13s 5½d; (6) 2l 15s 4d.

Willm. Peacocke—(2) —; (3) 1 house, 1 outhouse, M. 24 ac., P.G. 20; (4) 1l 13s 4d; (5) 16s 8d; (6) 3l 18s.

John Coates of ye barnes—(2) —; (3) 1 house, 5 outhouses, M. 22 ac., P.G. 10; (4) 1l 5s; (5) 12s 6d; (6) 3l 0s 8d.

   Idem—(2) —; (3) 1 house, M. 8 ac., P.G. 3; (4) 6s 10d; (5) 3s 5d; (6) 1l 0s 8d.

Robert Hall—(2) —; (3) 1 house, 1 outhouse, M. 18 ac., P.G. 6; (4) 1l 13s 4d; (5) 8s 4d; (6) 2l 7s 4d.

James Coates, junr.—(2) —; (3) 1 house, 6 outhouses, M. 20 ac., P.G. 18; (4) 2l 14s 8d; (5) 13s 8d; (6) 3l 4s 8d.

John Heard—(2) —; (3) 1 house, 1 outhouse, M. 20 ac., P.G. 1; (4) 16s 2d; (5) 8s 1d; (6) 2l 4s.

   Idem—(2) —; (3) 1 house, 2 outhouses, M. 8 ac., P.G. 12; (4) 15s; (5) 7s 6d; (6) 1l 11s 6d.

William Collin—(2) —; (3) 1 house, 2 outhouses, M. 40 ac., P.G. 16; (4) 2l 10s 6d; (5) 1l 5s 3d; (6) 5l 4s 8d.

Anthony Scott—(2) —; (3) 1 house, 3 outhouses, M. 6 ac., P.G. 8; (4) 1l 10s; (5) 5s; (6) 1l 4s 8d.

Idem with Bryan Peacock, etc.—(2) —; (3) M. 6 ac.; (4) 12s 6d; (5) 2s 6d; (6) 12s.

Cutbert Heard—(2) —; (3) 1 house, 2 outhouses, M. 12 ac., P.G. 8; (4) 15s; (5) 7s 6d; (6) 1l 17s 2d.

   Idem—(2) —; (3) 1 house, 2 outhouses, M. 16 ac., P.G. 8; (4) 1l 6s 11d; (5) 6s 8¾d; (6) 1l 6s.

   Idem—(2) —; (3) 1 house, 1 outhouse, M. 40 ac.; (4) 2l; (5) 10s; (6) 3l 2s 6d.

   Idem—(2) —; (3) a Corne mill; (4) 8s 4d; (5) 3s 4d; (6) 1l.

John Scott—(2) —; (3) 1 house, 3 outhouses, M. 10 ac., P.G. 7; (4) 10s; (5) 5s; (6) 1l 13s 4d.

Cutbert Heard, junr—(2) —; (3) 1 house, 2 outhouses, M. 16 ac., P.G. 7; (4) 1l 11s 3d; (5) 10s 5d; (6) 2l 4s 8d.

John Hall—(2) —; (3) 1 outhouse, M. 10 ac., P.G. 4; (4) 12s 8d; (5) 6s 4d; (6) 1l 7s 10d.

Raph Cherry—(2) —; (3) 1 house, 1 outhouse, M. 12 ac., P.G. 6; (4) 1l 2s; (5) 5s 6d; (6) 1l 14s 6d.

Chrofer. Clarkson—(2) —; (3) 1 house, 2 outhouses, M. 12 ac., P.G. 8; (4) 18s 9d; (5) 6s 3d; (6) 1l 17s 2d.

Percivall Peacocke—(2) —; (3) 1 house, 2 outhouses, M. 30 ac., P.G. 14; (4) 1l 6s 8d; (5) 13s 4d; (6) 4l 1s 2d.

Bryan Peacocke—(2) —; (3) 1 house, 2 outhouses, M. 16 ac., P.G. 8; (4) 16ˢ 8ᵈ; (5) 8ˢ 4ᵈ; (6) 2ˡ 5ˢ 2ᵈ.

James Peacock, senʳ—(2) —; (3) 1 house, 2 outhouses, M. 24 ac., P.G. 8; (4) 16ˢ 8ᵈ; (5) 8ˢ 4ᵈ; (6) 2ˡ 19ˢ 4ᵈ.

Idem—(2) —; (3) 1 house, 2 outhouses, M. 30 ac.; (4) 1ˡ 2ˢ 6ᵈ; (5) 7ˢ 6ᵈ; (6) 2ˡ 7ˢ 6ᵈ.

Total—57 tenants; 51 houses, 119 outhouses, 1669 acres 1 rood of meadow, 488 pasture gates; fynes paid in 20 years, £96 16ˢ 7ᵈ; yearly rent, £31 4ˢ 11¼ᵈ; yearly value—£167 0ˢ 1ᵈ.

Improvemᵗ—£135 15ˢ 1¾ᵈ.

---

2. Newforest.[1] [p. 34

Rowland Hall—(2) —; (3) 1 house, 2 outhouses, M. 16 ac., P.G. 18; (4) 2ˡ 3ˢ 4ᵈ; (5) 10ˢ 10ᵈ; (6) 2ˡ 19ˢ 4ᵈ.

Willm. Bynkes—(2) —; (3) 1 house, 2 outhouses, M. 18 ac., P.G. 20; (4) 1ˡ 3ˢ; (5) 11ˢ 6ᵈ; (6) 3ˡ 3ˢ 2ᵈ.

Peter Ward—(2) —; (3) 1 house, 2 outhouses, M. 34 ac., P.G. 40½; (4) 5ˡ 16ˢ 8ᵈ; (5) 1ˡ 3ˢ 4ᵈ; (6) 6ˡ 6ˢ 9ᵈ.

Thomas Wynne—(2) —; (3) 1 house, 2 outhouses, M. 13 ac., P.G. 13; (4) 16ˢ; (5) 8ˢ; (6) 2ˡ 6ˢ.

Roger Bynkes—(2) —; (3) 1 house, 1 outhouse, M. 13 ac., P.G. 9½; (4) 11ˢ 4ᵈ; (5) 5ˢ 8ᵈ; (6) 1ˡ 18ˢ 6ᵈ.

George Wynne—(2) —; (3) 1 house, 4 outhouses, M. 20 ac., P.G. 21; (4) 1ˡ 16ˢ; (5) 12ˢ; (6) 3ˡ 8ˢ 8ᵈ.

Anthony Allen—(2) —; (3) 1 house, 1 outhouse, M. 10 ac., P.G. 19; (4) 2ˡ 3ˢ 4ᵈ; (5) 10ˢ 10ᵈ; (6) 2ˡ 16ˢ 4ᵈ.

Anthony Coates—(2) —; (3) 1 house, 2 outhouses, M. 9 ac. 2 r., P.G. 11; (4) 1ˡ 6ˢ 8ᵈ; (5) 6ˢ 8ᵈ; (6) 1ˡ 16ˢ 6ᵈ.

John Bynkes—(2) —; (3) 1 house, 3 outhouses, M. 36 ac., P.G. 28¼; (4) 2ˡ 7ˢ; (5) 15ˢ 8ᵈ; (6) 5ˡ 13ˢ 8¼ᵈ.

Robert Taylor—(2) —; (3) M. 7 ac., P.G. 4½; (4) 8ˢ; (5) 2ˢ 8ᵈ; (6) 18ˢ 1ᵈ.

Ralph Wagget—(2) —; (3) 1 house, 1 outhouse, M. 18 ac., P.G. 24; (4) 2ˡ; (5) 13ˢ 4ᵈ; (6) 3ˡ 11ˢ 8ᵈ.

Robert Wagget—(2) —; (3) 1 outhouse, M. 8 ac., P.G. 10½; (4) 17ˢ 6ᵈ; (5) 5ˢ 10ᵈ; (6) 1ˡ 13ˢ 9ᵈ.

Francis Mansfeild—(2) —; (3) 1 house, M. 6 ac., P.G. 6; (4) 10ˢ; (5) 3ˢ 4ᵈ; (6) 1ˡ 2ˢ 4ᵈ.

Thomas Wagget—(2) —; (3) 1 house, 2 outhouses, M. 22 ac., P.G. 24; (4) 2ˡ; (5) 13ˢ 4ᵈ; (6) 3ˡ 17ˢ 4ᵈ.

[1] A township in par. of Arkengarthdale. Sometime before 1171 Conan, earl of Richmond, granted the forestry of New Forest and Arkingarthdale, which at that time appears to have formed one forest, to Hervey, ancestor of the Fitz Hughs (*V.C.H., Yks., N.R.*, i, 37).

Anthony Binkes—(2) —; (3) 1 house, 2 outhouses, M. 18 ac.,
P.G. 20¼; (4) 1^l 3^s 4^d; (5) 11^s 8^d; (6) 3^l 7^s -½^d.

Trannian Binkes—(2) —; (3) 1 house, 1 outhouse, M. 29 ac.,
P.G. 18; (4) 1^l 1^s 8^d; (5) 10^s 10^d; (6) 4^l 6^s 4^d.

Edward Binkes, jun^r—(2) —; (3) 1 house, 1 outhouse, M. 26 ac.,
P.G. 27½; (4) 3^l 16^s 8^d; (5) 15^s 4^d; (6) 4^l 10^s 3^d.

Sr Francis Boynton—(2) —; (3) 1 house, 1 outhouse, M. 44 ac.,
P.G. 24; (4) 8^l 1^s 6^d; (5) 2^l 13^s 10^d; (6) 6^l 3^s 4^d.

Edward Binkes—(2) —; (3) 1 house, ½ outhouse, M. 11 a., P.G. 9½;
(4) 17^s 6^d; (5) 5^s 10^d; (6) 1^l 13^s 8^d.

Total—19 tenants; 17 houses, 28½ outhouses, 349 acres 2 roods of meadow, 348½ pasture gates; fynes payd in 20 years, £38 19^s 6^d; yearly rent, £12 0^s 6^d; yearly value, £61 12^s 9^d.

Improvement, £49 12^s 3^d.

---

3. Hope.[1]   4. Crackpott.[2]

[3]Roger Peacocke—(2) —; (3) 1 house, 1 outhouse, M. 20 ac.,
P.G. 4; (4) 3^l 6^s 8^d; (5) 16^s 8^d; (6) 2^l 16^s 8^d.

Chrofer. Peacocke—(2) —; (3) 1 house, 3 outhouses, M. 20 ac.,
P.G. 4; (4) 1^l 13^s 4^d; (5) 16^s 8^d; (6) 3^l 6^s 8^d.

Parcivall Pinkny—(2) —; (3) 1 house, 2 outhouses, M. 16 ac.,
P.G. 5½; (4) 1^l 0^s 10^d; (5) 10^s 5^d; (6) 3^l 0^s 10^d.

Bryan Pinkney—(2) —; (3) 1 house, 2 outhouses, M. 16 ac.,
P.G. 5½; (4) 2^l 1^s 8^d; (5) 10^s 5^d; (6) 3^l 0^s 10^d.

Chrofer. Pinkny, jun^r—(2) —; (3) 1 house, 1 outhouse, M. 18 ac.,
P.G. 6½; (4) 2^l 10^s; (5) 12^s 6^d; (6) 3^l 9^s 2^d.

Anthony Pinkny—(2) —; (3) 1 house, 3 outhouses, M. 50 ac.,
P.G. 18; (4) 3^l 6^s 8^d; (5) 1^l 13^s 4^d; (6) 4^l 9^s 4^d.

James Pinkny—(2) —; (3) 1 house, 2 outhouses, M. 20 ac., P.G. 6½; (4) 1^l 5^s; (5) 12^s 6^d; (6) 3^l 12^s.

Richard Slaughter—(2) —; (3) 1 house, 1 outhouse, M. 10 ac.,
P.G. 2; (4) 1^l 13^s 4^d; (5) 8^s 4^d; (6) 1^l 14^s 2^d.

George Foggythwait—(2) —; (3) 2 houses, 1 outhouse, M. 26 ac.,
P.G. 2; (4) 5^l; (5) 1^l 5^s; (6) 3^l 12^s 2^d.

Leonard Peacock—(2) —; (3) 1 house, 1 outhouse, M. 8 ac.,
P.G. 2; (4) 16^s 8^d; (5) 8^s 4^d; (6) 1^l 8^s 8^d.

James Fryer—(2) —; (3) 1 house, ½ outhouse, M. 12 ac., P.G. 4;
(4) 1^l 17^s; (5) 12^s 6^d; (6) 2^l 6^s 8^d.

Miles Granger—(2) —; (3) 1 house, ½ outhouse, M. 12 ac., P.G. 4;
(4) 2^l 10^s; (5) 12^s 6^d; (6) 2^l 6^s 8^d.

[1] A township in par. of Barningham.
[2] In the tnshp. and par. of Grinton.
[3] " Hope " in the margin.

[1]Richard Garthe—(2) —; (3) 1 house, 3 outhouses, M. 34 ac., P.G. 38; (4) 11^l 13^s 4^d; (5) 1^l 13^s 4^d; (6) 6^l 14^s 2^d.

   Idem—(2) —; (3) 2 houses, 4 outhouses, M. 34 ac., P.G. 37; (4) 6^l 13^s 4^d; (5) 1^l 13^s 4^d; (6) 6^l 14^s 2^d.

   Idem—(2) —; (3) M. 7 ac., P.G. 6; (4) 13^s 4^d; (5) 3^s 4^d; (6) 1^l 15^s 6^d.

George Blaides—(2) —; (3) 2 houses, 3 outhouses, M. 50 ac., P.G. 52; (4) 9^l 6^s 8^d; (5) 2^l 6^s 8^d; (6) 10^l 17^s.

William Blades—(2) —; (3) 1 house, 2 outhouses, M. 16 ac., P.G. 18; (4) 3^l 6^s 8^d; (5) 16^s 8^d; (6) 3^l 10^s 4^d.

   Total—19 tenants; 21 houses, 33 outhouses, 399 acres of meadow, 226 pasture gates; fynes payd in 20 years, £61 14^s 6^d; yearly rent, £16 13^s 4^d; yearly value, £66 12^s 4^d.

   Improvement, £49 19^s 0^d.

---

3. Certeyne tenements in Helaw,[2] Reathe,[3] ę Harkerside.[4]

[5]Anthony Wilson—(2) —; (3) 1 house, 2 outhouses, M. 6 ac., P.G. 1; (4) 14^s; (5) 7^s; (6) 1^l 0^s 6^d.

Leonard Hutchinson—(2) —; (3) 1 outhouse, M. 7 ac.; (4) 1^l 5^s 8^d; (5) 6^s 10^d; (6) 1^l 10^s.

Richard Robinson—(2) —; (3) 1 house, 2 outhouses, M. 12 ac., P.G. 4; (4) 18^s; (5) 9^s; (6) 1^l 17^s 10^d.

[6]Mathew Alderson—(2) —; (3) 1 house, 3 outhouses, M. 40 ac., P.G. 3; (4) 4^l 5^s 10^d; (5) 1^l 14^s 4^d; (6) 5^l 11^s 6^d.

   Idem—(2) —; (3) 1 house, M. 10 ac., P.G. 2; (4) 1^l 7^s 4^d; (5) 6^s 10^d; (6) 1^l 11^s 6^d.

Richard Metcalfe—(2) —; (3) 2 houses, 3 outhouses, M. 24 ac., P.G. 4; (4) 1^l 12^s 4^d; (5) 16^s 2^d; (6) 3^l 13^s.

Anthony Metcalfe—(2) —; (3) 1 house, 1 outhouse, M. 4 ac., P.G. 1½; (4) 5^s 6^d; (5) 2^s 9^d; (6) 14^s 6^d.

John Tysdale—(2) —; (3) 1 house, 1 outhouse, M. 4 ac.; (4) 3^s 6^d; (5) 1^s 9^d; (6) 9^s 6^d.

[7]Willm. Robinson—(2) —; (3) 1 house, 2 outhouses, M. 22 ac., P.G. 5; (4) 1^l 18^s; (5) 19^s; (6) 3^l 7^s 6^d.

James or Chrofer. Heard—(2) —; (3) 1 house. M. 12 ac., P.G. 3½; (4) 1^l 16^s; (5) 9^s; (6) 1^l 17^s 9^d.

---

[1] " Crackpot " in the margin.

[2] Healaugh in the townships of Melbecks and Reeth, par. Grinton.

[3] In par. of Grinton.

[4] In tnshp. and par. of Grinton.

[5] " Helaw " in the margin.

[6] " Reath " in the margin.

[7] " Harkerside " in the margin.

James Heard, jun^r—(2) —; (3) 1 house, 1 outhouse, M. 12 ac., P.G. 3; (4) 1^l 7^s; (5) 9^s; (6) 1^l 17^s.

Tho. or Chrofer. Heard—(2) 27 years; (3) 1 house, M. 4 ac.; (4) 13^s 4^d; (5) 3^s 4^d; (6) 12^s.

Idem—(2) —; (3) 1 house; (4) 8^d; (5) 4^d; (6) 1^s 6^d.

Total—13 tenants; 13 houses, 16 outhouses, 157 acres of meadow, 27 pasture gates; fynes payd in 20 years, £16 7^s 2^d; yearly rent, £6 5^s 4^d; yearly value, £24 4^s 1^d. Improvem^t—£17 18^s 9^d.

James Heard, jun.r—(2) —; (3) 1 house, 1 outhouse, M. 12 ac., P.G. 3; (4) 1l 7s; (5) 9s; (6) 1l 17s.

Tho. or Chrofer. Heard—(2) 27 years; (3) 1 house, M. 4 ac.; (4) 13s 4d; (5) 3s 4d; (6) 12s.

Idem—(2) —; (3) 1 house; (4) 8d; (5) 4d; (6) 1s 6d.

Total—13 tenants; 13 houses, 16 outhouses, 157 acres of meadow, 27 pasture gates; fynes payd in 20 years, £16 7s 2d; yearly rent, £6 5s 4d; yearly value, £24 4s 1d. Improvemt—£17 18s 9d.

Demeasnes.

[p. 35]

	£	s.	d.
Sr Robert Stapleton[1] and Sr John Mallory,[2] knights, hold by leasse from Q. Eliz. the lead ℮ cole mynes[3] within Arkengarthdale payeng the yearly rent of	03	10	00
They are worth yearly	£10	00	00

	£	s.	d.
[4]Phillip Brumskell hath the disposing of the Impropriation of Bowes payeng the yearly rent of	01	13	04
It is worth yearly	13	06	08

[4]Sr Henry Compton hath a leasse of Argengarth Church parcell of the late dissolved Monastery of Eggleston at ye rent of	09	10	02½
It is worth yearly	26	13	04

The Summary of the whole Lordship of Richmond	Demeasnes		£	s.	d.
		The yearly rent	34	13	10½
		The yearly value	80	00	00
		The Improvement	45	06	01½
	Tenement Lands	The number of Tennants—209			
		Meadow ℮ arrable land—4343 acres			
		Beastgates Pasture—1387			
		Fynes paid in 20 yeares past	£290	18^s	08½^d

[1] Sir Robert Stapleton of Wighill, d. 1607, son and heir of Sir Robert S. of Wighill, d. 1557, by his wife Elizabeth, dau. of Sir William Mallory of Studley (Chetwynd-Stapleton, H. E., *The Stapletons of Yorkshire*, p. 310).

[2] Sir John Mallory, born before 1585, eldest son of Sir William Mallory of Studley, by his wife Ursula, dau. of George Gale of York, master of the mint there (Walbran, J. R., *Memoirs of the Lords of Studley*, pp. 11–13).

[3] On the Patent Roll for 1625 these are described as now or late in the tenure of Ambrose Appleby, gent., at a rent of £3 10s.

[4] " Not ye Cities " in the margin.

		£	s.	d.
	The yearly rent	£092	12ˢ	05¾ᵈ
	The yearly value	£562	00ˢ	11ᵈ
	The Improvement	£469	08ˢ	05¼ᵈ
Freehold	The number of Tenants—27			
	The free rent £004 15ˢ 08½ᵈ			
	and one pound of Cummin seed			

The yearly rent £092 12ˢ 05¾ᵈ
The yearly value £562 00ˢ 11ᵈ
The Improvement £469 08ˢ 05¼ᵈ

Freehold | The number of Tenants—27
The free rent £004 15ˢ 08½ᵈ
and one pound of Cummin seed

[p. 36

Reprizes and deductions yearly out of the two Lordshipps.

Fees.

	£	s.	d.
The Bailife of the franchises ꝑ liberties of both Mannors ꝑ Steward ꝑ cheif forester	50	00	00
for charges in Keeping the Courts	08	00	00
The Steward's Clarke of the Courts of all the Libertyes	03	06	08
The feodary	01	00	00
The Bailife of the Towneship of Midleham 3ˡˡ, and the Grave there 40ˢ	05	00	00
The Keeper of Wanlas Parke[1]	03	00	08
The Bowebearer of ye forest of Wensladale and Keeper of Bardell[2]	01	00	08
The Keeper of Radell[3] and Crakedale[4]	01	10	00
The Graves of Hawes quarter	01	00	00
The Grave of Bainbrigge	01	00	00
The Grave of Worton and the Barony	01	03	04
The Pinder of Worton	00	02	00
The Cryer of the Leet and Keeping the Pinfold of Bainbrigge	00	04	02
The Bowbearer of Bishopsdale and Coverdale Chace	02	00	00
The Keeper of the Heyning,[5] Burton, Walden and Aisgarth	03	00	00

[1] NE. of Swinithwaite and in par. of West Witton, known as the park of West Witton in the thirteenth century (*V.C.H.*, *N.R.*, i, 286).

[2] Bardale, a valley running down from the hills to Marsett and in the township of Bainbridge.

[3] Raydale, a valley to the east of Bardale, and in the tnshp. of Bainbridge.

[4] Cragdale, a valley to the east of Raydale, known as Crakedale in 1307 (Place Name Society, v, 263).

[5] This place is not easy to identify. The herbage of the Hyghnyng in Thoralby is mentioned in an Inq. P.M., 1298 (*Yorkshire Inquisitions*, iii, 70— Y.A.S., Rec. Ser., xxxi); and under Thoralby "the herbage of the two closes of West henning and Middle Hennington." In a forest eyre of 1530 mention is made of the chace of Heminges Walden (*V.C.H.*, *Yks.*, i, 512).

	£	s.	d.
The Grave of Montforts Lands[1]	00	13	04
One of the Keepers of ye game in Bpsdale Chace	02	00	00
The other Keeper	01	04	00
The Paliser[2] of Bishops dale Carre being a frith[3] for the deare	00	05	00
The Keeper of Coverdale Chace	03	00	08
The Grave of Carleton ℘ Coverdale	01	06	08
The Bailife ℘ forester of Kettlewell ℘ Collector of the rents there, for wᶜʰ he hath yᵉ occupacon of a peece of ground called Berkenthwait ℘ a horse gate in Scale Parke ℘ a fee of	01	10	04
The Bailife of Cracall	03	00	08
The Surveyor of both Lordships	06	13	04
The Bowbearer ℘ Keepers of New forest[4]	04	06	08
The Grave of Bowes	01	02	06

Total—£106 10ˢ 02ᵈ.

The Generall Abstract of both the Lordshipps.[5]

		£	s.	d.
Demeasnes.	The yearly rent is	134	09	10½
	The yearly value is	754	18	04
	The Improvemᵗ is	620	08	05½
Tenement Lands.	The number of Tennants is 962			
	The quantity of Land is 15,599 acres			
	The number of beast gates is 7271			
		£	s.	d.
	Fynes paid in 20 yeares past	2048	12	06½
	The yearly rent is	690	02	00½
	Deduct the fees *ut sup.*	106	10	02
	Rests cleere in rents	583	11	10½
	The yearly value is	3398	17	04
	The Cleere Improvemᵗ is	2078	15	03½
Freehold.	The number of Tennants—95			
	The free rent	005	03	04½
	and a payre of gloves ℘ a pound of cumyn seed			

[1] These included lands at the Heyning, Burton Walden and Aysgarth.

[2] Paliser, a maker of palings or fences; one who has charge of a park (*N.E.D.*).

[3] A deer park (*N.E.D.*).

[4] In par. of Arkengarthdale.

[5] Middleham and Richmond.

J

Out Common.	The out Common to these Lo^{pps} are worth a full third of the tenements ꝑ knowne grounds wch after that proporcon is yearly	1389	11	10
	W^{ch} added to the former Improvem^t of the demeasne ꝑ tent lands as aforesaid is	4713	15	07

[p. 37

Some Observacons concerning these two Lordshipps.

Castles.	There are three Castles wthin these Lordships, viz. Midleham, Richmond ꝑ Bowes—ruined.
Markets.	There are three Market Townes, Midleham, ꝑ Ketlewell within ye Lo^p of Midleham, ꝑ Richmond within that Lordship.
Churches.	In the Lo^p of Midleham are fyve Churches, viz

1. Midleham in the King's guift
2. Coverham, an Impropriation in the guift of S Freeman, etc
3. Kettlewell, an Impropriation in the guift of Bernard Calvert
4. Aisgarth, an Impropriation in the guift of Trinity Colledg in Cambridge
5. West Witton, an Impropriation in the King's guift, in leasse to Sr Henry Slingsby

In the Lo^p of Richmond are 2 Churches, viz.

1. Bowes, an Impropriation in the guift of Philip Brumskill.
2. Arkengarth, an Impropriation in the King's guift, in leasse to Sr Henry Compton

Woods.	There are few or no woods or tymber trees in the two Lo^{pps} besides the woods growing in Radale, Bishops dale Chace ꝑ the Heaning; the rest are in hedgrowes ꝑ consist of Ashe, Hasel, Hollings ꝑ the like
Mynes.	There are in the two Lo^{pps} mynes of Coale ꝑ Lead in diverse places, but of small value.
Estates.	There are no Copieholders in the Lo^{pps}, but freeholders, lessees ꝑ tenants at will
Quality.	The greatest part of these two Lo^{pps} consists of Medow and Pasture, ꝑ Out Commons, wth a small quantity of Arrable land, it being not able to beare Corne for ye coldnes of the soyle and the length of

winter there.[1] The best sort of Meadow is worth 5^s ye acre, the second sort 2^s 6^d, the third 12^d. The best pasture is worth 3^s 4^d the acre, the second 18^d, ℗ the third 4^d. The best arrable is worth 4^s the acre, the second 2^s, and the third 12^d. And after this proporcon all the lands in this Survey were valued.

The Tennants of these Mannors have long tyme before the 14th of Q. Elizabeth chalenged a Customary estate in the nature of Copiehold to them ℗ theyre heyres in all theyre Severall Tenementes, paieing a fyne of a peny only at death or alienacon of Lord or Tennant. In wch. 14th yeare that Custome was taken away, ℗ leasses for 40 yeares were graunted to them seuerally of theyre severall tenementes. In consideracon of two yeares rent payd for a fyne. In theyre Leasses are these Clauses or Condicions. The Tennants at the death of Lord or Tennant or upon renewing theyre Leasses to pay two yeares rent of the yearly value in the name of a fyne, ℗ one yeares value or rent at every alienacion. They are to doe suit ℗ service at Midleham, Bainbrigg, etc., according to Custome. They are not to alienate for longer then theyre owne lives ℗ sixe yeares after theyre decease wthout consent of the Steward, Auditor, Receyvor, ℗ Surveyor, or any three of them whereof the steward to be one. They are also to doe all services for the prince as in former tymes according to Custome. The Queene covenanted to grant to them ℗ theyre eldest sons surviving new leasses at the end of the 40 yeares under the same rents ℗ covenants ℗ for the like terme.

The Tennants of these Lo^{pps} have diverse names of holdings as they terme them.

1 Some have leasses for 40 yeares taken about the 8th yeare of K. James (1610), wth a covenant for like terme for 40 yeares more after the expiracon of the present terme payeng two yeares old rent for a fyne to the Crowne.

   1 But these Tennants when they renewed theyre leasses, besides the fyne of two yeares old rent, paye foure yeares like fyne for composicon, wch they say was for confirmacon

   2 They gave to Sr Tho. Metcalfe (then High Steward of the said Mannors) two yeares more as a gratuity to procure his assistance to renew theyre leasses, wch eight yeares fyne was an absolute breach (as is conceyved) of that custome, wch they pretend to be so strong, ℗ is confirmed by a decree in the Exchequer Court, in the 37th of Q. Eliz.

[1] This accounts for the low valuation of the arable land.

2 Other Tennants have leasses of 40 yeares also beginning about the same tyme wth the former, wth like covenants ę condicons, saving that the covenant for renewing for 40 yeares more is left out

3 Others have leasses but for 21 yeares absolute, expired long since.

4 Others have leasses for lives,

5 And others have no estate at all, but these are very few.

Yet all these severall sorts of Tennants pretend to hold by one ę the same custome.

It is conceyved that they cannot hold by lease ę custome too.

[p. 38

It is reported that the Lord Duke of Lennox ę Richmond, Lodowick, had land wthin these Lo^pps of the same custome as was pretended but he overthrew them in a suit of law in the Exchequer Court.

The Lordship of Berna Castle[1] was formerly held in the same nature, ę was also the land of K. Richard the third. But the tennants therof yealderd themselves w^thout suit (as is said) ę now hold altogither by speciall graunt, w^thout pretence of that covenant.

The Cheife Custome they pretend (in nature of copiehold) was this ę inserted into the first graunts ę leasses they tooke for 40 yeares about the 13th or 14th of Q. Eliz., That so often as occasion should require they should be ready to attend the Lord Wardens of the Marches against Scotland wth horse ę men well furnished for warre at theyre owne charge as long as need should require, wch was an unlimited service. But the Tennants now say, they were to serve but 14 dayes at theyre owne charge, and afterwards at the charge of the Soveraigne.

But this service ceassed at the coming in of K. James, ę therefore it is conceyved that theyre customes then fayled—for *cessante causa vel ratione legis, cessat lex*

It is supposed that they were all formerly tenants at will till the 13th or 14th of Q. Eliz. for they cannot or will not shew any deed, graunt or copie before that tyme.

That there leasses should be good for 40 yeares more after theyre present terme, as all one as if they had a graunt for 80 yeares, w^ch (as is conceyved) theyre graunt will not amount unto

Lastly it is the opinion of many, that the Covenant for renewing theyre leasses was vacated by the purchase made by the City. And one reason may be, because the fynes due at the Princes death cannot be claymed by the City, ę so a great part of the consideracon for that covenant is taken away

---

[1] Barnard Castle.

[1]These 2 Lo^pps have in them about 980 tennants besides 95 freeholders.

The first sort hold (as is before) 15,599 acres, wch being all or the greatest part enclosed were valued at 6^s 8^d the acre.

The beastgates pasture being 7271 are valued at 4^s the gate for summering only

Besides they have vast ℮ large commons ℮ mounteynes wch they call theyre fells wch considering the quantity by the former survey are a full third part as good as theyre other grounds ℮ enclosures, ℮ at least are quodruple to them in number of acres, though farre short of theyre goodnes.

The mynes are taken of the King, since the Cities contract, by Humfry Wharton, receyvor here

The enclosures are most of them rich grounds ℮ lye all in the dales encompast wth mounteynes, moores and fells

The fynes *post mortem*, ℮ alienacon would be demaunded of Sr George Vane, who hath receyved them of late yeares, not-w^thstanding Mr Sollicitors report to the Committee for the revenue that they were due to the City.

By the survey the lands are thus rated   The true value of them is
The best meadow at   5^s   ye acre   16^s
The second sort at   2^s 6^d   ,,   ,,   12^s
The beast gates at   4^s   6^s 8^d
And according to these rates it is conceyved the Surveyors made theyre Improvem^t of every particuler in the two Lordships

---

[p. 39
[This page contains an index to each subdivision in the two lordships.]

[p. 40
The severall tenants of these two Mannors in these divisions being in number 962, have tyme out of mind (as is in part touched before) chalenged before the 14th yeare of Q. Elizabeth's raigne a Customary Estate in the nature of a Copiehold to them ℮ theyre heyres in all theyre severall tenements yeilding theyre annuall rents and payeng for fyne a peny only at ye death or alienacon of Lord or Tennant. In wch 14th yeare that Custome was taken away, and leases for 40 yeares (some under the Great Seale, others under the Exchequer Seale) were graunted to them respectively in maner ℮ forme ℮ under such clauses ℮ condicons as are here-after breifly explained viz. The Graunt is in consideracon of two

[1] In the margin—" 5199 13   4
                1454   4   –
                6653 17   4
                2217 19   1
                8871 16   5 "

yeares rent payd for a fyne. The *Habendum* is for 40 yeares. The rent dayes are at the feasts of the Annunciation of our Lady, ꝑ St. Michael the Arch Angell. The Tenants are to pay at the death of the Lord or Tenant, and at the renewing of theyre leasse a double rent of the yearly value in the name of a fyne, ꝑ at every alienacon one yeares value or rent. The Tennants are to doe suit ꝑ service at Midleham, Bainbrigg, etc. according to the Custome. They likewise covenant eyther by themselves or other sufficient men to inhabite, occupie, ꝑ manure theyre severall tenements during the terme. Not to lett, sell, or alien theyre tenements or any part therof for any longer terme then theyre owne lives, ꝑ six yeares after theyre decease (if the terme of theyre leasse doe so long continue) w^{th}out the consent of the Cheife Steward, Auditor, Receyvor and Surveyor or any three of them, whereof the Steward to be one. They are likewise to doe all services for the Prince as in former tymes according to custome. They are likewise bound to repayre at theyre owne charge and so to leave the same at the end of theyre terme. They have liberty given them to take sufficient houseboot, hedgboot, fyreboot, ploughboot ꝑ cartboot to be spent on the premises only, and tymber for repayring theyre houses by assignement. There is likewise a graunt from the Queene in theyre leasses that the tenants ꝑ theyre eldest sons (surviving the terme of that leasse) shall have new leasses under the same rents ꝑ covenants, ꝑ for the same terme, so long as the tenants shall observe the covenants accordingly. And lastly, there is a proviso, that if the rent be not payd w^{th}in 40 dayes, the leasse to be voyd.

INDEX OF PERSONS.

An asterisk (*) indicates that the name occurs more than once on a page.

The letter *n* indicates that the name occurs in a footnote.

Roman numerals indicate that the name occurs in the Introduction.

INDEX OF PLACES.

An asterisk (*) indicates that the name occurs more than once on a page.

The letter *n* indicates that the name occurs in a footnote.

Roman numerals indicate that the name occurs in the Introduction.

The ancient parish in which the more important places are situated is given in brackets.

INDEX TO FIELD NAMES.